3 Mathematics

Curriculum Associates

Project Manager: Lynn Tauro
Cover Design: Matthew Pollock
Book Design: Pat Lucas and Scott Hoffman

ISBN 978-0-7609-6829-1

North Billerica, MA 01862

15 14 13 12 11 10 9 8 7 6

Table of Contents

To the Student v

PRETEST 1

INSTRUCTION

BIG IDEA 1: DEVELOP UNDERSTANDINGS OF MULTIPLICATION AND DIVISION AND STRATEGIES FOR BASIC MULTIPLICATION FACTS AND RELATED DIVISION FACTS.

Lesson	Title	Page	NGSSS
Lesson 1	Multiplication	31	MA.3.A.1.1
Lesson 2	Division	39	MA.3.A.1.1
Lesson 3	Multiplication and Division as Inverse Operations	47	MA.3.A.1.3
Lesson 4	Number Properties	55	MA.3.A.1.2

BIG IDEA 2: DEVELOP AN UNDERSTANDING OF FRACTIONS AND FRACTION EQUIVALENCE.

Lesson	Title	Page	NGSSS
Lesson 5	Modeling Fractions	63	MA.3.A.2.1
Lesson 6	Equivalent Fractions	71	MA.3.A.2.4
Lesson 7	Comparing and Ordering Fractions	77	MA.3.A.2.2, MA.3.A.2.3

BIG IDEA 3: DESCRIBE AND ANALYZE PROPERTIES OF TWO-DIMENSIONAL SHAPES.

Lesson	Title	Page	NGSSS
Lesson 8	Triangles	85	MA.3.G.3.1
Lesson 9	Quadrilaterals	91	MA.3.G.3.1
Lesson 10	Other Shapes	97	MA.3.G.3.1
Lesson 11	Composing and Decomposing Polygons	103	MA.3.G.3.2
Lesson 12	Congruent Figures and Symmetry	109	MA.3.G.3.3

Supporting Idea: Algebra			NGSSS
Lesson 13	Patterns	117	MA.3.A.4.1

Supporting Idea: Geometry and Measurement			NGSSS
Lesson 14	Length	125	MA.3.G.5.2
Lesson 15	Perimeter	133	MA.3.G.5.1
Lesson 16	Time	139	MA.3.G.5.3

Supporting Idea: Number and Operations			NGSSS
Lesson 17	Comparing, Ordering, and Representing Numbers	145	MA.3.A.6.1
Lesson 18	Estimation	151	MA.3.A.6.1
Lesson 19	Problem Solving	157	MA.3.A.6.2

Supporting Idea: Data Analysis			NGSSS
Lesson 20	Frequency Tables	165	MA.3.S.7.1
Lesson 21	Pictographs	173	MA.3.S.7.1
Lesson 22	Bar Graphs	181	MA.3.S.7.1
Lesson 23	Line Plots	189	MA.3.S.7.1

Post Test 195

To the Student

All students need strong math skills. ***Florida Ready—Mathematics*** will help you develop the math skills every third grader should know. Florida calls these skills the Next Generation Sunshine State Standards (NGSSS). Each lesson in this book teaches the specific skills, or benchmarks, that make up the NGSSS. Learning the NGSSS in this book will make you a better math student. It will also help you do well on any math test you may take.

Your teacher will tell you what lessons you will work on in this book. Each lesson has five parts. Your teacher will guide you through the first two parts. You will work on the other parts on your own. You will try to solve math problems. **Think About It** questions may help you understand problems. **Hints** may help you solve them. The problems are just like the ones you will see on a math test. Most are multiple-choice problems. Others will ask you to record your answer in a grid.

Florida Ready—Mathematics has two practice tests: a pretest and a post test. In each practice test, you will respond to 50 math items. These items cover a variety of math concepts.

Taking these practice tests will help you become familiar with the kinds of questions you may find on a math test. Your teacher will explain how you will do the practice tests and how to record your answers. Be sure to follow the directions in each practice test. As you complete the practice tests, answer the questions carefully. Record your answers in your book.

As you work on the multiple-choice questions in both the instruction book and practice tests, use the Tips for Answering Multiple-Choice Questions below. They can make you a better test-taker.

Tips for Answering Multiple-Choice Questions

- Read each question carefully before you try to answer it.
- Be sure you know what the question is asking you to do.
- Read all the answer choices for multiple-choice questions before you choose your answer. Then cross out any answer choices that you know are wrong.
- Think about the answer choices that are left. Choose the one you think is correct.
- Circle the letter of the correct answer choice or fill in the answer bubble.
- Read the question again. Then check that your answer makes sense.

1 If $4 \times 8 = 32$, what does 8×4 equal?

Ⓐ 32

Ⓑ 36

Ⓒ 44

Ⓓ 48

2 Point *A* on the number line below represents the mixed number $1\frac{3}{4}$. Which mixed number is equal to $1\frac{3}{4}$?

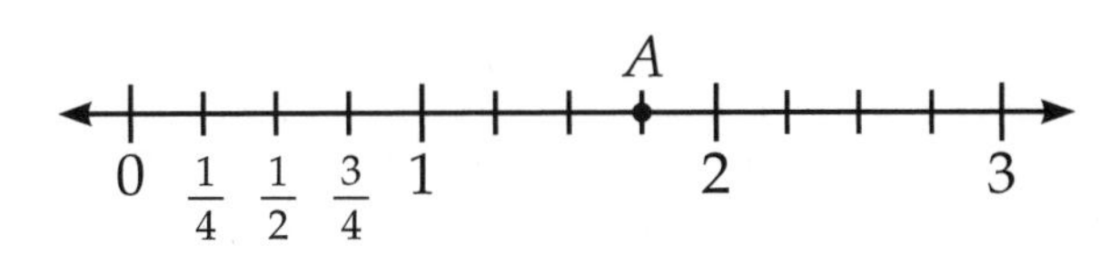

Ⓕ $1\frac{2}{5}$

Ⓖ $1\frac{6}{9}$

Ⓗ $1\frac{9}{12}$

Ⓘ $1\frac{5}{8}$

Go On

3 Anton made turkey sandwiches for a picnic. He used 3 slices of turkey for 1 sandwich, 6 slices for 2 sandwiches, and 9 slices for 3 sandwiches. If he continued this pattern, how many slices did he use for 5 sandwiches?

Sandwiches	1	2	3	4	5
Slices	3	6	9		

Ⓐ 12

Ⓑ 15

Ⓒ 16

Ⓓ 20

4 Which figure shows a line of symmetry?

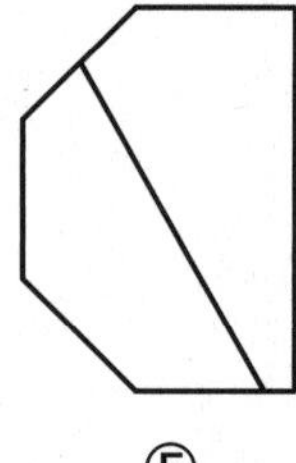

Ⓕ

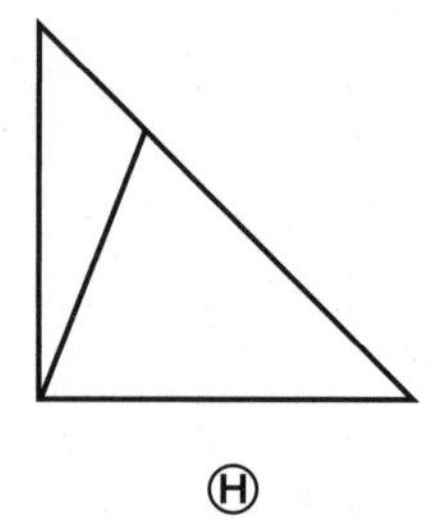

Ⓗ

Ⓖ

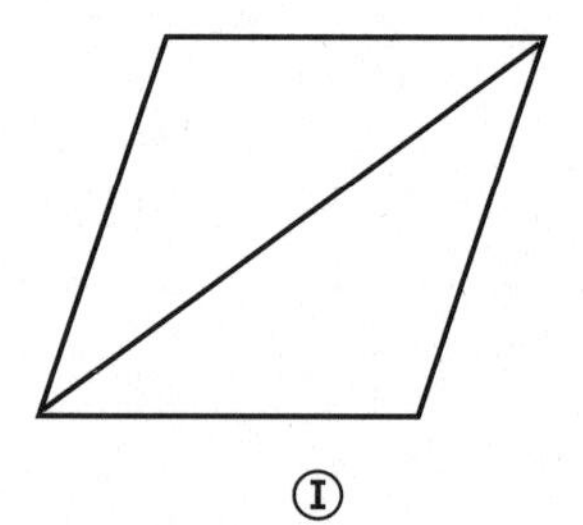

Ⓘ

Go On

5 Eda planted 4 rows of tomatoes with 6 plants in each row. She wrote this number sentence to find how many plants there were in all.

$6 + 6 + 6 + 6 = \square$

Which multiplication sentence also shows the total number of tomato plants?

Ⓐ $6 \times 6 = 36$

Ⓑ $6 + 4 = 10$

Ⓒ $5 \times 6 = 30$

Ⓓ $4 \times 6 = 24$

6 The figures below represent two fractions.

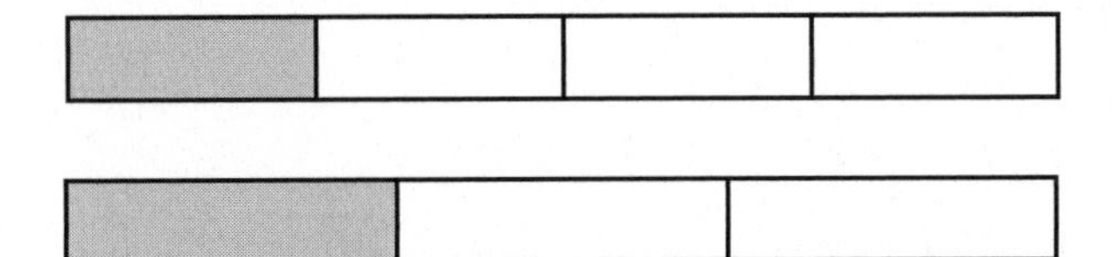

Which of the following correctly compares the values of the fractions?

Ⓕ $\frac{1}{4} < \frac{1}{3}$

Ⓖ $\frac{1}{4} > \frac{1}{3}$

Ⓗ $\frac{1}{3} = \frac{1}{4}$

Ⓘ $\frac{1}{3} < \frac{1}{4}$

7 Which shape is a pentagon?

Ⓐ 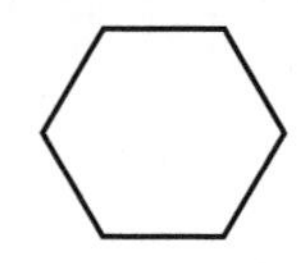

Ⓑ 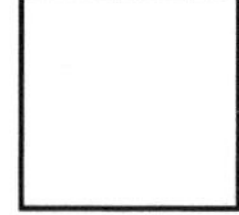

Ⓒ 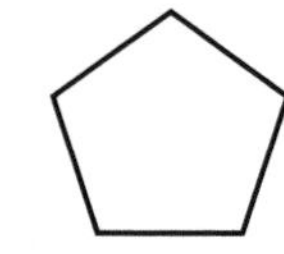

Ⓓ 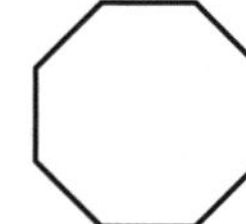

8 Do not use a ruler to answer this question. Which is the most reasonable estimate of the length of this pencil?

Ⓕ 12 centimeters

Ⓖ 12 inches

Ⓗ 3 centimeters

Ⓘ 3 inches

Go On

9 Each section of a fence has some long boards and some short boards, as shown in this picture.

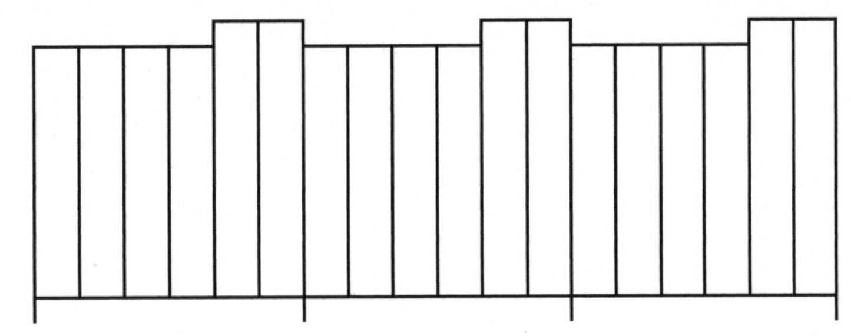

If 2 more sections are added, how many total long boards and short boards will there be?

Ⓐ 20 long boards, 20 short boards

Ⓑ 10 long boards, 20 short boards

Ⓒ 6 long boards, 12 short boards

Ⓓ 2 long boards, 4 short boards

10 What type of triangle has all different side lengths?

Ⓕ right

Ⓖ equilateral

Ⓗ isosceles

Ⓘ scalene

11 Elsa saves dimes, nickels, and quarters. She has 290 dimes, 132 nickels, and 85 quarters. About how many coins does Elsa have in all?

Ⓐ 300

Ⓑ 400

Ⓒ 500

Ⓓ 600

12 The line plot below shows the prices of all of the different pizzas sold at North End Pizza.

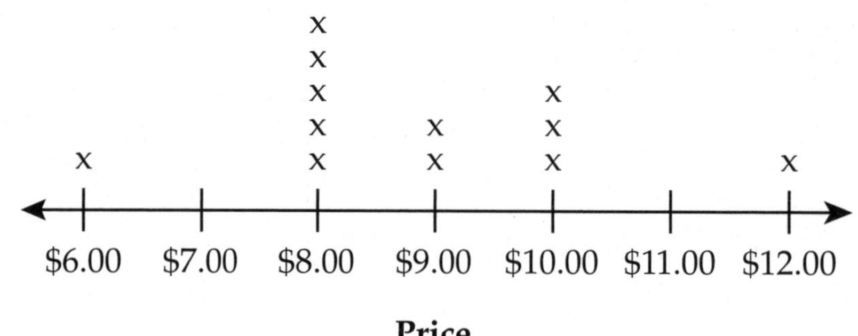

How many pizzas cost $10 or more?

Ⓕ 2

Ⓖ 3

Ⓗ 4

Ⓘ 5

Go On

13 Oscar did this division problem.

$\square \div 4 = 9$

Which problem could he do to check his answer?

Ⓐ $4 \times 9 = \square$

Ⓑ $9 - 4 = \square$

Ⓒ $9 \div 4 = \square$

Ⓓ $9 + 4 = \square$

14 Which figure shows $\frac{1}{2}$ shaded?

Ⓕ 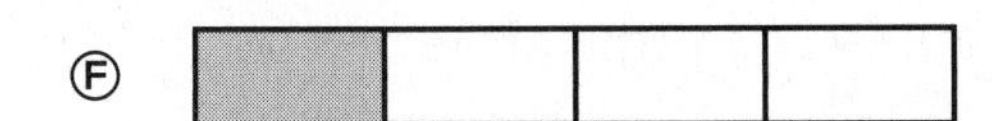

Ⓖ

Ⓗ

Ⓘ

Go On

15 Which sentence describes a trapezoid?

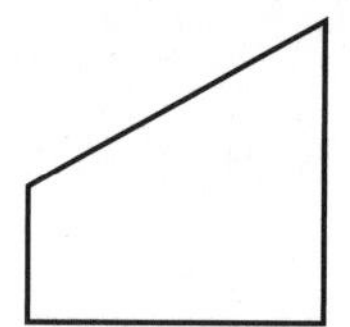

Ⓐ It has 1 pair of parallel sides.

Ⓑ It has no equal angles.

Ⓒ It has 4 equal sides.

Ⓓ It has 2 pairs of parallel sides.

16 What is the rule that could be used to find the missing numbers in this table?

Y	2	4	6	8
Z	6	12		

Ⓕ Multiply the numbers in row Y by 2.

Ⓖ Multiply the numbers in row Y by 3.

Ⓗ Add 4 to the numbers in row Y.

Ⓘ Add 8 to the numbers in row Y.

Go On

17 Dylan, Wendy, Sophia, and Matt each ordered the same size pizza. Dylan's pizza was cut into 6 pieces. Wendy's pizza was cut into 10 pieces. Sophia's pizza was cut into 4 pieces. Matt's pizza was cut into 8 pieces. If each child ate 2 pieces of pizza, who ate the most pizza?

Ⓐ Dylan

Ⓑ Wendy

Ⓒ Sophia

Ⓓ Matt

18 This clock shows the time that Lynsay leaves from home for school.

This clock shows the time that Lynsay gets to school.

What part of an hour does it take for Lynsay to get from home to school?

Ⓕ $\frac{1}{4}$

Ⓖ $\frac{1}{2}$

Ⓗ $\frac{3}{4}$

Ⓘ 1

19 Aryl has forgotten the correct order of the three numbers of the combination for his bicycle lock. He does remember that the digits of the combination included 2, 3, and 8. How many different orders of the three numbers are there?

Ⓐ 3

Ⓑ 6

Ⓒ 9

Ⓓ 27

20 All of the shapes below have lines of symmetry except which one?

Ⓕ 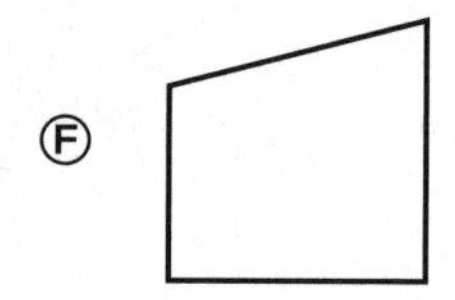

Ⓖ 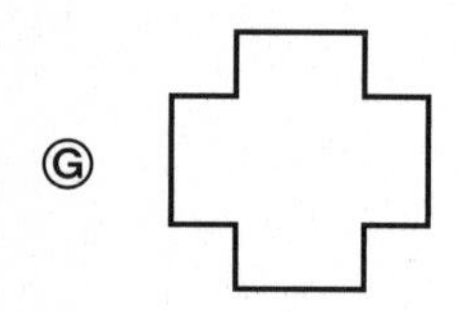

Ⓗ 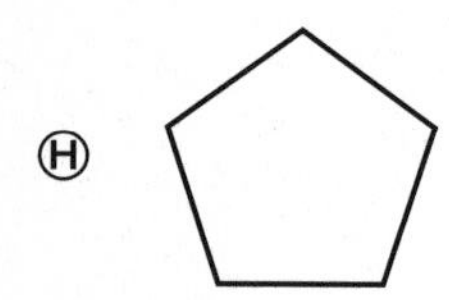

Ⓘ 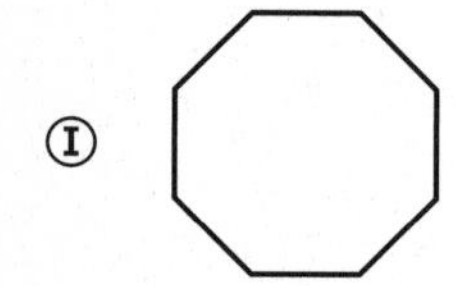

Go On

21 The bar graph below shows the favorite breakfast drinks of some third-grade students.

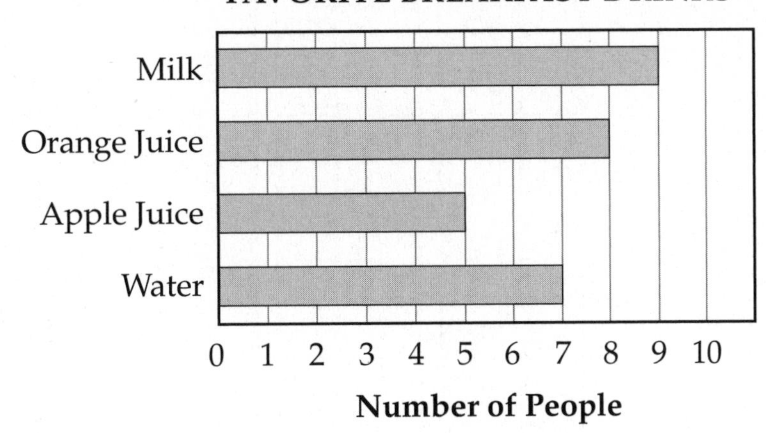

Which chart matches the data in the graph?

Ⓐ

Drink	Milk	Orange Juice	Apple Juice	Water
Number of People	7	5	8	9

Ⓑ

Drink	Milk	Orange Juice	Apple Juice	Water
Number of People	9	8	5	8

Ⓒ

Drink	Milk	Orange Juice	Apple Juice	Water
Number of People	9	17	22	29

Ⓓ

Drink	Milk	Orange Juice	Apple Juice	Water
Number of People	9	8	5	7

Go On

22 What multiplication sentence is shown by this array?

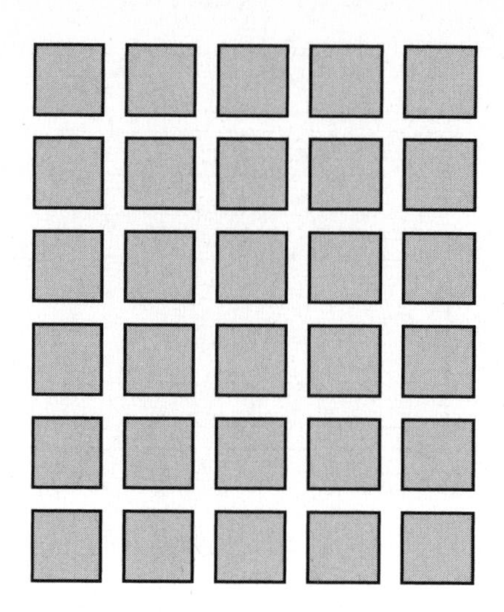

Ⓕ $6 \times 6 = 36$

Ⓖ $5 \times 6 = 30$

Ⓗ $5 \times 5 = 25$

Ⓘ $5 \times 4 = 20$

23 Which mixed number shows the shaded part of these figures?

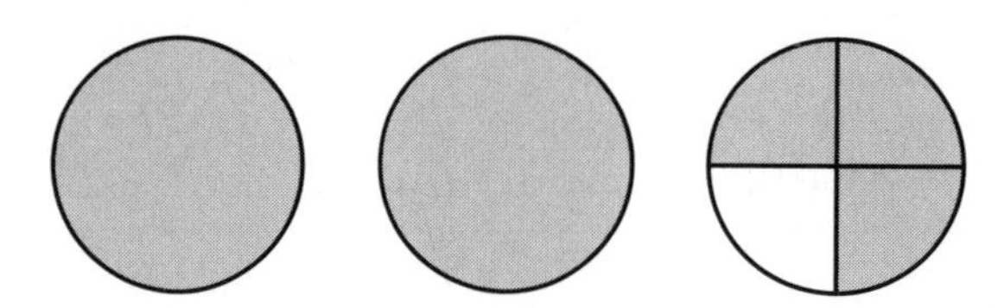

Ⓐ $2\frac{3}{4}$

Ⓑ $2\frac{2}{3}$

Ⓒ $2\frac{1}{4}$

Ⓓ $1\frac{3}{4}$

Go On

24 Below is a diagram of Jade's garden. She will make a stone path in a straight line from point *A* to point *B*. What is the name of the two smaller shapes that this path will form?

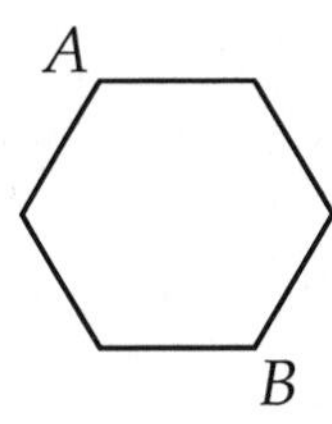

Ⓕ trapezoid

Ⓖ rectangle

Ⓗ triangle

Ⓘ hexagon

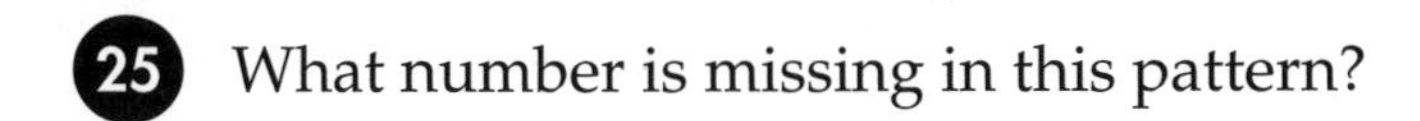

25 What number is missing in this pattern?

3, 6, ____, 12, 15, 18

Ⓐ 8

Ⓑ 9

Ⓒ 10

Ⓓ 21

Go On

26 Eva has three different bows, a box, and a gift bag.

Which shows all the different combinations Eva can make using one bow and one box or bag?

Ⓕ 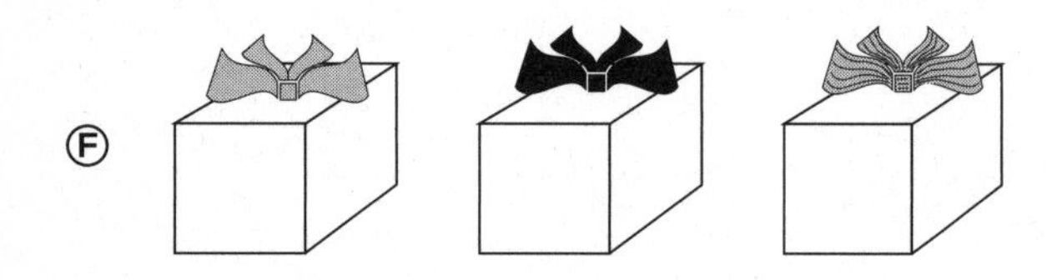

Ⓖ 

Ⓗ 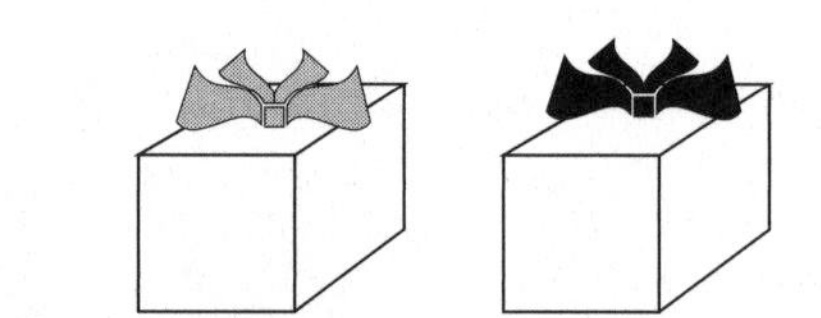

Ⓘ 

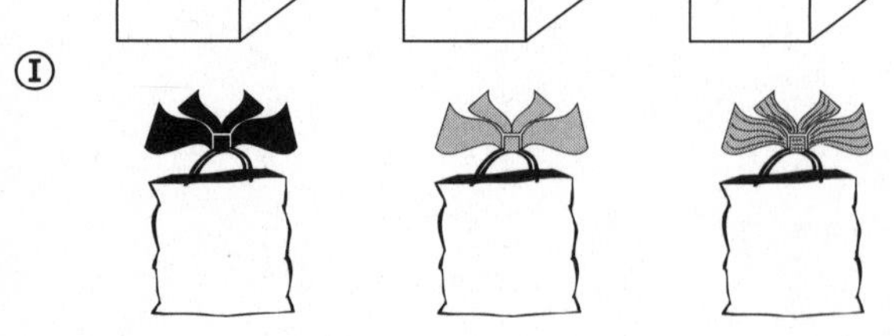

Go On

27 Caleb drew the rectangle below. Use your ruler to measure the rectangle. What is the perimeter of the rectangle?

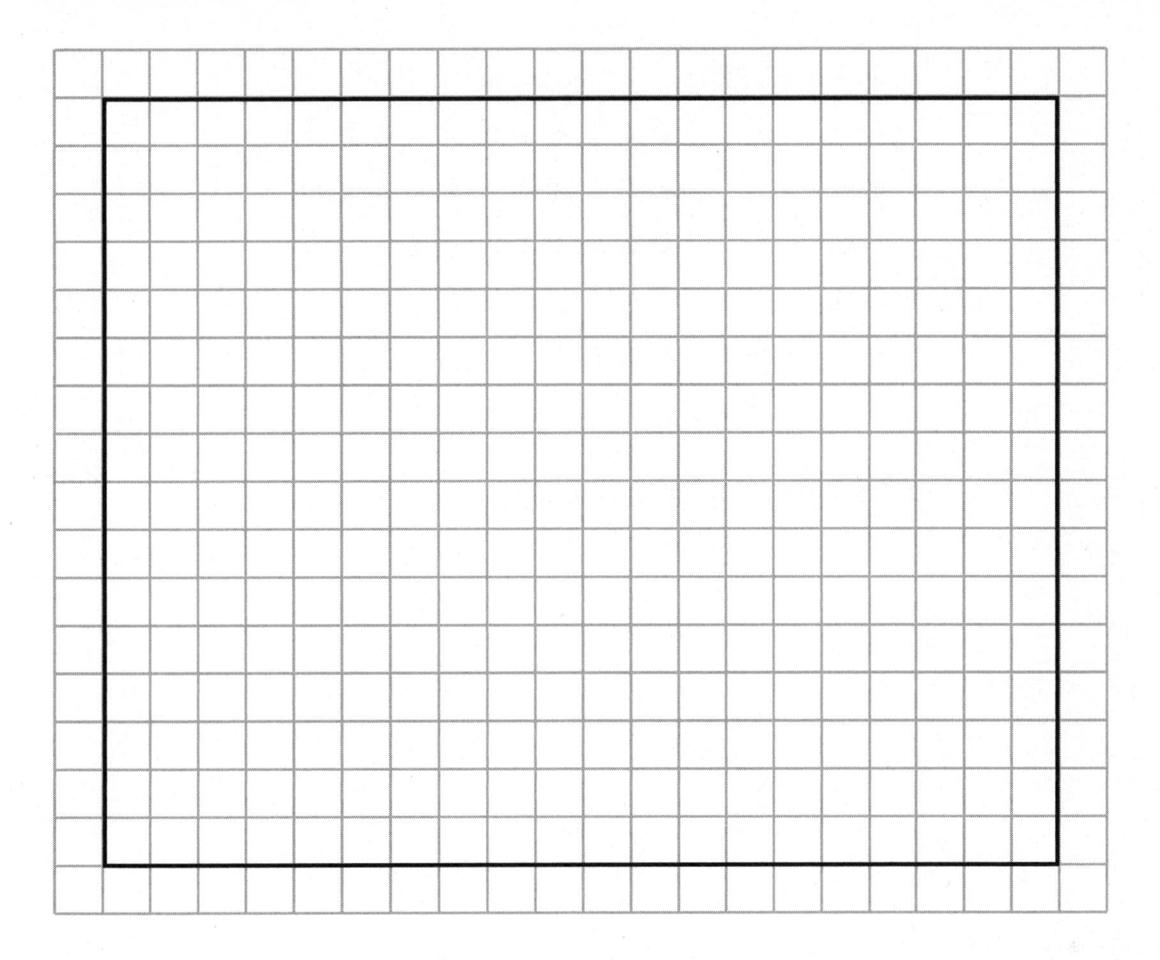

Ⓐ 4 inches

Ⓑ 9 inches

Ⓒ 18 inches

Ⓓ 20 inches

 The pictograph shows the most common types of pets owned by third graders at Lincoln Elementary School.

Kind of Pet	Number of Pets
Dog	▲▲▲▲▲▲▲▲▲▲▲▲
Cat	▲▲▲▲▲▲▲▲▲▲▲
Fish	▲▲▲▲▲▲▲▲▲
Guinea Pig	▲▲▲▲▲▲▲▲
Bird	▲▲▲▲

Each ▲ stands for 2 pets.

How many more cats than guinea pigs are there?

Ⓕ 3

Ⓖ 6

Ⓗ 17

Ⓘ 34

29 Jamie has 24 photos that she wants to put on her display case. The case has 3 shelves. Jamie wants to put the same number of photos on each shelf. Which number sentence shows that P equals the number of photos that she should put on each shelf?

Ⓐ $3 + P = 24$

Ⓑ $24 + 3 = P$

Ⓒ $24 - 3 = P$

Ⓓ $24 \div 3 = P$

Go On

30 Which pair of figures shows fractional parts that are equal?

Ⓕ 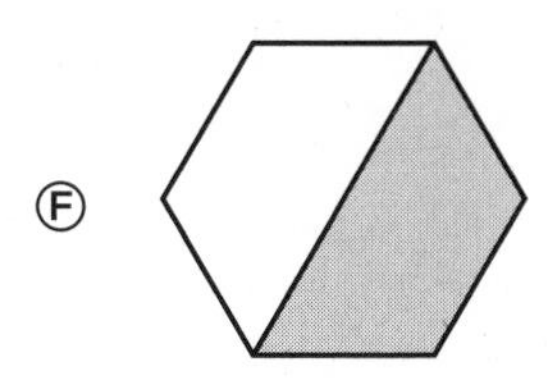 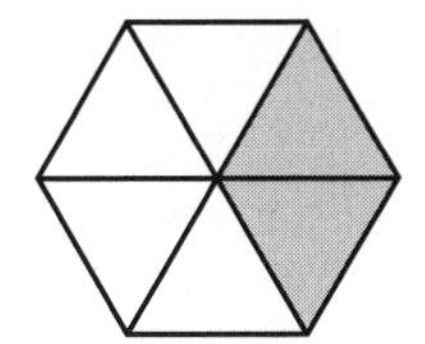

Ⓖ 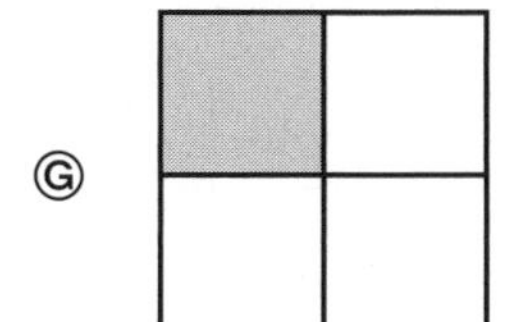 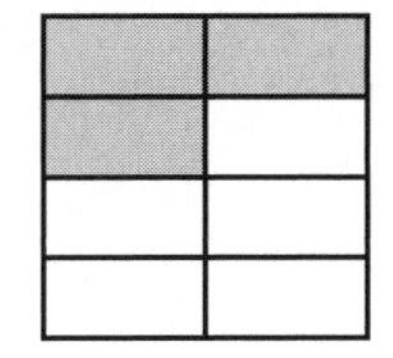

Ⓗ 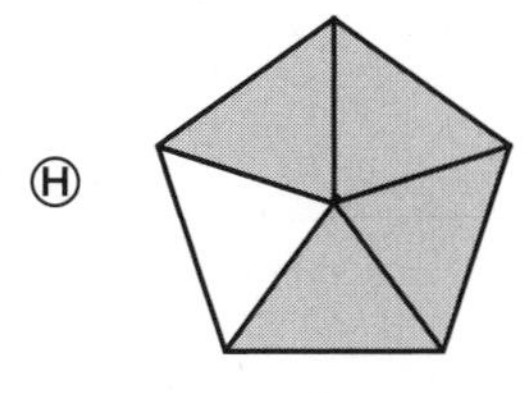 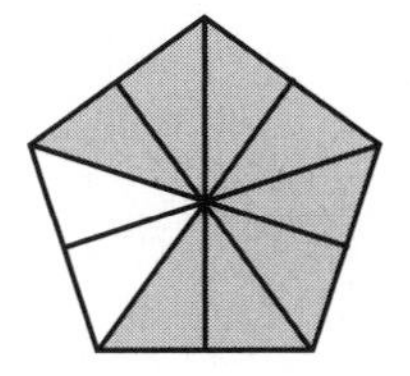

Ⓘ 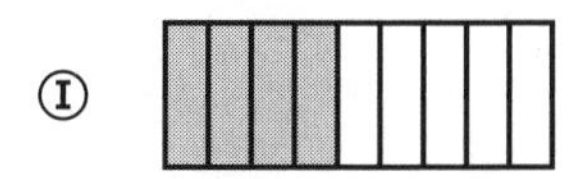 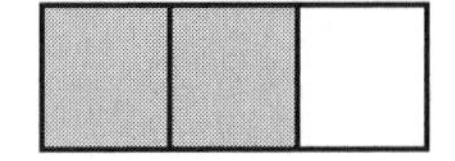

31 The students in Lori's math class lined up in the back of the classroom to play a question and answer game. For each question that a student answered correctly, he or she got to move ahead 2 steps. For each question that a student answered incorrectly, he or she had to move back 1 step. Lori answered 4 questions correctly and 2 questions incorrectly. How many steps ahead of the starting line was Lori after these 6 questions?

Ⓐ 2

Ⓑ 4

Ⓒ 6

Ⓓ 8

32 Four students each added a row to the design of table tennis balls. How many table tennis balls should be put in row 4?

Row 1	○○○○○○○○○○○○
Row 2	○○○○○○○○○
Row 3	○○○○○○
Row 4	

Ⓕ 2

Ⓖ 3

Ⓗ 4

Ⓘ 6

33 Jeff has a sticker on his notebook that is the same size and shape as the figure below. His sticker has a perimeter of 12 centimeters.

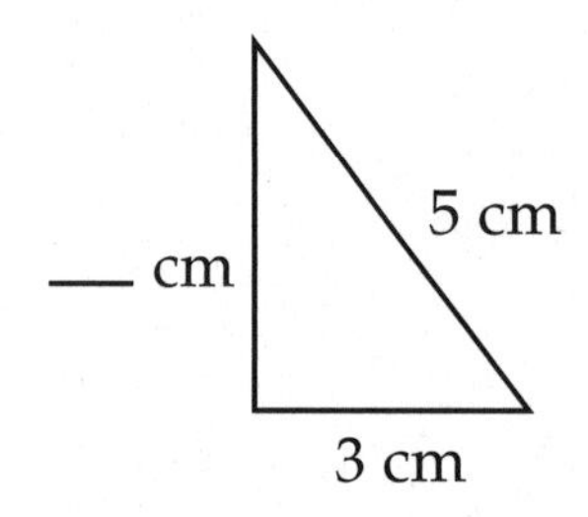

What is the missing measure?

Ⓐ 4 centimeters

Ⓑ 5 centimeters

Ⓒ 6 centimeters

Ⓓ 8 centimeters

Go On

34 Which pair of clocks show the same time?

Ⓕ

Ⓗ

Ⓖ

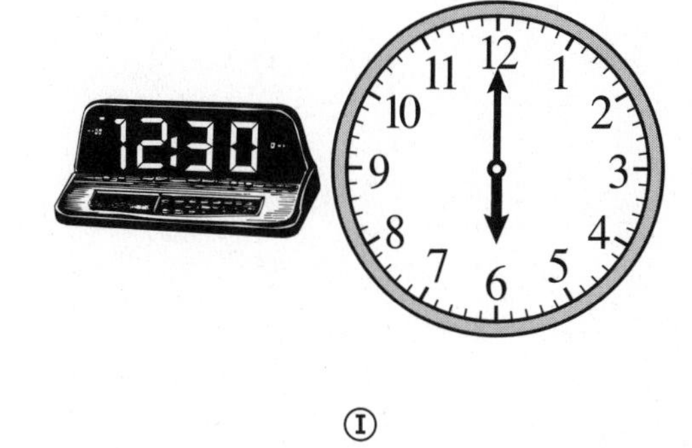

Ⓘ

35 $24 \div 1 =$

Ⓐ 25

Ⓑ 24

Ⓒ 1

Ⓓ 0

Go On

36 Which pair of shapes appears to be congruent?

Ⓕ

Ⓖ 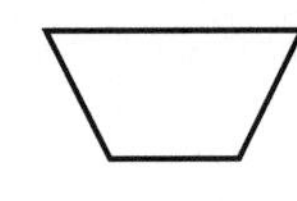

Ⓗ 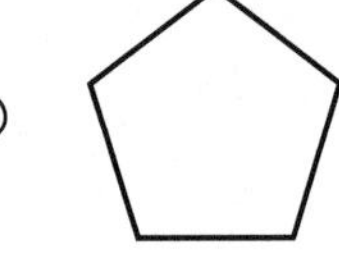 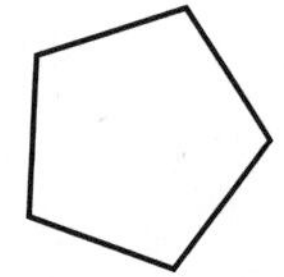

Ⓘ 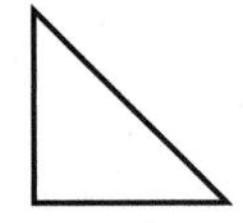

37 The figure below is shaded to represent a fraction.

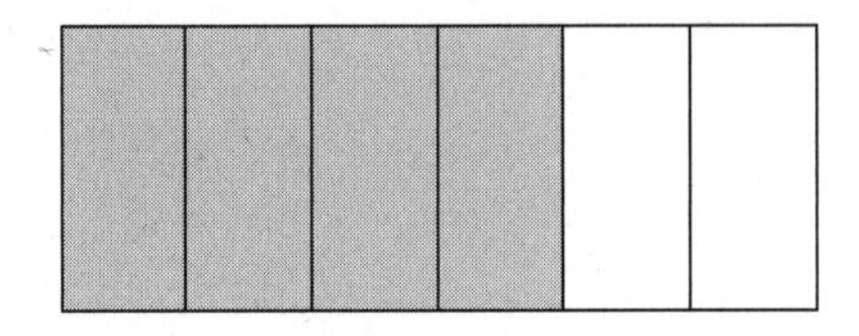

Which fraction has a value equal to the figure above?

Ⓐ $\frac{2}{3}$

Ⓑ $\frac{1}{2}$

Ⓒ $\frac{1}{4}$

Ⓓ $\frac{1}{3}$

Go On

38 Angie spun a spinner 20 times. She landed on red 4 times, on yellow 5 times, and on blue 11 times. Which tally chart shows these results?

Ⓕ

Color	Tally
red	𝍸 𝍸
yellow	𝍸 ||
blue	|||

Ⓖ

Color	Tally
red	||||
yellow	𝍸
blue	𝍸 𝍸 |

Ⓗ

Color	Tally
red	𝍸 ||
yellow	𝍸 |
blue	𝍸 ||

Ⓘ

Color	Tally
red	||
yellow	||
blue	𝍸 𝍸𝍸 |

Go On

39 The dentist gives out a toothbrush and a floss sample to all people who have their teeth cleaned. Toothbrushes are purple, blue, red, or green. The floss comes in cherry, mint, or bubblegum flavors. How many different combinations of color and flavor are possible?

Ⓐ 5

Ⓑ 6

Ⓒ 9

Ⓓ 12

40 What fraction of this group of circles is black?

   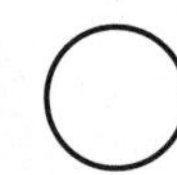    

Ⓕ $\frac{7}{8}$

Ⓖ $\frac{7}{10}$

Ⓗ $\frac{5}{8}$

Ⓘ $\frac{1}{8}$

Go On

41 Luke has 9 baseball cards that he wants to give away to 3 friends. Which shows one way that each friend will get the same number of cards?

Ⓐ 

Ⓑ 

Ⓒ 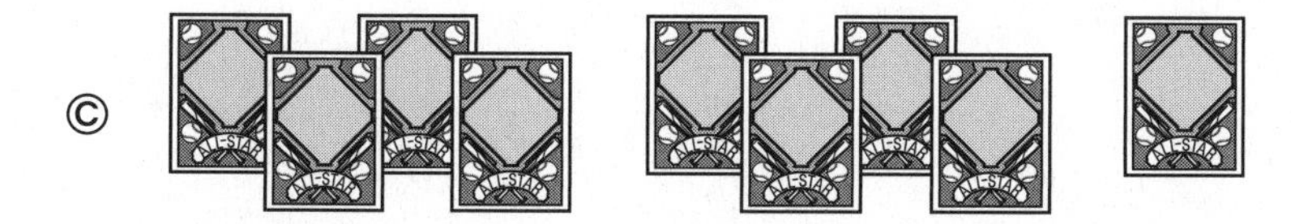

Ⓓ 

42 Which shape **always** has 4 right angles?

Ⓕ rhombus

Ⓖ kite

Ⓗ rectangle

Ⓘ trapezoid

43 The model below shows $1\frac{1}{4}$ shaded.

Which model shows a mixed number that is **less** than $1\frac{1}{4}$?

Ⓐ 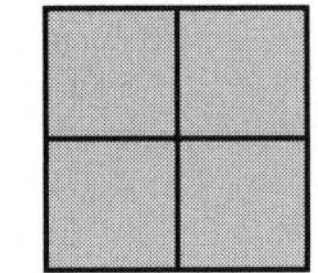 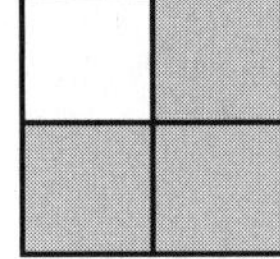

Ⓑ 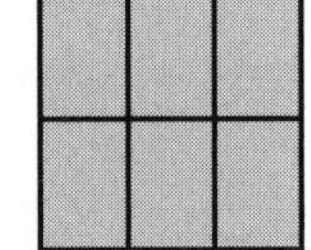 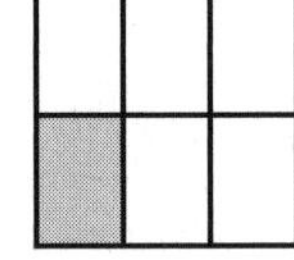

Ⓒ 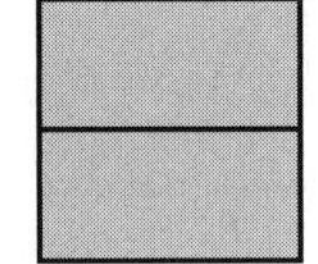 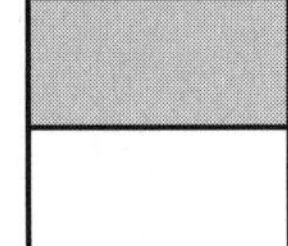

Ⓓ 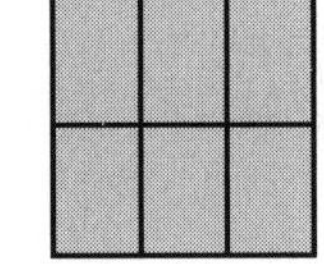 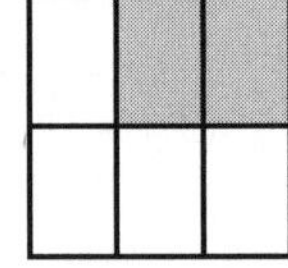

44 Students at Johnson Elementary School raised more than $2,500 at the annual fair. Which statement about $2,500 is true?

Ⓕ $2,200 > $2,500

Ⓖ $2,309 > $2,500

Ⓗ $2,489 > $2,500

Ⓘ $2,532 > $2,500

Go On

45 The objects below are sorted into two groups. What is true about how they are sorted?

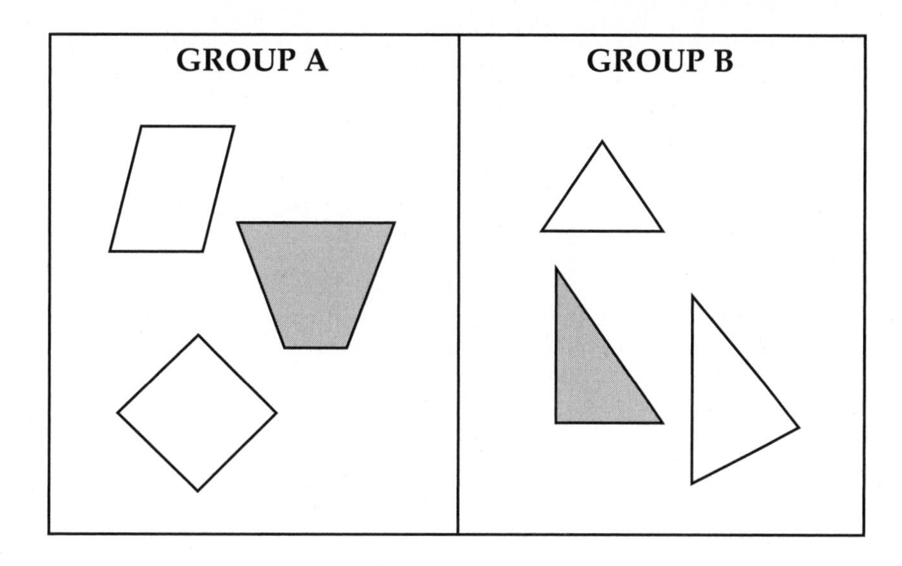

Ⓐ The objects are sorted by size.

Ⓑ The objects are sorted by color and size.

Ⓒ The objects are sorted by the number of sides.

Ⓓ The objects are sorted by color and the number of sides.

Go On

46 Students started this graph to show the number of pages that they read during silent reading.

Student	Number of Pages
Tony	□ □ □ □
Flora	□ □ □ □ □
Lee	
Rudy	□ □ □ □ □ □
Janna	□ □ □ □ □ □ □

Each □ stands for 2 pages.

If Lee read 12 pages, which group of symbols is needed to complete the graph?

Ⓕ □ □ □

Ⓖ □ □ □ □ □ □

Ⓗ □ □ □ □ □ □ □ □

Ⓘ □ □ □ □ □ □ □ □ □ □ □ □

47 Which number must go in the box?

$(3 \times 8) \times 7 = 3 \times (\square \times 7)$

Ⓐ 8

Ⓑ 21

Ⓒ 24

Ⓓ 56

Go On

48 The figure below is a model for the division sentence $48 \div 6 = 8$.

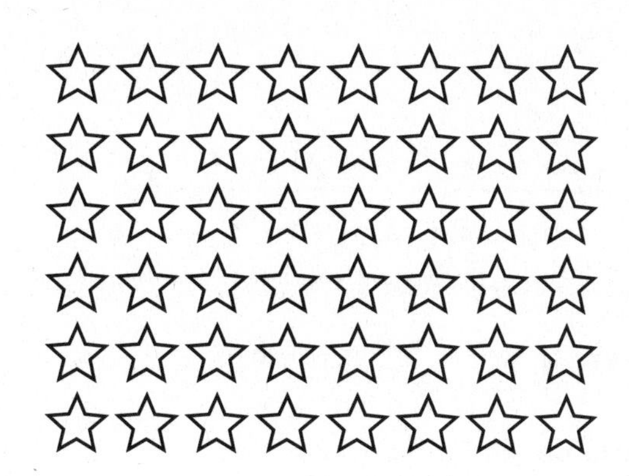

Which multiplication sentence is modeled by the same figure?

Ⓕ $8 \times 4 = 32$

Ⓖ $6 \times 6 = 36$

Ⓗ $6 \times 8 = 48$

Ⓘ $8 \times 8 = 64$

49 Look at the fraction models.

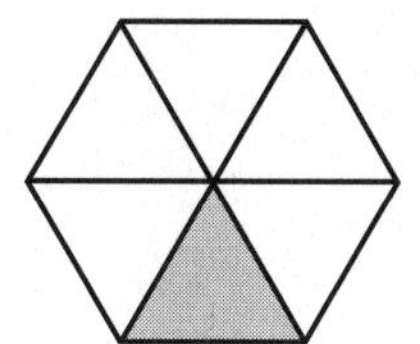 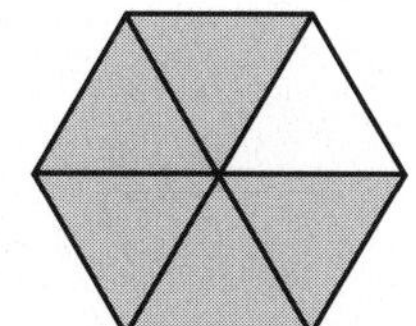 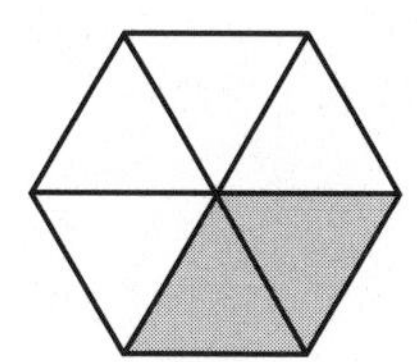 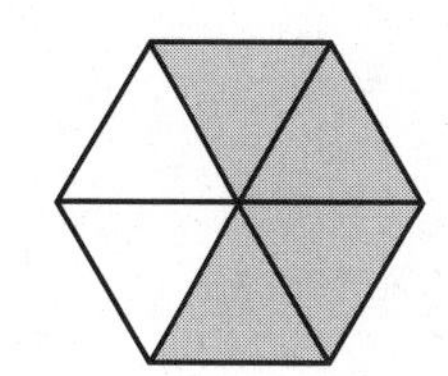

Which list shows the fractions in order from **least** to **greatest**?

Ⓐ $\frac{5}{6}, \frac{4}{6}, \frac{2}{6}, \frac{1}{6}$

Ⓑ $\frac{1}{6}, \frac{2}{6}, \frac{4}{6}, \frac{5}{6}$

Ⓒ $\frac{1}{6}, \frac{2}{6}, \frac{5}{6}, \frac{4}{6}$

Ⓓ $\frac{2}{6}, \frac{1}{6}, \frac{4}{6}, \frac{5}{6}$

50 Jared cut out two shapes, as shown below.

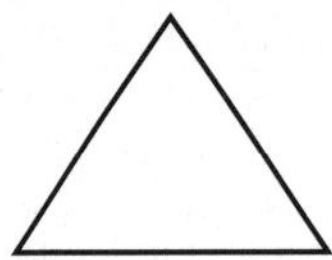
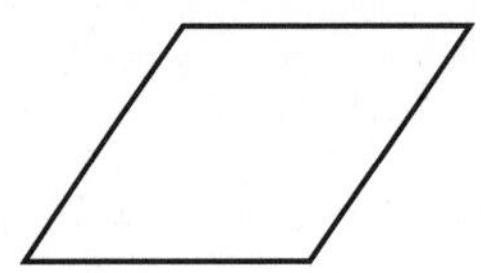

Which of the following shapes could Jared make if he combined the two shapes, without overlapping?

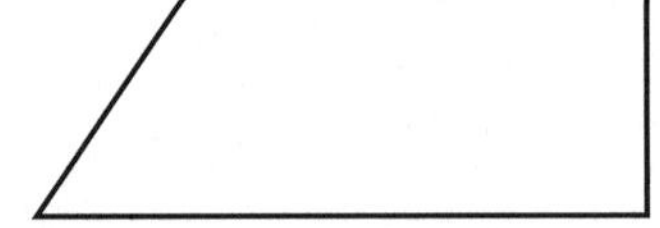

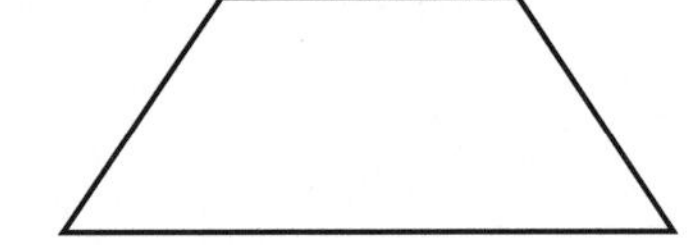

This is the end of the Mathematics Test.
Until time is called, go back and check your work or answer questions you did not complete. When you have finished, close your Test Book.

Lesson 1
Multiplication

NGSSS

MA.3.A.1.1: Model multiplication and division including problems presented in context: repeated addition, multiplicative comparison, array, how many combinations, measurement, and partitioning.

Introduction

In this lesson, you will learn different ways to multiply numbers. You will also review single-digit multiplication facts.

In math, an **operation** tells you what to do with numbers. You might add (+), subtract (–), multiply (×), or divide (÷). An **expression** is a combination of numbers and math operations. It is what you see on one side of an equals sign. 2×2 is an example of an expression.

An **equation** is a number sentence that includes an equals sign. It shows the value of an expression. $2 \times 2 = 4$ is an example of an equation.

In a multiplication number sentence, the numbers you multiply are called **factors**. The answer to a multiplication problem is called the **product**.

You can write a multiplication number sentence to represent the picture below.

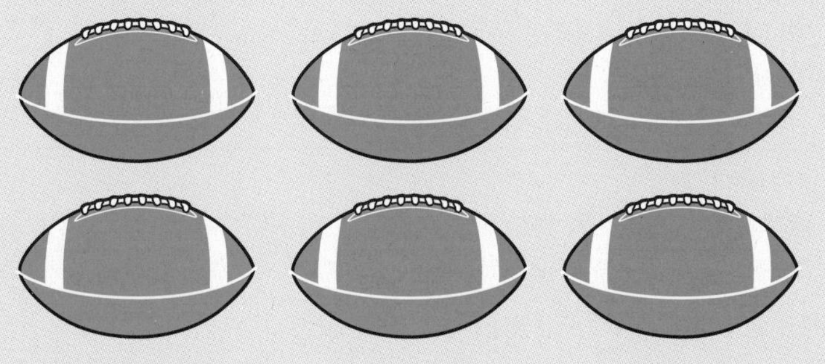

There are 2 rows of footballs, and each row has 3 footballs in it. There are 6 footballs altogether. So, $2 \times 3 = 6$.

Modeled Instruction

EXAMPLE 1

John laid his toy cars out in 5 rows. There are 3 cars in each row. How many toy cars does John have?

Follow these steps to solve the problem.

Step 1 Draw a picture to solve the problem.

There are 5 rows of toy cars and 3 cars in each row.

Step 2 Count the total number of toy cars.

There are 15.

SOLUTION: John has 15 toy cars.

Try It! **Use what you know to solve these problems.**

1 Shawn put apples on the counter in 2 rows. There are 5 apples in each row. How many apples did he buy? ________________

2 Lara drew 3 rows of triangles. She put 4 triangles in each row. How many triangles did she draw? ________________

EXAMPLE 2

Caleb and his classmates are sitting in 5 rows. There are 4 students in each row. How many students are in Caleb's class?

Follow these steps to solve the problem.

Step 1 Find the number of rows and the number of students in each row.

There are 5 rows of 4 students.

Step 2 Add the number of students in each row to itself, once for each row.

This is called repeated addition.

$$4 + 4 + 4 + 4 + 4 = 20$$

4	4	4	4	4
↑	↑	↑	↑	↑
row 1	row 2	row 3	row 4	row 5

SOLUTION: There are 20 students in Caleb's class.

Try It! **Use what you know to solve these problems.**

1 Mrs. Jenkins planted flowers in 3 rows. She planted 7 flowers in each row. How many flowers did she plant? ________________

2 Sandra got a new box of crayons with 4 rows and 8 crayons in each row. How many crayons are in the box? ________________

EXAMPLE 3

Allison is having toast with jam for breakfast. She can choose white or wheat bread. She can also choose raspberry, strawberry, or apricot jam. How many different combinations of bread and jam are possible?

Follow these steps to solve the problem.

Step 1 Find the number of kinds of bread and jam.

There are 2 kinds of bread and 3 kinds of jam.

Step 2 Determine how many combinations are possible for each kind of bread.

There are 3 combinations for each kind of bread: raspberry, strawberry, and apricot.

Step 3 Multiply by the number of kinds of bread.

3×2

SOLUTION: There are 6 possible combinations of bread and jam.

Try It! **Use what you know to solve these problems.**

1 How many different combinations of one fruit and one vegetable are possible with 5 kinds of fruit and 2 kinds of vegetables? ______________________

2 How many different combinations of one swimsuit and one beach towel are possible with 3 different swimsuits and 3 different beach towels? ______________________

Guided Instruction

Read the Think About It to understand the problem. Then solve the problem.

Think About It

You can draw an array to help you find the answer.

Gabby put a pan of cookies in the oven. There are 4 rows of cookies with 6 cookies in each row. How many cookies are on the pan?

A 10

B 16

C 24

D 28

EXPLANATION:

You need to multiply 4 by 6 to find the total number of cookies.

CORRECT ANSWER:

Answer choice **C** is correct.

INCORRECT ANSWERS:

Read why the other choices are not correct.

A 10 is not correct because that is the answer to $4 + 6$, not 4×6.

B 16 is not correct because that is the answer to 4×4, not 4×6.

D 28 is not correct because that is the answer to 4×8, not 4×6.

Guided Practice

Hints

Use repeated addition or multiply to find the answer.

Draw a picture or multiply to find the answer.

Use repeated addition or multiply to find the answer.

Solve each problem. Use the Hints to help you. Then explain how you found your solution.

1 Shanti is 9 years old. Her mom is 4 times Shanti's age. How old is Shanti's mom?

Solution: ______________________________

Explanation: ______________________________

____

____

2 Karina has a rock collection. She put her rocks in 6 rows with 5 rocks in each row. How many rocks does Karina have?

Solution: ______________________________

Explanation: ______________________________

____

____

3 There are 7 bags of apples on the shelf. There are 8 apples in each bag. How many apples are there altogether?

Solution: ______________________________

Explanation: ______________________________

____

____

PAIR SHARE

With your partner, share and discuss your answers and supporting details.

FL Math Practice

1 Chris has posters on his bedroom wall. He has 2 rows of posters with 3 posters in each row. How many posters does Chris have on his wall?

Ⓐ 2

Ⓑ 3

Ⓒ 5

Ⓓ 6

2 Clark lined up his stickers below.

Which expression can be used to find the total number of stickers Clark has?

Ⓕ 3×3

Ⓖ $3 + 5$

Ⓗ 3×5

Ⓘ 3×8

3 A grocery store is selling cherries. There are 3 cherries in each bunch. If Sam buys 8 bunches, how many cherries will he get?

Ⓐ 11

Ⓑ 24

Ⓒ 28

Ⓓ 32

4 Seth scored 7 points in a basketball game. Mike scored 4 times as many points as Seth. How many points did Mike score?

Ⓕ 28

Ⓖ 24

Ⓗ 21

Ⓘ 11

5 Which of the following is equivalent to 5×8?

Ⓐ $5 + 5 + 5 + 5 + 5$

Ⓑ $8 + 8 + 8 + 8 + 8$

Ⓒ $5 + 8 + 5 + 8 + 5 + 8 + 5$

Ⓓ $8 + 8 + 8 + 8 + 8 + 8 + 8 + 8$

6 How many different combinations of one color of socks and one color of shoes can be made from 3 different colors of socks and 4 different colors of shoes?

Ⓕ 7

Ⓖ 10

Ⓗ 12

Ⓘ 15

7 Mariah runs 8 laps around the track each day. How many laps has she run after 6 days?

Ⓐ 14

Ⓑ 42

Ⓒ 44

Ⓓ 48

8 Which multiplication expression is equivalent to $3 + 3 + 3 + 3 + 3 + 3$?

Ⓕ 3×3

Ⓖ 6×3

Ⓗ $6 + 6$

Ⓘ 3×5

9 Trish lined up her crayons below.

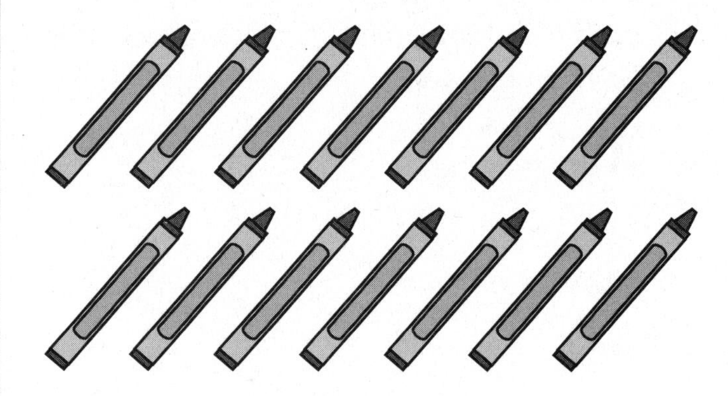

Which expression can be used to find the total number of crayons Trish has?

Ⓐ $2 + 7$

Ⓑ 2×2

Ⓒ 7×7

Ⓓ 7×2

10 Jamie has 9 pennies. Andrew has 6 times as many pennies as Jamie. How many pennies does Andrew have?

Ⓕ 63

Ⓖ 54

Ⓗ 45

Ⓘ 15

Lesson 2
Division

NGSSS

MA.3.A.1.1: Model multiplication and division including problems presented in context: repeated addition, multiplicative comparison, array, how many combinations, measurement, and partitioning.

Introduction

In this lesson, you will use single-digit division facts to solve problems. You will also learn about grouping, repeated subtraction, arrays, and equal sharing as ways to divide.

When you take a set of objects and split them into groups of a certain size, you are **grouping**. If all of the objects fit into **equal-sized groups**, the numbers divide evenly. If there are any left over, there is a **remainder**. The answer to a division problem is called the **quotient**.

- **Divide 9 cookies into groups of 3.**

There are no cookies left over, so there is no remainder. $9 \div 3 = 3$

Repeated subtraction is another way to divide. Start with a certain number and subtract a number again and again until you cannot subtract it any more. The number of times you subtracted is the quotient. If you end with 0, the numbers divide evenly. If not, there is a remainder.

- **Use repeated subtraction to find $12 \div 4$.**

$12 - 4 = 8$ (1 time)
$8 - 4 = 4$ (2 times)
$4 - 4 = 0$ (3 times)

You can subtract 3 times before you get 0. $12 \div 4 = 3$

EXAMPLE 1

A principal handed out Good Citizen awards to 3 third-grade classrooms. He gave the same number of awards to each class. Write a number sentence that shows how many Good Citizen awards he gave to each class.

Follow these steps to solve the problem.

Step 1 Count the total number of Good Citizen awards: 12.

Step 2 Find the number of classrooms the principal handed out awards to: 3.

Step 3 Count the number of awards in each class: 4.

Step 4 Write what the model shows in words. There were 12 awards given equally to 3 classrooms. Each class received 4 awards.

Step 5 Write a number sentence that shows how many awards were given to each class: $12 \div 3 = 4$.

SOLUTION: The number sentence $12 \div 3 = 4$ shows there were 4 awards given to each class.

Try It! **Use what you know to solve this problem.**

1 The model below shows triangles arranged in 2 equal groups. Write a number sentence that shows how many triangles are in each group. ______________________

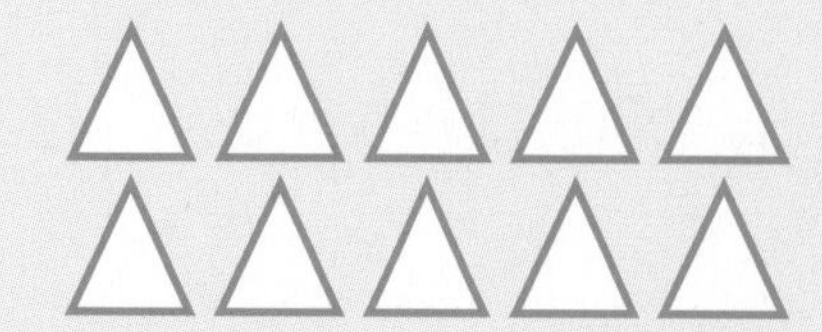

EXAMPLE 2

Mr. Jameson wants to divide his class into groups for a project. There are 20 students in the class. Mr. Jameson wants as many groups of 3 students as possible. How many groups of 3 students will there be?

Follow these steps to solve the problem.

Step 1 Find the number of students in the class and the number in each group. There are 20 students in the class and 3 in each group.

Step 2 Use repeated subtraction to solve the problem. Start with the number of students in the class and subtract the number in each group until you get 0 or cannot subtract any more. Count the number of times you subtracted.

$20 - 3 = 17$ (1 time)
$17 - 3 = 14$ (2 times)
$14 - 3 = 11$ (3 times)
$11 - 3 = 8$ (4 times)
$8 - 3 = 5$ (5 times)
$5 - 3 = 2$ (6 times)

Step 3 Look for a remainder. After subtracting 3 as many times as possible, 2 is left. So the remainder is 2.

SOLUTION: There will be 6 groups of 3 students.

Try It! **Use what you know to solve these problems.**

1 Lucas has 21 books to put on shelves. Each shelf holds 7 books. How many shelves will Lucas need? ____________________

2 Hannah walked 10 miles last week. If she walked the same number of miles each day for 5 days, how many miles did she walk each day? ____________________

EXAMPLE 3

Eli has 15 pennies. He divided them into 3 equal stacks. How many pennies are in each stack?

Follow these steps to solve the problem.

Step 1 Find the number of pennies and the number of stacks. There are 15 pennies divided into 3 equal stacks.

Step 2 Use equal sharing to solve the problem. Label one penny in the picture with a 1 to show it is in the first stack. Then label another penny with a 2 and another with a 3, since there are 3 stacks. Continue labeling pennies 1 through 3 until they all have a number.

Step 3 Count the number of pennies in each stack.

SOLUTION: There are 5 pennies in each stack.

Try It! **Use what you know to solve this problem.**

1 Max and Nora have 8 apples to share between the 2 of them. How many apples will each child receive? ____________

Read the Think About It to understand the problem. Then solve the problem.

Think About It

This is a division question because it is asking about grouping. Try drawing a picture or using repeated subtraction to help you solve the problem.

Nicole bought 28 stickers at a store. The stickers came on sheets with 4 stickers on each sheet. How many sheets of stickers did she buy?

A 4

B 7

C 8

D 14

EXPLANATION:

To get the answer, divide the total number of stickers by the number on each sheet. You can draw a picture of 28 stickers. Group the stickers by 4s. Then count the groups. There are 7 groups. You can also start with 28 and subtract 4 until you cannot subtract any more. Then count the number of times you subtracted. You can subtract 7 times.

CORRECT ANSWER:

Answer choice **B** is correct.

INCORRECT ANSWERS:

Read why the other choices are not correct.

A There are 4 stickers on a sheet, not 4 sheets of stickers.

C If she bought 8 sheets, she would have 32 stickers.

D She would have 14 sheets if there were 2 stickers on a sheet.

Guided Practice

Hints

Split the chocolates into 2 equal groups. How many chocolates are there in each group?

Draw a picture or use repeated subtraction to find the answer.

Use grouping, an array, or repeated subtraction to find the answer.

PAIR SHARE

With your partner, share and discuss your answers and supporting details.

Solve each problem. Use the Hints to help you. Then explain how you found your solution.

1 There are 12 chocolates in a package. If 2 people split the package of chocolates evenly, how many will each person get?

Solution: ______________________________

Explanation: ______________________________

____

2 Olivia is selling wrapping paper for school. The wrapping paper comes on rolls. There are 4 rolls of paper in each box. She sold 36 total rolls of wrapping paper. How many boxes of wrapping paper did she sell?

Solution: ______________________________

Explanation: ______________________________

____

3 Madeleine has a box of crayons. There are 8 rows of crayons in the box, and there are 48 total crayons. How many crayons are in each row?

Solution: ______________________________

Explanation: ______________________________

____

1 Dana has a photo album. The album holds 40 pictures. Each page holds 5 pictures. How many pages are in the album?

Ⓐ 5

Ⓑ 6

Ⓒ 8

Ⓓ 10

2 A tennis coach has 18 tennis balls. She puts them in groups of 6.

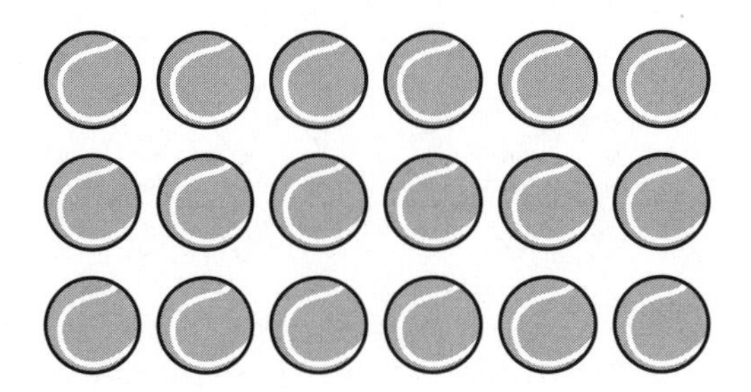

How many groups are there?

Ⓕ 3

Ⓖ 6

Ⓗ 9

Ⓘ 18

3 There are 24 books on 3 shelves in a bookcase. Each shelf has the same number of books on it. Which number sentence shows how many books are on each shelf?

Ⓐ $24 - 3 = 21$

Ⓑ $8 + 3 = 11$

Ⓒ $24 \div 2 = 12$

Ⓓ $24 \div 3 = 8$

4 On Saturday, 7 families are going to the park. Each family has the same number of people. There are 42 people going to the park. How many people are in each family?

Ⓕ 8

Ⓖ 6

Ⓗ 5

Ⓘ 4

5 The picture below shows the number of circles Ramon made. He drew the circles in 4 equal rows.

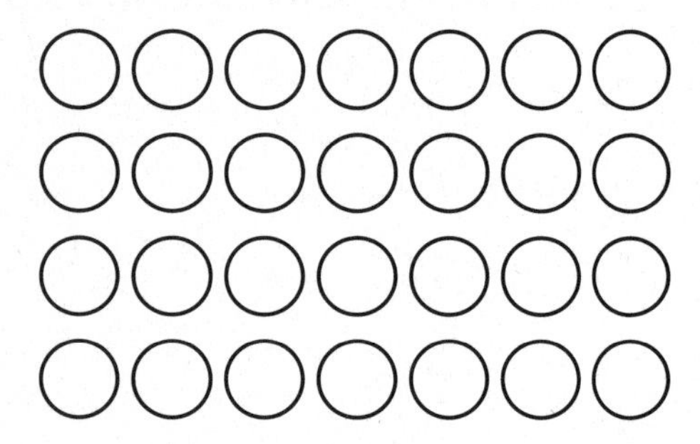

Which number sentence shows how many circles are in each row?

Ⓐ $4 + 7 = 11$

Ⓑ $28 \div 4 = 7$

Ⓒ $28 \div 2 = 14$

Ⓓ $28 - 7 = 21$

6 Kayla plays the flute. To practice, she plays the same number of songs every day. In the last 9 days, she played 54 songs. How many songs does Kayla play each day?

Ⓕ 6

Ⓖ 7

Ⓗ 8

Ⓘ 9

7 Caden's class is going on a field trip. There are 27 students in the class. The tour guide asked the students to get in groups of 9. How many groups are there?

Ⓐ 3

Ⓑ 4

Ⓒ 6

Ⓓ 18

8 The model below shows hearts arranged in 2 equal groups.

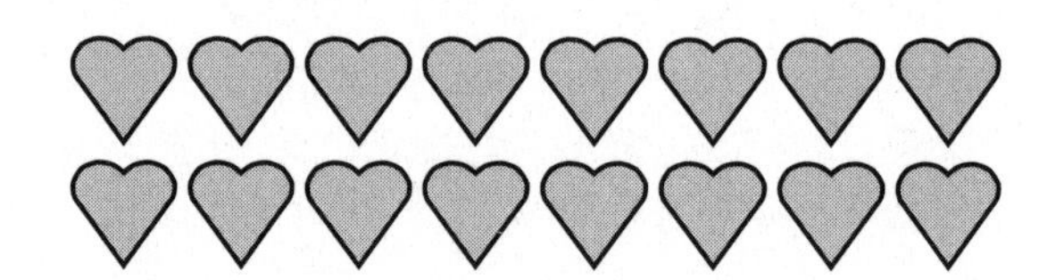

Which number sentence shows how many hearts are in each group?

Ⓕ $14 \div 2 = 7$

Ⓖ $16 \div 2 = 8$

Ⓗ $16 - 2 = 14$

Ⓘ $8 \times 3 = 24$

Lesson 3

Multiplication and Division as Inverse Operations

NGSSS

MA.3.A.1.3: Identify, describe, and apply division and multiplication as inverse operations.

Introduction

Multiplication and division are **inverse operations**, or opposites. When you multiply, you combine equal-sized groups to find the total. When you divide, you start with the total and break it into equal-sized groups. You can use inverse operations to make an equation easier to solve. You can also use inverse operations to check your answer.

- **Rewrite and solve the equation $\square \times 7 = 35$ using inverse operations.**

Step	Result
Identify the operation that is opposite of the one in the equation.	division
Identify the number in the equation that shows the total.	35
Divide the total by the other number in the equation.	$35 \div 7 = \square$
Solve the division problem.	$35 \div 7 = 5$

So, 5 goes in the $\square$ in the original equation: $5 \times 7 = 35$

- **Check the answer to the division problem $24 \div 3 = 8$.**

Step	Result
Identify the operation that is opposite of the one in the equation.	multiplication
Identify the number in the equation that shows the total. This number should be the product when checking the answer.	24
Multiply the other two numbers from the original equation.	8×3
Solve the multiplication problem.	$8 \times 3 = 24$

So, $24 \div 3 = 8$ is correct.

EXAMPLE 1

Jamie planted 32 flowers in her flower garden. She planted the same number of flowers in each row. She planted 4 rows. Write an equation that could be used to find the number of flowers in each row.

Follow these steps to solve the problem.

Step 1 This problem involves a total number and equal-sized groups. Either multiplication or division could be used to solve the problem. In this example, you will write a multiplication equation.

Step 2 Find the number of rows. This is one of the factors.

4

Step 3 Find the number of flowers in each row. This is the other factor.

Use a variable like ◯ because you do not know the number of flowers in each row.

Step 4 Find the total number of flowers. This is the product.

32

SOLUTION: The equation $4 \times ◯ = 32$ could be used to find the number of flowers in each row.

Try It! **Use what you know to solve this problem.**

1 Jeff has 6 bags of marbles. There are the same number of marbles in each bag. Altogether, Jeff has 42 marbles. Write an equation that could be used to find the number of marbles in each bag. ______________________________

EXAMPLE 2

What equation is the inverse of $a \times 3 = 18$?

Follow these steps to solve the problem.

Step 1 Identify the operation that is the opposite of the one used in the original equation. The original equation uses multiplication, so the opposite is division.

Step 2 Identify which number in the original equation shows the total. This will be the first number of the new division equation.

18

Step 3 Divide by one of the factors from the original multiplication equation.

$18 \div 3$

Step 4 Use the other factor as the quotient in the new division equation.

$18 \div 3 = a$

SOLUTION: $18 \div 3 = a$ is the inverse of $a \times 3 = 18$.

Try It! **Use what you know to solve these problems.**

1 What equation is the inverse of $9 \times \square = 54$? ______________

2 What equation is the inverse of ___ $\times 8 = 48$? ______________

3 What equation is the inverse of $2 \times a = 14$? ______________

EXAMPLE 3

Paul earned $49 this summer weeding his neighbor's garden. He was paid the same amount each time, and he weeded the garden 7 times. He wrote the equation 49 ÷ ___ = 7 to determine how much he was paid each time. Use inverse operations to find the answer.

Follow these steps to solve the problem.

Step 1 Identify the operation that is the opposite of the one used in the original equation. The original equation uses division, so the opposite is multiplication.

Step 2 Identify which number in the original equation shows the total. This will be the product in the new multiplication equation.

49

Step 3 Multiply the other number and the variable to complete the equation.

$7 \times$ ___ $= 49$

Step 4 Determine what number belongs in the blank.

$7 \times 7 = 49$

SOLUTION: Paul earned $7 each time he weeded the garden.

Try It!

Use what you know to solve this problem.

1 Emma has 21 coins. She put the same number of coins into each of 3 jars. She wrote the equation $21 \div c = 3$ to find out how many coins were in each jar. Use inverse operations to find the answer. ______________________

Guided Instruction

Read the Think About It to understand the problem. Then solve the problem.

Think About It

Which operation is the inverse of division?

Gabe solved the problem $24 \div 4 = 6$. Which equation could he use to check his answer?

A $24 \div 6 = 4$

B $8 \times 3 = 24$

C $20 + 4 = 24$

D $6 \times 4 = 24$

EXPLANATION:

The equation will use multiplication because it is the opposite of division. It will also use the same numbers as the original equation: 24, 4, and 6.

CORRECT ANSWER:

Answer choice **D** is correct.

EXPLANATION:

Read why the other answer choices are not correct.

A $24 \div 6 = 4$ is not correct because it does not use the inverse operation.

B $8 \times 3 = 24$ is not correct because it does not contain the same numbers as the original equation.

C $20 + 4 = 24$ is not correct because it does not use the inverse operation or contain the same numbers as the original equation.

Hints

The total number of pieces of pie is 64. Be sure to put the total at the correct place in the equation you write.

What numbers will the division equation include?

Use inverse operations to write a division number sentence to find the answer.

Solve each problem. Use the Hints to help you. Then explain how you found your solution.

1 Molly's mom baked some pies for the bake sale at school. She cut each pie into 8 pieces. Altogether, there are 64 pieces of pie. Write an equation that could be used to find the number of pies Molly's mom baked.

Solution: ______________________

Explanation: ______________________

____

____

2 Will solved the multiplication problem $4 \times 9 = 36$. Write a division equation that Will could use to check his answer.

Solution: ______________________

Explanation: ______________________

____

____

3 In Lily's art class, the students sit in groups at tables. There are 4 students at each table. There are 20 students in the class. Lily wrote the equation $\square \times 4 = 20$ to determine how many tables there are. Use inverse operations to find the answer.

Solution: ______________________

Explanation: ______________________

____

____

PAIR SHARE

With your partner, share and discuss your answers and supporting details.

FL Math Practice

1 A group of 18 students is getting on a bus. Each seat on the bus holds 2 people. Which equation could be used to find the number of seats needed to hold all 18 students?

Ⓐ $18 \times 2 = s$

Ⓑ $18 + 2 = s$

Ⓒ $2 \times s = 18$

Ⓓ $2 + s = 18$

2 Mason bought some bunches of bananas at the grocery store. There were 6 bananas in each bunch. Altogether, there are 36 bananas. He wrote the equation below to help him find out how many bunches he bought.

$$\square \times 6 = 36$$

How many bunches of bananas did Mason buy?

Ⓕ 4

Ⓖ 6

Ⓗ 8

Ⓘ 9

3 Which equation is the inverse of $8 \times 5 = 40$?

Ⓐ $40 \div 8 = 5$

Ⓑ $40 - 8 = 32$

Ⓒ $5 \times 8 = 40$

Ⓓ $4 \times 10 = 40$

4 Alissa has 27 stickers. She wants to divide them evenly among 3 of her friends. She wrote the equation below to help her figure out how many to give to each friend.

$$27 \div \_\_\_ = 3$$

How many stickers should Alissa give to each friend?

Ⓕ 6

Ⓖ 7

Ⓗ 8

Ⓘ 9

5 Which equation is the inverse of $t \div 4 = 4$?

Ⓐ $4 + 4 = t$

Ⓑ $4 \times 4 = t$

Ⓒ $4 \times t = 16$

Ⓓ $4 \div 4 = t$

6 Mikayla solved the multiplication problem $9 \times 8 = 72$. Which number sentence can she use to check her answer?

Ⓕ $9 + 8 = 17$

Ⓖ $8 \times 8 = 81$

Ⓗ $72 - 8 = 64$

Ⓘ $72 \div 8 = 9$

7 Which equation is the inverse of $8 \times 2 = \bigcirc$?

Ⓐ $\bigcirc - 2 = 8$

Ⓑ $\bigcirc \times 2 = 8$

Ⓒ $\bigcirc \div 2 = 8$

Ⓓ $\bigcirc + 2 = 8$

8 Kate has been on vacation for 28 days. She wants to figure out how many weeks she has been on vacation. There are 7 days in a week. Which equation could be used to find the number of weeks that Kate has been on vacation?

Ⓕ $28 \div \square = 7$

Ⓖ $28 \times 7 = \square$

Ⓗ $\square \div 7 = 28$

Ⓘ $7 + \square = 28$

9 Corbin solved the division problem $10 \div 5 = 2$. Which number sentence can he use to check his answer?

Ⓐ $2 + 5 = 7$

Ⓑ $5 - 2 = 3$

Ⓒ $2 \times 5 = 10$

Ⓓ $10 - 5 = 5$

Lesson 4
Number Properties

NGSSS

MA.3.A.1.2: Solve multiplication and division fact problems by using strategies that result from applying number properties.

Introduction

In this lesson, you will learn about multiplication and division number properties. You can apply these number properties to help you solve multiplication and division problems.

- **The following table shows number properties for multiplication and division.**

Number Property	What It Says	Examples
Commutative Property for Multiplication	The order of factors does not change the product.	$3 \times 5 = 5 \times 3$ $a \times b = b \times a$
Associative Property for Multiplication	The grouping of factors does not change the product.	$(2 \times 3) \times 4 = 2 \times (3 \times 4)$ $(a \times b) \times c = a \times (b \times c)$
Distributive Property	You can use addition and multiplication to break a problem into parts.	$6 \times (2 + 5) = (6 \times 2) + (6 \times 5)$ $a \times (b + c) = (a \times b) + (a \times c)$
Identity Property for Multiplication	The product of any number and 1 is the number.	$9 \times 1 = 9$ $a \times 1 = a$
Zero Property for Multiplication	The product of any number and 0 is 0.	$8 \times 0 = 0$ $a \times 0 = 0$
Identity Property for Division	The quotient of any number divided by 1 is the number.	$5 \div 1 = 5$ $a \div 1 = a$

EXAMPLE 1

Write an expression equivalent to 6×8.

Follow these steps to solve the problem.

Step 1 Rewrite the expression.

6×8

Step 2 Change the order of the numbers in the expression.

8×6

Step 3 Check to see that the expressions are equivalent.

$6 \times 8 = 8 \times 6$

$48 = 48$

SOLUTION: 8×6 is an equivalent expression to 6×8.
This shows the commutative property of multiplication.

Try It! **Use what you know to solve these problems.**

1 Write an expression equivalent to 5×4. ____________________

2 Write an expression equivalent to 3×7. ____________________

3 Write an expression equivalent to 2×9. ____________________

EXAMPLE 2

Write an expression equivalent to $(5 \times 2) \times 4$.

Follow these steps to solve the problem.

Step 1 Rewrite the expression without any parentheses.

$5 \times 2 \times 4$

Step 2 Insert parentheses around a different pair of numbers in the expression.

$5 \times (2 \times 4)$

Step 3 Check to see that the expressions are equivalent.

$$(5 \times 2) \times 4 = 5 \times (2 \times 4)$$
$$10 \times 4 = 5 \times 8$$
$$40 = 40$$

SOLUTION: $5 \times (2 \times 4)$ is an equivalent expression to $(5 \times 2) \times 4$. This shows the associative property of multiplication.

Try It! **Use what you know to solve these problems.**

1 Write an expression equivalent to $(3 \times 6) \times 1$. ______________

2 Write an expression equivalent to $7 \times (2 \times 5)$. ______________

3 Write an expression equivalent to $(2 \times 4) \times 9$. ______________

EXAMPLE 3

Write an expression equivalent to $6 \times (5 + 2)$.

Follow these steps to solve the problem.

Step 1 Rewrite the expression.

$6 \times (5 + 2)$

Step 2 Rewrite the expression using the distributive property. Multiply each number in the parentheses by 6 and add them together.

$(6 \times 5) + (6 \times 2)$

Step 3 Check to see that the expressions are equivalent.

$$6 \times (5 + 2) = (6 \times 5) + (6 \times 2)$$
$$6 \times 7 = 30 + 12$$
$$42 = 42$$

SOLUTION: $(6 \times 5) + (6 \times 2)$ is an equivalent expression to $6 \times (5 + 2)$.

Try It! **Use what you know to solve these problems.**

1 Write an expression equivalent to $3 \times (9 + 4)$. ______________

2 Write an expression equivalent to $2 \times (7 + 7)$. ______________

3 Write an expression equivalent to $5 \times (8 + 3)$. ______________

Read the Think About It to understand the problem. Then solve the problem.

Think About It

This problem asks you to find an equivalent expression. You may have to use more than one number property to find the answer.

Which expression is equal to $(6 \times 3) \times 8$?

A $(6 + 3) \times 8$

B $3 \times (6 \times 8)$

C 9×8

D $6 \times (3 + 8)$

EXPLANATION:

Look for an expression that uses the same numbers and symbols but has the numbers in a different order and parentheses around a different pair of numbers. You will be using the associative property of multiplication.

CORRECT ANSWER:

Answer choice **B** is correct.

INCORRECT ANSWERS:

A The expression $(6 + 3) \times 8$ is not correct because it has a + instead of a × between the 6 and the 3.

C The expression 9×8 is not correct because the numbers inside the parentheses were added to get 9 and not multiplied.

D The expression $6 \times (3 + 8)$ is not correct because it has a + instead of a × between the 3 and the 8.

Guided Practice

Hints

You don't have to actually multiply to find the answer. Use what you know to write an equivalent expression.

Use the number from the opposite side of the equal sign to figure out what goes in the blank.

Check to see if the two sides are equal. Then figure out why or why not for the explanation.

PAIR SHARE

With your partner, share and discuss your answers and supporting details.

Solve each problem. Use the Hints to help you. Then explain how you found your solution.

1 Martin has a scrapbook with 8 pages. There are 5 photos on each page. He used the expression 8×5 to find the total number of photos in the scrapbook. Write an expression equivalent to 8×5.

Solution: ______________________________

Explanation: ______________________________

____

____

2 What number goes in the blank to make the following number sentence true? Rewrite the entire number sentence on the solution line.

$\_\_\_ \div 1 = 6$

Solution: ______________________________

Explanation: ______________________________

____

____

3 Is the following number sentence correct?

$(7 + 9) \times 2 = 9 \times 11$

Solution: ______________________________

Explanation: ______________________________

____

____

FL Math Practice

1 Molly wrote the number sentence below.

$8 \times \_\_ = 0$

What number goes in the blank to make the number sentence true?

Ⓐ 0

Ⓑ 1

Ⓒ 8

Ⓓ 16

2 Which number sentence is true?

Ⓕ $4 \div 1 = 0$

Ⓖ $1 \div 4 = 4$

Ⓗ $4 \div 1 = 4$

Ⓘ $4 \div 0 = 0$

3 Aiden wrote the expression below.

$7 \times (1 \times 8)$

Which expression is equivalent to Aiden's expression?

Ⓐ 7×8

Ⓑ 7×9

Ⓒ $7 \times (1 + 8)$

Ⓓ $(7 + 1) \times 8$

4 Marco has 2 packages of red napkins and 4 packages of blue napkins. There are 8 napkins in each package. He wrote the following expression to find the total number of napkins.

$(2 + 4) \times 8$

Which expression is equivalent to Marco's expression?

Ⓕ $6 + 8$

Ⓖ 8×8

Ⓗ $8 + 8$

Ⓘ $16 + 32$

5 Which statement is correct?

Ⓐ $6 \times 4 = 4 + 6$

Ⓑ $6 \times 4 = 4 \times 6$

Ⓒ $6 \times 4 = 3 + 2 \times 4$

Ⓓ $6 \times 4 = 6 \times 2 + 2$

6 Trina has 7 crayons in her desk. She also has 4 other boxes of crayons with 8 crayons in each box. The expression below represent the total number of crayons Trina has.

$7 + (4 \times 8)$

Which expression also represents the total number of crayons Trina has?

Ⓕ $7 + 12$

Ⓖ $(7 \times 4) + (7 \times 8)$

Ⓗ $(7 + 4) \times (7 + 8)$

Ⓘ $(4 \times 8) + 7$

7 Which number sentence is true?

Ⓐ $5 \times 1 = 1$

Ⓑ $5 \times 1 = 5$

Ⓒ $5 \times 5 = 1$

Ⓓ $5 \times 5 = 5$

8 Missy wrote the expression below.

$4 \times (9 \times 6)$

Which expression is equivalent to Missy's expression?

Ⓕ 4×15

Ⓖ 13×6

Ⓗ $(4 \times 9) \times (4 \times 6))$

Ⓘ $(6 \times 4) \times 9$

9 Ava needs to solve the multiplication problem 6×9. She rewrote the problem to help her solve it using smaller parts. Which of the following shows how Ava could have rewritten the problem?

Ⓐ $9 \times 3 + 3$

Ⓑ $6 \times (5 + 4)$

Ⓒ $6 \times 9 \times 1$

Ⓓ $9 \times (1 \times 6)$

Lesson 5
Modeling Fractions

NGSSS

MA.3.A.2.1: Represent fractions, including fractions greater than one, using area, set, and linear models.

Introduction

A **fraction** stands for part of a whole or part of a set. Think about cutting a pie into slices. Each slice is a part of the whole. Think about a pair of shoes. Each shoe is part of the set.

The **numerator** tells the number of parts of the whole that are special in some way. It is the top number. The **denominator** tells the total number of equal parts in the whole. It is the bottom number.

Look at the circle below. It has 4 equal parts. There is 1 shaded part. The numerator tells about the shaded part. The denominator tells the total number of equal parts in the whole circle.

$$\frac{\text{numerator}}{\text{denominator}} = \frac{1}{4}$$

A fraction that is greater than one can be written as a **mixed number**. A mixed number has a whole number part and a fraction part.

- **To find the mixed number represented by the figure below:**

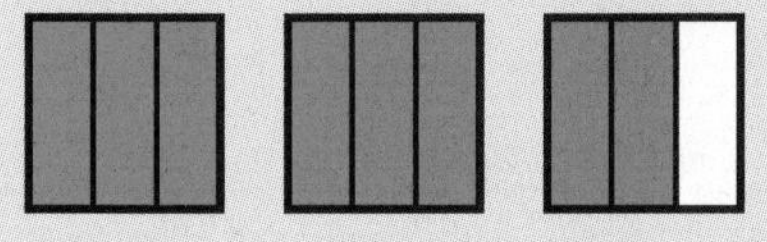

Find the number of whole squares that are shaded.	2
Find the fraction of the third square that is shaded.	$\frac{2}{3}$
Write the whole number and fraction parts together.	$2\frac{2}{3}$

So, the mixed number $2\frac{2}{3}$ represents the figure above.

EXAMPLE 1

What fraction of this set of buttons is white?

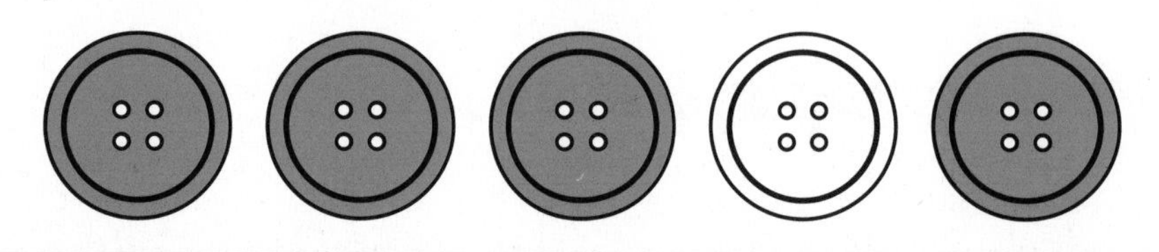

Follow these steps to solve the problem.

Step 1 Find the total number of equal parts in the set.

There are 5 buttons in the whole set.

Step 2 Find the number of white parts in the set.

There is 1 white button in the set.

Step 3 Write this as a fraction.

$$\frac{\text{numerator}}{\text{denominator}} = \frac{\text{number of white buttons}}{\text{total number of buttons}} = \frac{1}{5}$$

SOLUTION: The fraction of the set that is white is $\frac{1}{5}$.

Try It! **Use what you know to solve this problem.**

1 What fraction of the T-shirts are red? ______________

EXAMPLE 2

What fraction of the circle is shaded?

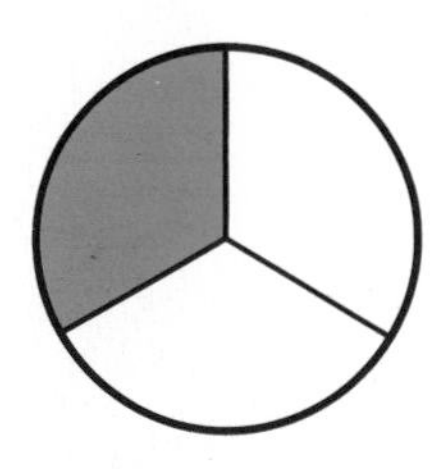

Follow these steps to solve the problem.

Step 1 Find the total number of equal parts in the circle.

There are 3 equal parts.

Step 2 Find the number of shaded parts in the circle.

There is 1 shaded part.

Step 3 Write this as a fraction.

$$\frac{\text{numerator}}{\text{denominator}} = \frac{\text{number of shaded parts}}{\text{total number of parts}} = \frac{1}{3}$$

SOLUTION: The circle is $\frac{1}{3}$ shaded.

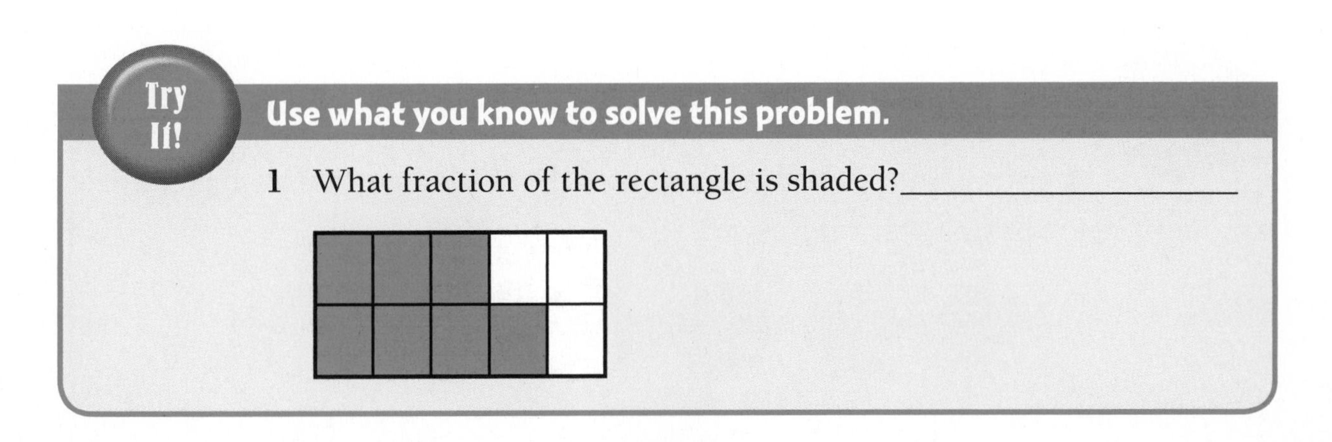

Modeled Instruction

EXAMPLE 3

What mixed number represents the shaded portion of the figure below?

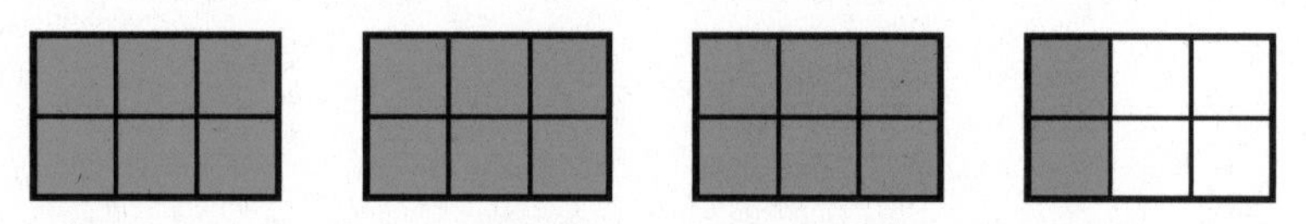

Follow these steps to solve the problem.

Step 1 Find the number of whole rectangles that are shaded.

There are 3 whole rectangles shaded.

Step 2 Find the fraction of the fourth rectangle that is shaded.

$\frac{2}{6}$ of the fourth rectangle is shaded.

Step 3 Write the whole number and fraction parts of the mixed number together: $3\frac{2}{6}$.

SOLUTION: The mixed number $3\frac{2}{6}$ represents the shaded portion of the figure.

Try It! **Use what you know to solve this problem.**

1 What mixed number represents the shaded portion of the figure below? ______________________

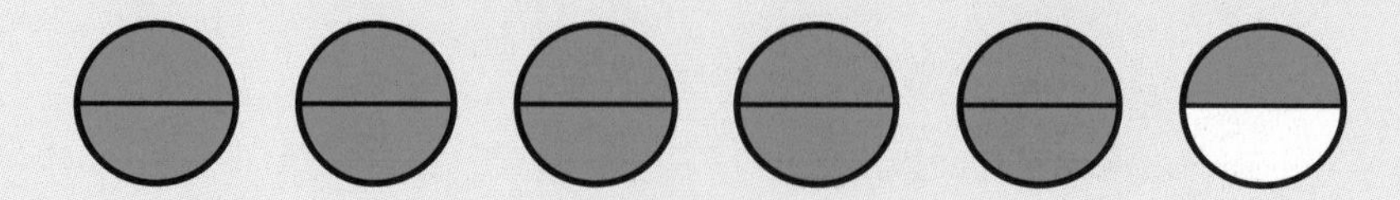

**Read the Think About It to understand the problem.
Then solve the problem.**

Think About It

Can any of the circles be combined to form another whole?

Sue drew four circles and shaded parts of each one.

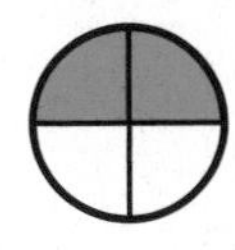 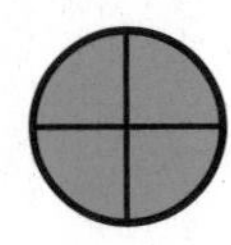 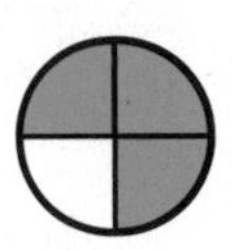 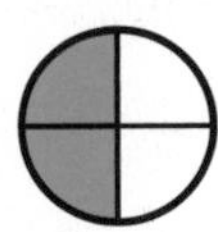

What mixed number is represented by the shading of the four circles above?

A $2\frac{1}{2}$

B $3\frac{3}{4}$

C $2\frac{3}{4}$

D $3\frac{1}{2}$

EXPLANATION:

You can combine the first and fourth circles to make one whole. There is one other whole circle shaded, and $\frac{3}{4}$ of another circle shaded.

CORRECT ANSWER:

Answer choice **C** is correct.

INCORRECT ANSWERS:

A is not correct because there are more than $2\frac{1}{2}$ circles shaded.

B is not correct because there are fewer than $3\frac{3}{4}$ circles shaded.

D is not correct because there are fewer than $3\frac{1}{2}$ circles shaded.

Guided Practice

Hints

How many ties are there total? That will be your denominator.

Read the question again. Are you looking for the shaded or the unshaded sections?

What two whole numbers is point *A* between? How many equal parts is the line divided into between these whole numbers?

Solve each problem. Use the Hints to help you. Then explain how you found your solution.

1 What fraction of the ties have stripes?

Solution: ______________________________

Explanation: ______________________________

____

2 What fraction of the rectangle is not shaded?

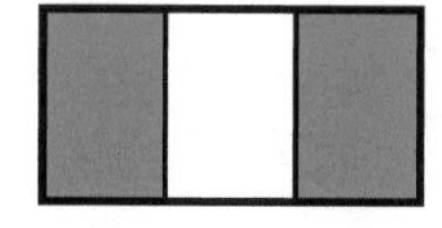

Solution: ______________________________

Explanation: ______________________________

____

3 Look at the number line below. What mixed number is represented by point *A*?

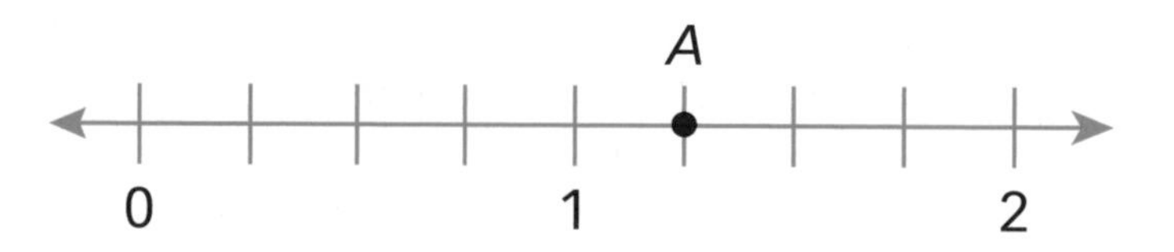

Solution: ______________________________

Explanation: ______________________________

____

With your partner, share and discuss your answers and supporting details.

FL Math Practice

1 Which set is $\frac{4}{7}$ shaded?

Ⓐ 

Ⓑ

Ⓒ 

Ⓓ

2 Isaiah drew two squares and shaded parts of each square.

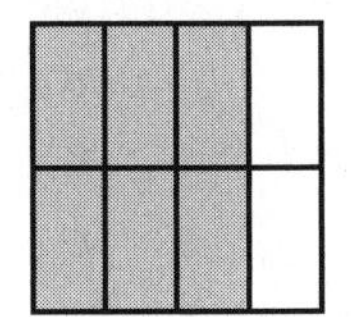 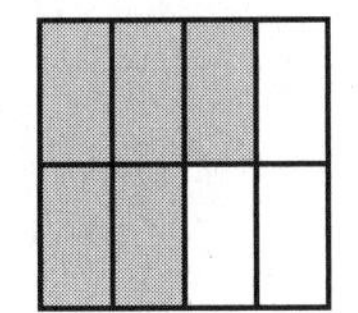

What mixed number is represented by the shading of the two squares above?

Ⓕ $1\frac{5}{8}$

Ⓖ $1\frac{3}{8}$

Ⓗ $2\frac{1}{8}$

Ⓘ $1\frac{1}{8}$

3 What mixed number is represented by point *B* on the number line below?

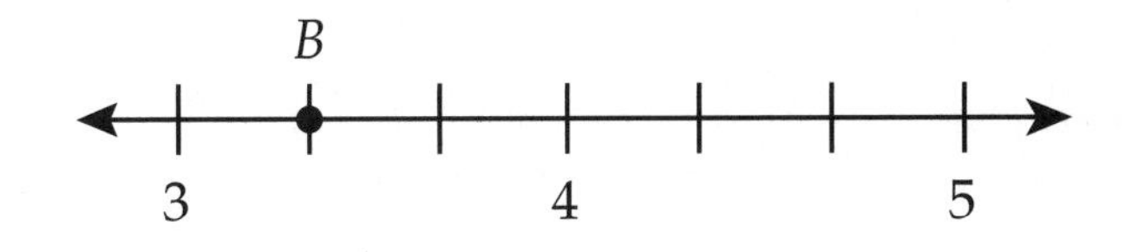

Ⓐ $3\frac{1}{3}$

Ⓑ $3\frac{1}{2}$

Ⓒ $3\frac{2}{3}$

Ⓓ $4\frac{1}{3}$

4 Which set shows $\frac{5}{8}$ of the balloons shaded?

Ⓕ 

Ⓖ 

Ⓗ 

Ⓘ 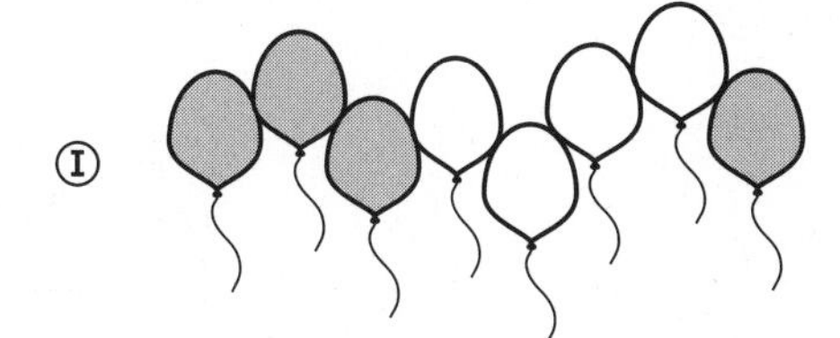

5 What fraction is represented by point M on the number line below?

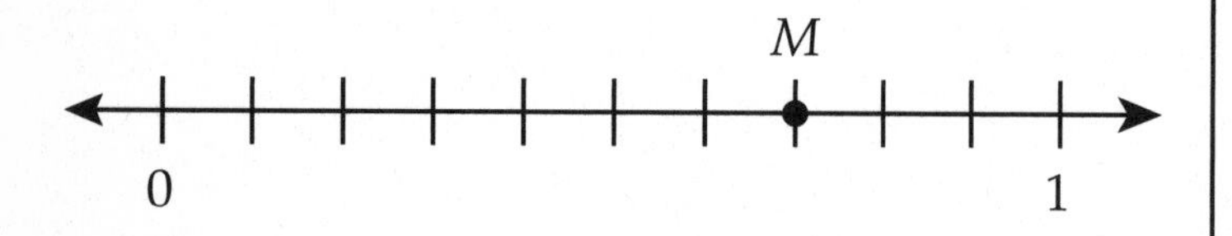

Ⓐ $\frac{8}{11}$

Ⓑ $\frac{8}{10}$

Ⓒ $\frac{7}{10}$

Ⓓ $\frac{7}{9}$

6 Mr. Scott gave his students a list of 6 books to read.

Student	Set of Books
Anthony	
Emma	
Lauren	
Jaiden	

Which student read $\frac{4}{6}$ of the books?

Ⓕ Anthony

Ⓖ Emma

Ⓗ Lauren

Ⓘ Jaiden

7 Which figure shows $\frac{3}{9}$ shaded?

Ⓐ 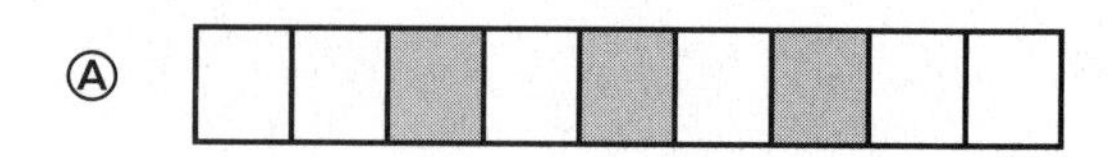

Ⓑ 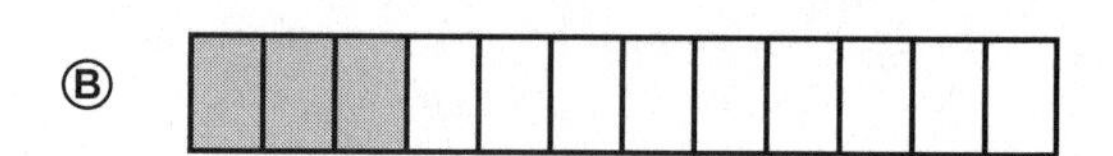

Ⓒ 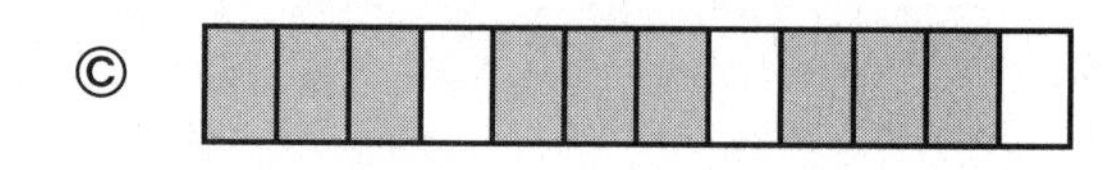

Ⓓ 

8 What fraction is represented by the shaded portion of the figure below?

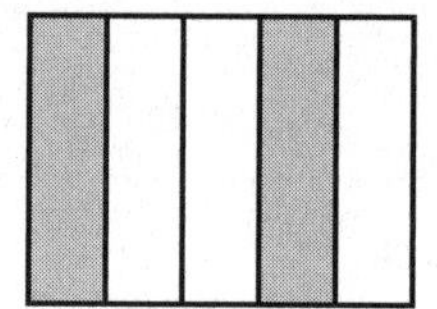

Ⓕ $\frac{1}{3}$

Ⓖ $\frac{2}{5}$

Ⓗ $\frac{2}{3}$

Ⓘ $\frac{3}{5}$

Lesson 6

Equivalent Fractions

NGSSS

MA.3.A.2.4: Use models to represent equivalent fractions, including fractions greater than 1, and identify representations of equivalence.

Introduction

Equivalent fractions are fractions that show the same amount, or are equal to each other.

- **Look at the fractions $\frac{1}{2}$ and $\frac{2}{4}$ below.**

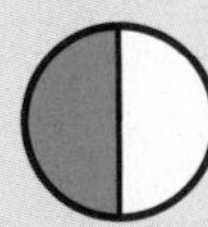
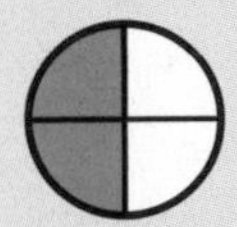

Each circle has the same area shaded. Each circle is divided into a different number of equal parts, so each circle shows a different fraction. The fractions are equivalent: $\frac{1}{2} = \frac{2}{4}$.

- **You can use multiplication to help you find equivalent fractions.**

Step	Result
Start with the fraction you are given.	$\frac{1}{2}$
Multiply the numerator and denominator by the same number.	$\frac{1 \times 2}{2 \times 2}$
Write the equivalent fraction.	$\frac{2}{4}$

So, $\frac{1}{2}$ is equivalent to $\frac{2}{4}$.

- **You can use division to help you find equivalent fractions.**

Step	Result
Start with the fraction you are given.	$\frac{2}{4}$
Divide the numerator and denominator by the same number.	$\frac{2 \div 2}{4 \div 2}$
Write the equivalent fraction.	$\frac{1}{2}$

So, $\frac{2}{4}$ is equivalent to $\frac{1}{2}$.

Modeled Instruction

EXAMPLE 1

The fraction $\frac{1}{4}$ is shaded in the model on the left. Shade an equivalent fraction in the model on the right.

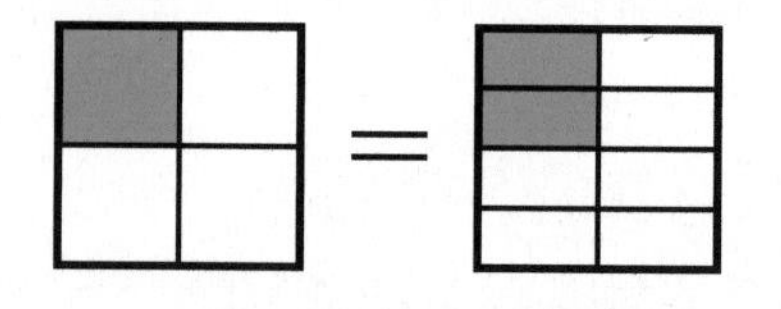

Follow these steps to solve the problem.

Step 1 Write the fraction you are given.

$\frac{1}{4}$

Step 2 Multiply the numerator and denominator by the same number.

$\frac{1 \times 2}{4 \times 2}$

Step 3 Complete the multiplication.

$\frac{1 \times 2}{4 \times 2} = \frac{2}{8}$

Step 4 Write the equivalent fraction and shade the model.

$\frac{2}{8}$

SOLUTION: The fraction $\frac{2}{8}$ is equivalent to $\frac{1}{4}$.

Try It! **Use what you know to solve this problem.**

1 Look at the fraction $\frac{1}{3}$ in the model.

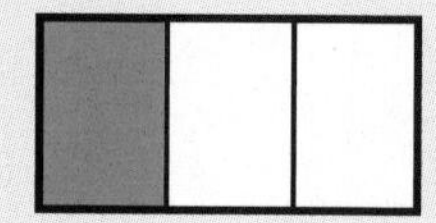

Write two fractions that are equivalent to $\frac{1}{3}$. ____________________

EXAMPLE 2

The mixed number $1\frac{6}{10}$ is shaded in the model on the left. Shade an equivalent mixed number in the model on the right.

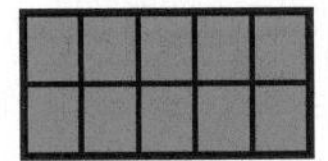 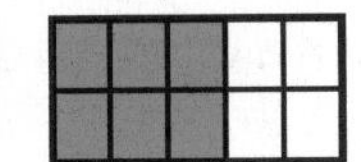 =  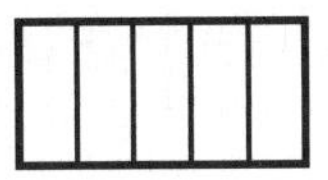

Follow these steps to solve the problem.

Step 1 Write the mixed number you are given.

$1\frac{6}{10}$

Step 2 Divide the numerator and denominator of the fraction part by the same number.

$\frac{6 \div 2}{10 \div 2}$

Step 3 Complete the division.

$\frac{6 \div 2}{10 \div 2} = \frac{3}{5}$

Step 4 Write the equivalent mixed number and shade the model.

$1\frac{3}{5}$

SOLUTION: The mixed number $1\frac{3}{5}$ is equivalent to $1\frac{6}{10}$. 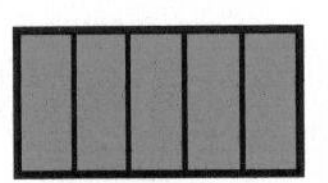 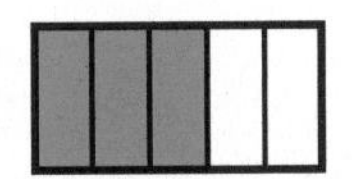

Try It! **Use what you know to solve this problem.**

1 Look at the mixed number $2\frac{8}{12}$ in the model.

Write two mixed numbers that are equivalent to $2\frac{8}{12}$. ________

Read the Think About It to understand the problem. Then solve the problem.

Think About It

What number could you divide both the numerator and denominator by to find an equivalent fraction?

Ty bought 6 pieces of fruit at the store. He noticed that $\frac{4}{6}$ of the fruit were bananas, as shown below.

Which fraction is equal to $\frac{4}{6}$?

A $\frac{1}{3}$

B $\frac{1}{2}$

C $\frac{2}{3}$

D $\frac{3}{4}$

EXPLANATION:

Divide the numerator and denominator by 2 to find an equivalent fraction.

CORRECT ANSWER:

Answer choice **C** is correct.

INCORRECT ANSWERS:

Read why the other answer choices are not correct.

A $\frac{1}{3}$ is not correct because it is equivalent to $\frac{2}{6}$.

B $\frac{1}{2}$ is not correct because it is equivalent to $\frac{3}{6}$.

D $\frac{3}{4}$ is not correct because it is equivalent to $\frac{6}{8}$.

Guided Practice

Hints

When finding an equivalent mixed number, the whole number part stays the same. Then find an equivalent fraction to the fraction part of the number.

Use the models to help you. Check your answer using multiplication or division.

PAIR SHARE

With your partner, share and discuss your answers and supporting details.

Solve each problem. Use the Hints to help you. Then explain how you found your solution.

1 The figure below shows how much pizza is left after Emily's class had a pizza party.

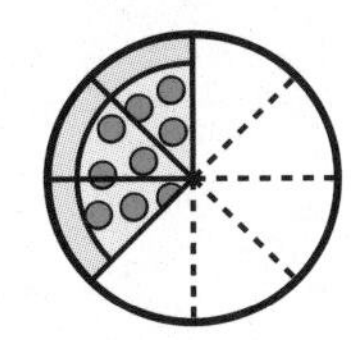

Write a mixed number that is equivalent to $1\frac{3}{8}$.

Solution: ______________________________

Explanation: ______________________________

____

____

2 Bradley divided his paper into thirds and colored $\frac{2}{3}$ of the paper.

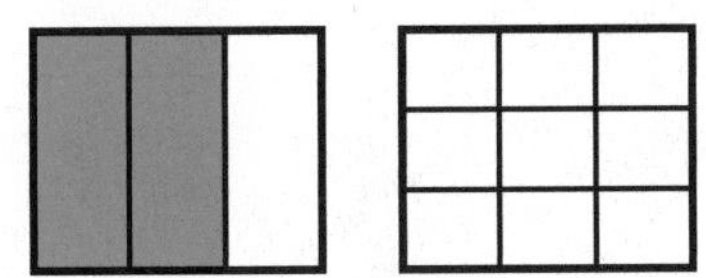

Megan divided her paper into ninths. The amount she colored is equal to the amount Bradley colored. What fraction did Megan color? Shade the fraction on the figure above and write the fraction on the solution line.

Solution: ______________________________

Explanation: ______________________________

____

____

1 There are $2\frac{6}{12}$ cartons of eggs in Mya's refrigerator.

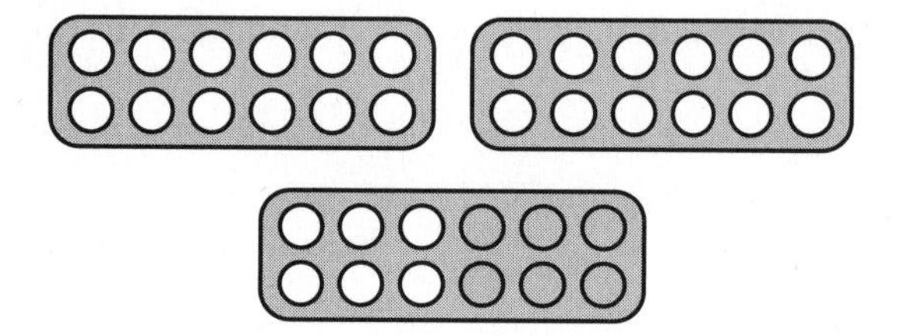

Which mixed number is equivalent to $2\frac{6}{12}$?

Ⓐ $2\frac{1}{3}$

Ⓑ $2\frac{2}{8}$

Ⓒ $2\frac{1}{6}$

Ⓓ $2\frac{1}{2}$

2 Which fraction is equivalent to $\frac{3}{4}$?

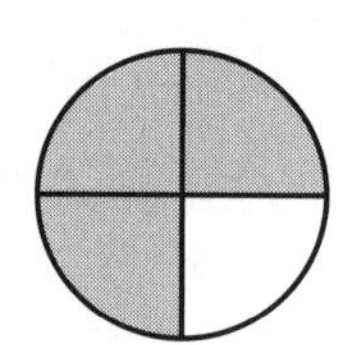

Ⓕ $\frac{9}{16}$

Ⓖ $\frac{12}{16}$

Ⓗ $\frac{2}{8}$

Ⓘ $\frac{7}{8}$

3 The number line below is divided into tenths.

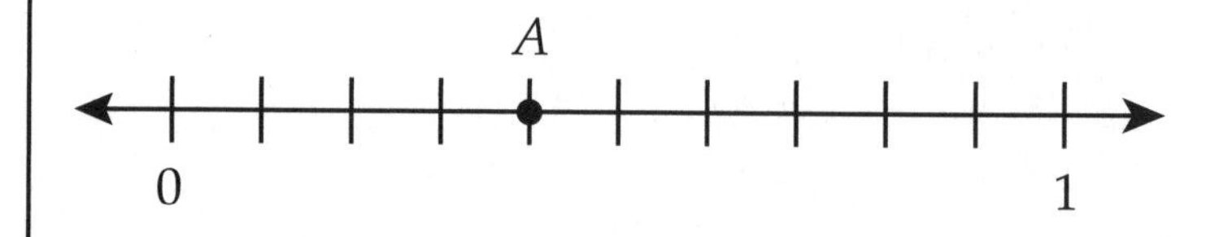

Point A represents the fraction $\frac{2}{5}$. Which fraction is equivalent to $\frac{2}{5}$?

Ⓐ $\frac{2}{10}$

Ⓑ $\frac{3}{10}$

Ⓒ $\frac{4}{10}$

Ⓓ $\frac{6}{10}$

4 Which fraction is equivalent to $\frac{3}{6}$?

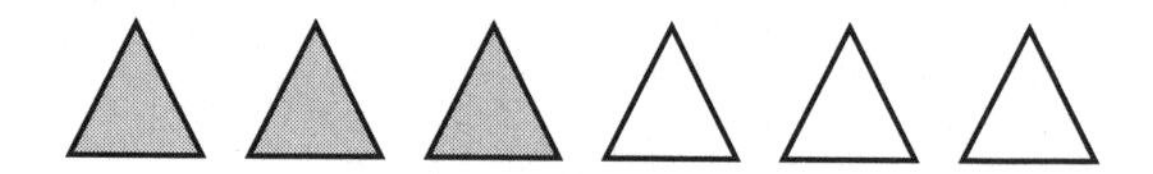

Ⓕ $\frac{1}{3}$

Ⓖ $\frac{2}{5}$

Ⓗ $\frac{6}{9}$

Ⓘ $\frac{6}{12}$

Lesson 7

Comparing and Ordering Fractions

NGSSS

MA.3.A.2.2: Describe how the size of the fractional part is related to the number of equal sized pieces in the whole.

MA.3.A.2.3: Compare and order fractions using models and strategies.

Introduction

In this lesson, you will compare and order fractions and mixed numbers.

When you compare and order fractions, think about the number of equal-sized parts that the whole is divided into, and about the size of those parts. The more parts a whole is divided into, the smaller each part is.

- **Look at the rectangles below.**

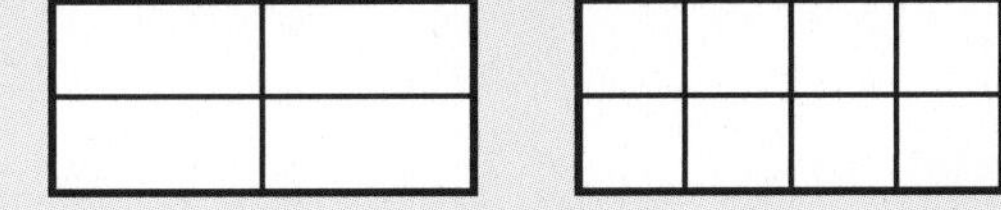

The rectangle on the left is divided into fourths. The rectangle on the right is divided into eighths. The fractional parts are larger in the rectangle on the left than in the rectangle on the right.

One part of the left rectangle is greater than one part of the right rectangle. Or, $\frac{1}{4}$ is greater than $\frac{1}{8}$.

- **You can use benchmark fractions to help you solve problems.**

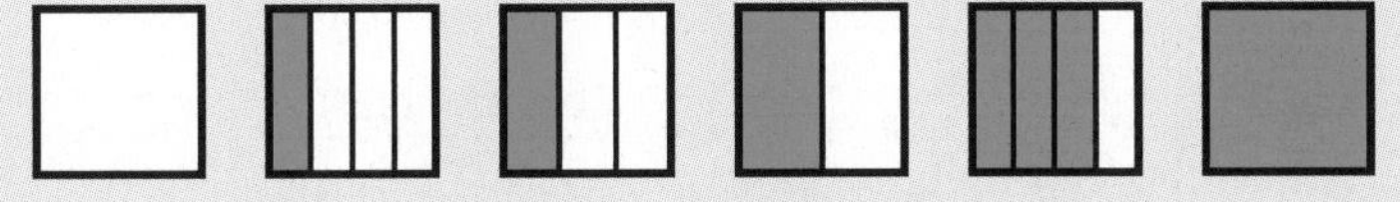

You can compare a fraction to 0, $\frac{1}{4}$, $\frac{1}{3}$, $\frac{1}{2}$, $\frac{3}{4}$, or 1 to help you understand how large or small the fraction is.

Modeled Instruction

EXAMPLE 1

Use $<$ or $>$ to compare the fractions $\frac{3}{10}$ and $\frac{5}{10}$.

Follow these steps to solve the problem.

Step 1 Look at the fractions to determine what strategy to use to compare them.

The fractions have the same denominator, so they have equal-sized parts. You can compare the numerators to see how the fractions compare to each other.

Step 2 Compare the numerators.

3 is less than 5.

Step 3 Compare the fractions.

$\frac{3}{10}$ is less than $\frac{5}{10}$.

SOLUTION: The fractions $\frac{3}{10}$ and $\frac{5}{10}$ can be compared as follows: $\frac{3}{10} < \frac{5}{10}$.

Try It!

Use what you know to solve these problems.

1 Use $<$ or $>$ to compare $\frac{3}{4}$ and $\frac{1}{4}$. ____________________

2 Use $<$ or $>$ to compare $\frac{7}{8}$ and $\frac{4}{8}$. ____________________

3 Use $<$ or $>$ to compare $\frac{2}{6}$ and $\frac{5}{6}$. ____________________

4 Use $<$ or $>$ to compare $\frac{7}{12}$ and $\frac{6}{12}$. ____________________

EXAMPLE 2

Use < or > to compare the fractions $\frac{3}{4}$ and $\frac{3}{9}$.

Follow these steps to solve the problem.

Step 1 Look at the fractions to determine what strategy to use to compare them.

The fractions have the same numerator, so you can use the denominators to see how the fractions compare to each other.

Step 2 Compare the denominators.

4 is less than 9. A whole that is divided into 4 equal parts will have larger fractional parts than a whole that is divided into 9 equal parts. Since the numerators are the same, the fraction with the smaller denominator is greater.

Step 3 Compare the fractions.

$\frac{3}{4}$ is greater than $\frac{3}{9}$.

SOLUTION: The fractions $\frac{3}{4}$ and $\frac{3}{9}$ can be compared as follows: $\frac{3}{4} > \frac{3}{9}$.

Use what you know to solve these problems.

1 Use < or > to compare $\frac{2}{6}$ and $\frac{2}{3}$. ____________

2 Use < or > to compare $\frac{4}{5}$ and $\frac{4}{10}$. ____________

3 Use < or > to compare $\frac{5}{7}$ and $\frac{5}{8}$. ____________

4 Use < or > to compare $\frac{10}{16}$ and $\frac{10}{12}$. ____________

Modeled Instruction

EXAMPLE 3

Use < or > to compare the fractions $\frac{2}{10}$ and $\frac{11}{12}$.

Follow these steps to solve the problem.

Step 1 Look at the fractions to determine what strategy to use to compare them.

The fractions can both be easily compared to $\frac{1}{2}$, so you can use $\frac{1}{2}$ as a benchmark fraction.

Step 2 Compare each fraction to $\frac{1}{2}$.

$\frac{1}{2}$ is equal to $\frac{5}{10}$, so $\frac{2}{10}$ is less than $\frac{1}{2}$.

$\frac{1}{2}$ is equal to $\frac{6}{12}$, so $\frac{11}{12}$ is greater than $\frac{1}{2}$.

Step 3 Compare the fractions.

Since $\frac{2}{10}$ is less than $\frac{1}{2}$ and $\frac{11}{12}$ is greater than $\frac{1}{2}$, that means that $\frac{2}{10}$ is less than $\frac{11}{12}$.

SOLUTION: The fractions $\frac{2}{10}$ and $\frac{11}{12}$ can be compared as follows: $\frac{2}{10} < \frac{11}{12}$.

Try It! **Use what you know to solve these problems.**

1 Use < or > to compare $\frac{3}{4}$ and $\frac{1}{8}$. ______________

2 Use < or > to compare $\frac{1}{3}$ and $\frac{3}{5}$. ______________

3 Use < or > to compare $\frac{4}{6}$ and $\frac{2}{12}$. ______________

4 Use < or > to compare $\frac{4}{8}$ and $\frac{13}{16}$. ______________

**Read the Think About It to understand the problem.
Then solve the problem.**

Think About It

Which mixed number has a greater area shaded?

Figure A represents the mixed number $1\frac{2}{4}$. Figure B represents the mixed number $1\frac{1}{3}$.

Figure 1 Figure 2

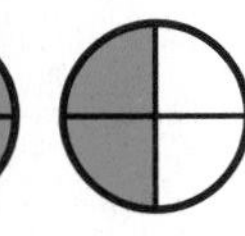
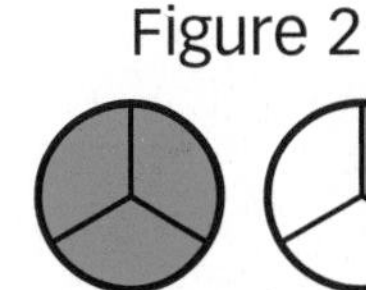

Which inequality below correctly compares the mixed numbers?

A $1\frac{2}{4} < 1\frac{1}{3}$

B $1\frac{2}{4} > 1\frac{1}{3}$

C $1\frac{4}{2} < 1\frac{3}{1}$

D $1\frac{4}{2} > 1\frac{3}{1}$

EXPLANATION:

Compare the total amount of each mixed number that is shaded.

CORRECT ANSWER:

Answer choice **B** is correct.

INCORRECT ANSWERS:

Read why the other answer choices are not correct.

A $1\frac{2}{4} < 1\frac{1}{3}$ is not correct because $1\frac{2}{4}$ is greater that $1\frac{1}{3}$.

C $1\frac{4}{2} < 1\frac{3}{1}$ is not correct because the mixed numbers are written incorrectly.

D $1\frac{4}{2} > 1\frac{3}{1}$ is not correct because the mixed numbers are written incorrectly.

Guided Practice

Hints

The denominator in all three fractions is the same. What do you need to compare to put the fractions in order?

The size of the wholes is the same, but there are a different number of slices in each pizza. Draw a picture to help you see which has larger slices.

Look at the models of the fractions to see how they compare to each other.

Solve each problem. Use the Hints to help you. Then explain how you found your solution.

1 Put the fractions $\frac{5}{7}$, $\frac{2}{7}$, and $\frac{4}{7}$ in order from least to greatest.

Solution: ______________________________

Explanation: ______________________________

____

____

2 Mary and Nate each ordered a large pizza at Pizza Palace. Mary had her pizza cut into 10 slices. Nate had his pizza cut into 8 slices. Which person's slices of pizza were larger?

Solution: ______________________________

Explanation: ______________________________

____

____

3 The fractions $\frac{3}{5}$ and $\frac{6}{8}$ are shown below. Use $<$ or $>$ to compare the fractions.

Solution: ______________________________

Explanation: ______________________________

____

____

PAIR SHARE

With your partner, share and discuss your answers and supporting details.

1 Which inequality below is correct?

Ⓐ $\frac{2}{10} < \frac{1}{10}$

Ⓑ $\frac{4}{6} > \frac{2}{6}$

Ⓒ $\frac{3}{8} > \frac{5}{8}$

Ⓓ $\frac{10}{12} < \frac{7}{12}$

2 Which fraction pictured below is **less** than $\frac{1}{2}$?

Ⓕ 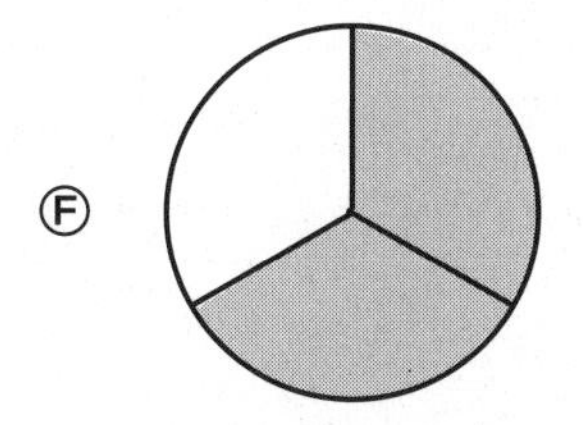

Ⓖ 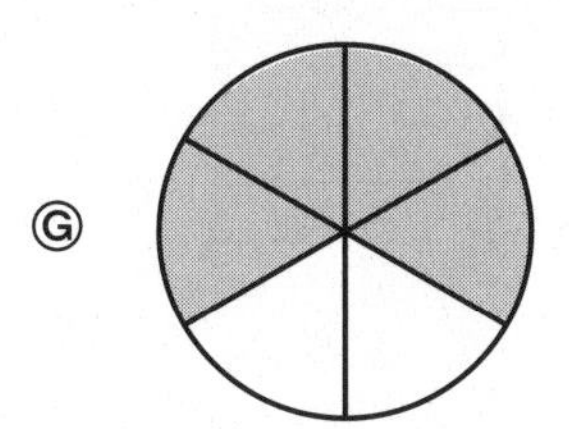

Ⓗ 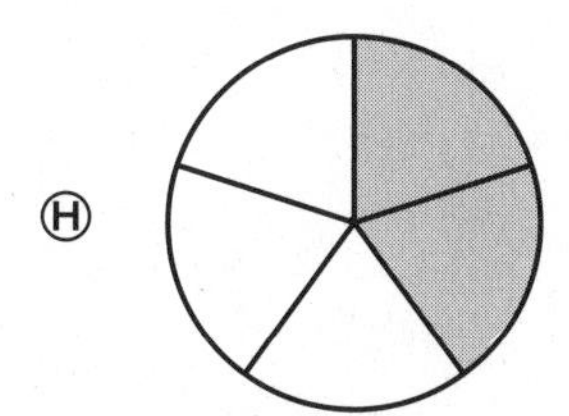

Ⓘ 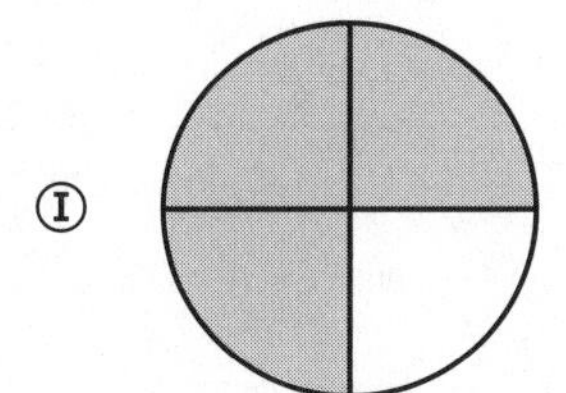

3 Brody and Taylor each have a set of marbles, which are pictured below. In Brody's set, $\frac{2}{3}$ of the marbles are black. In Taylor's set, $\frac{3}{4}$ of the marbles are black.

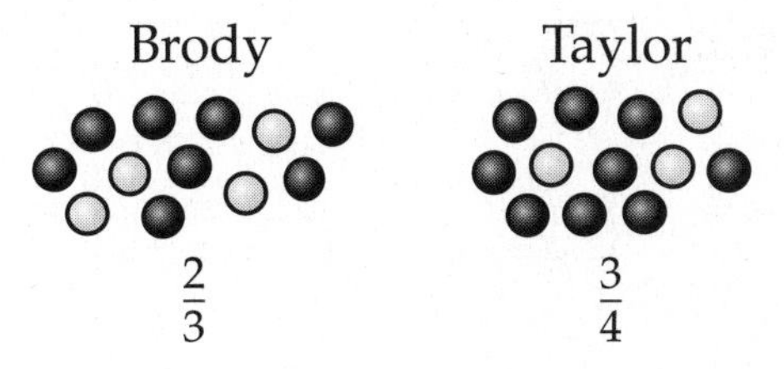

Which inequality correctly compares the fractions of the marbles that are black?

Ⓐ $\frac{2}{3} < \frac{3}{4}$

Ⓑ $\frac{2}{3} > \frac{3}{4}$

Ⓒ $\frac{4}{3} > \frac{2}{3}$

Ⓓ $\frac{4}{3} < \frac{2}{3}$

4 Ethan and Anna each ate some chocolate bars, which are pictured below. Ethan ate $1\frac{1}{2}$ chocolate bars. Anna ate $1\frac{2}{6}$ chocolate bars.

Ethan $1\frac{1}{2}$

Anna $1\frac{2}{6}$

Which inequality correctly compares the mixed numbers that are shown?

Ⓕ $1\frac{1}{2} > 1\frac{2}{6}$

Ⓖ $1\frac{1}{2} < 1\frac{2}{6}$

Ⓗ $1\frac{1}{2} > 1\frac{4}{6}$

Ⓘ $1\frac{1}{2} < 1\frac{4}{6}$

5 Which fraction is **greater** than $\frac{3}{4}$?

Ⓐ $\frac{2}{4}$

Ⓑ $\frac{9}{10}$

Ⓒ $\frac{1}{2}$

Ⓓ $\frac{2}{3}$

6 Four students were given a square piece of paper. Ross cut his paper into 5 equal parts, Rachel cut her paper into 8 equal parts, Monica cut her paper into 3 equal parts, and Joe cut his paper into 12 equal parts. Which student had the **smallest** pieces after cutting the paper?

Ⓕ Ross

Ⓖ Rachel

Ⓗ Monica

Ⓘ Joe

7 Which inequality correctly compares the fractions shown by the shaded parts below?

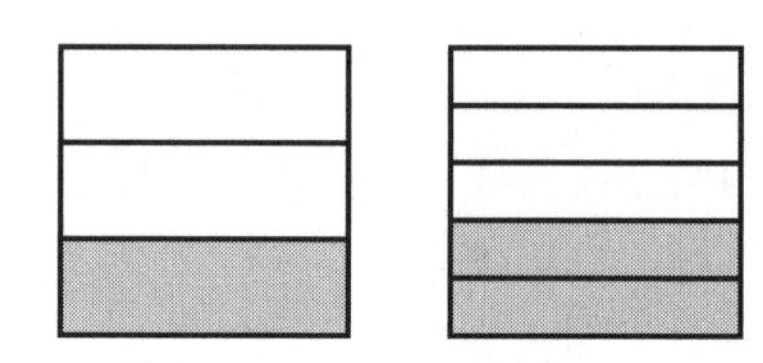

Ⓐ $\frac{2}{3} > \frac{3}{5}$

Ⓑ $\frac{2}{3} < \frac{3}{5}$

Ⓒ $\frac{1}{3} > \frac{2}{5}$

Ⓓ $\frac{1}{3} < \frac{2}{5}$

Lesson 8
Triangles

NGSSS

MA.3.G.3.1: Describe, analyze, compare, and classify two-dimensional shapes using sides and angles—including acute, obtuse, and right angles—and connect these ideas to the definition of shapes.

Introduction

In this lesson, you will learn about different kinds of triangles. A triangle is one type of polygon. **Polygons** are closed shapes made up of straight sides. They are named for the number of sides and angles they have. An **angle** is formed when two sides meet. If an angle looks like a square corner, it is called a right angle.

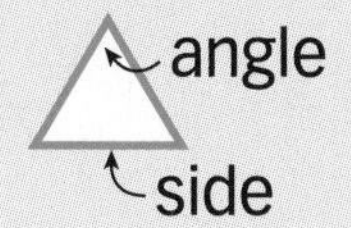

The table below shows some types of triangles.

Right	Equilateral	Isosceles	Scalene
A triangle with one right angle.	A triangle with all three sides the same length.	A triangle with exactly two sides the same length.	A triangle with sides of different lengths.

Modeled Instruction

EXAMPLE 1

What type of triangle is shown below?

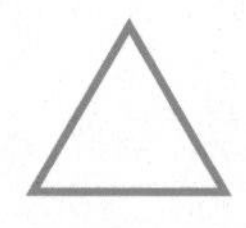

Follow these steps to solve the problem.

Step 1 Look at the angles of the triangle.

None of the angles look like a square corner, so the triangle does not have any right angles.

Step 2 Look at the sides of the triangle.

All of the sides are the same length.

SOLUTION: The triangle is an equilateral triangle.

Try It! **Use what you know to solve these problems.**

1 What type of triangle is shown below? ______________________

2 What type of triangle is shown below? ______________________

EXAMPLE 2

Circle all of the scalene triangles.

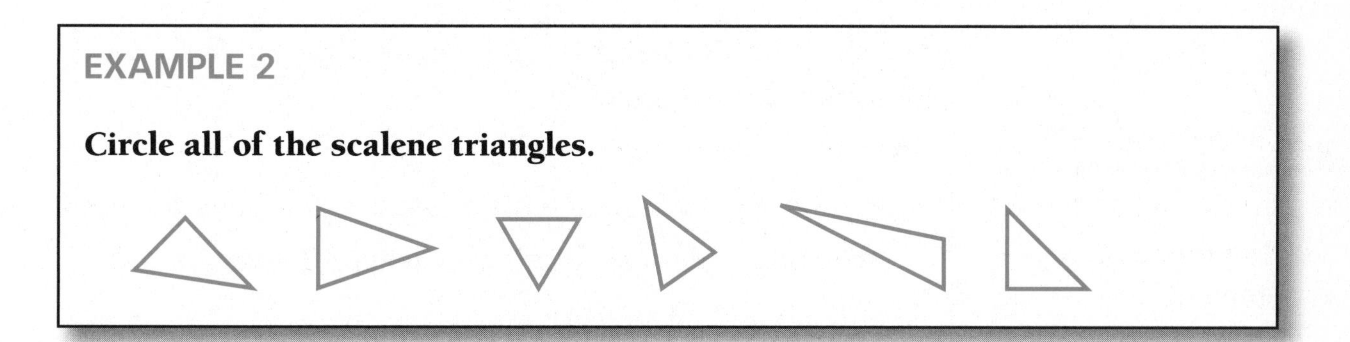

Follow these steps to solve the problem.

Step 1 Remember that the sides of a scalene triangle are all different lengths.

Step 2 Look at the sides of each triangle.

The first triangle has no sides the same length.
The second triangle has 2 sides the same length.
The third triangle has 3 sides the same length.
The fourth triangle has no sides the same length.
The fifth triangle has no sides the same length.
The sixth triangle has 2 sides the same length.

SOLUTION: The first, fourth, and fifth triangles are scalene triangles and should be circled.

Try It! **Use what you know to solve this problem.**

1 Circle all of the right triangles.

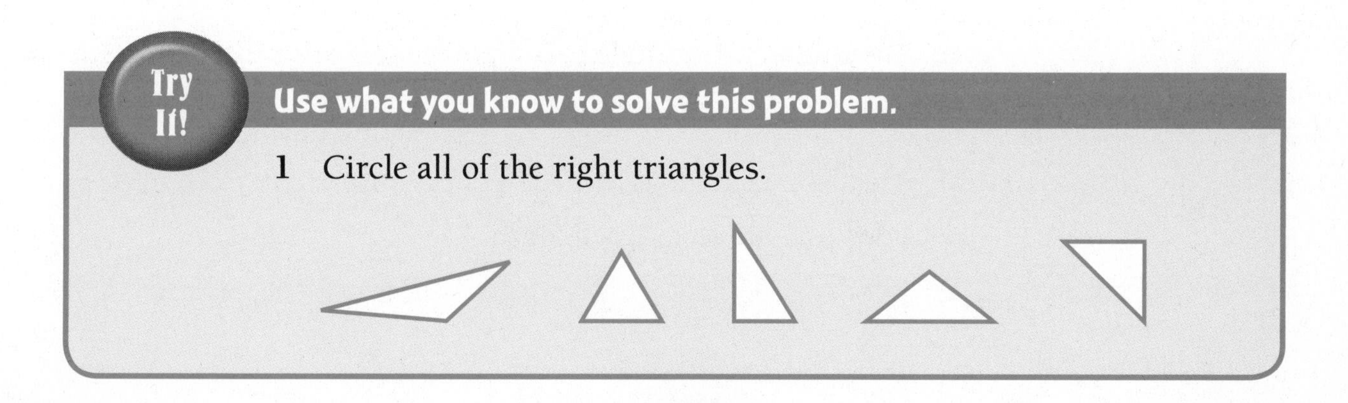

Read the Think About It to understand the problem. Then solve the problem.

Think About It

Be sure to choose the triangle that has two sides that are the same length, not three.

Evan drew a triangle with two sides the same length. The third side was a different length. What type of triangle did Evan draw?

A right

B equilateral

C isosceles

D scalene

EXPLANATION:

An isosceles triangle has exactly two sides that are the same length.

CORRECT ANSWER:

Answer choice **C** is correct.

INCORRECT ANSWERS:

Read why the other answer choices are not correct.

A A right triangle is not correct because it has a right angle and may or may not have any sides that are the same length.

B An equilateral triangle is not correct because it has three sides that are the same length.

D A scalene triangle is not correct because it does not have any sides that are the same length.

Guided Practice

Hints

Look at the lengths of each side. Determine if any of the sides are the same length.

Think about the names of the types of triangles. Which type begins with something that sounds like "equal"?

Sometimes a triangle can be described in more than one way.

PAIR SHARE

With your partner, share and discuss your answers and supporting details.

Solve each problem. Use the Hints to help you. Then explain how you found your solution.

1 What type of triangle is shown below?

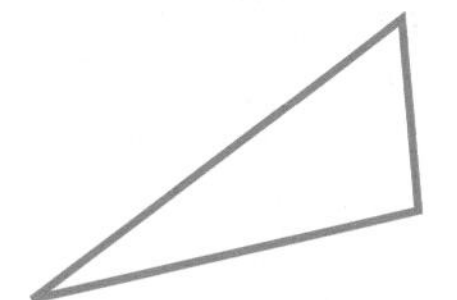

Solution: ______________________________

Explanation: ______________________________

____

____

2 What type of triangle has three sides of equal length?

Solution: ______________________________

Explanation: ______________________________

____

____

3 Rebecca says the triangle below is a right triangle. Jonah says it is an isosceles triangle. Who is correct?

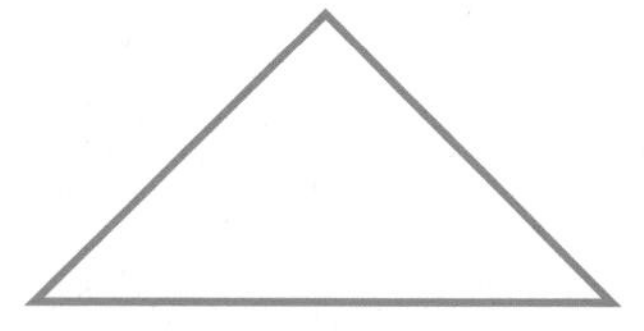

Solution: ______________________________

Explanation: ______________________________

____

____

FL Math Practice

1 Oscar saw the sign below while riding in the car with his mom.

Which type of triangle is the sign?

Ⓐ isosceles

Ⓑ equilateral

Ⓒ right

Ⓓ scalene

2 Which two words could be used to describe the following triangle?

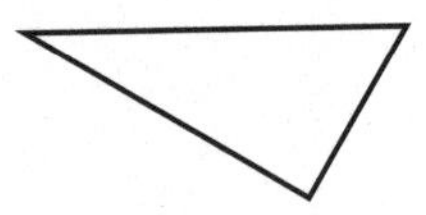

Ⓕ isosceles and scalene

Ⓖ equilateral and right

Ⓗ right and isosceles

Ⓘ scalene and right

3 Which type of triangle has three sides of different lengths?

Ⓐ equilateral

Ⓑ right

Ⓒ scalene

Ⓓ isosceles

4 Which of the following is an isosceles triangle?

Ⓕ 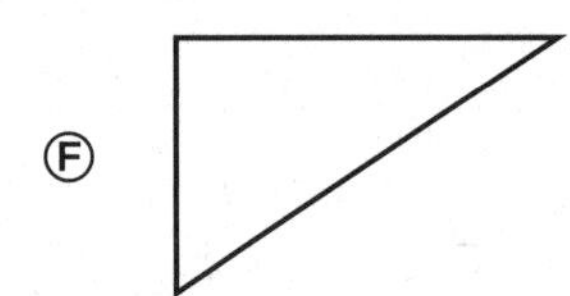

Ⓖ 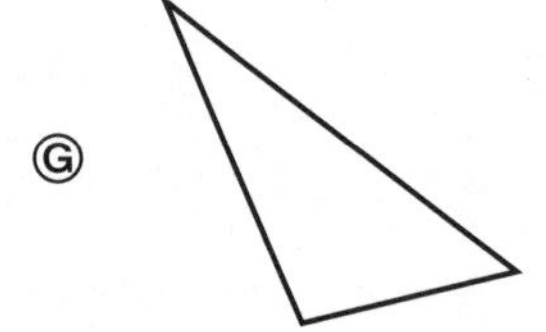

Ⓗ 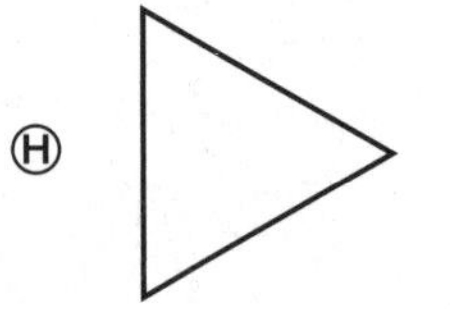

Ⓘ 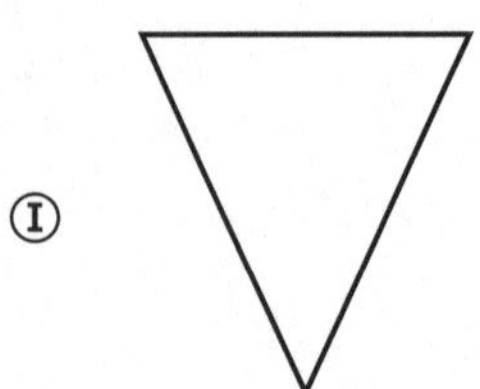

Lesson 9
Quadrilaterals

NGSSS

MA.3.G.3.1: Describe, analyze, compare, and classify two-dimensional shapes using sides and angles—including acute, obtuse, and right angles—and connect these ideas to the definition of shapes.

Introduction

In this lesson, you will learn about different kinds of quadrilaterals. A **quadrilateral** is a polygon with 4 sides and 4 angles.

To understand quadrilaterals, you need to know what some words mean. **Parallel** sides are made up of lines that would never meet if the lines were extended. **Perpendicular** sides meet to form a right angle. **Opposite** sides are across from each other. **Adjacent** sides are right next to each other. A **diagonal** can be drawn to connect opposite vertices of a quadrilateral.

The table below shows some types of quadrilaterals.

Parallelogram	Rectangle	Square
A quadrilateral with two sets of opposite sides that are parallel and equal	A quadrilateral with two sets of opposite sides that are equal and all right angles	A quadrilateral with all sides equal and all right angles

Rhombus	Trapezoid	Kite
A quadrilateral with two sets of opposite sides that are parallel and all sides equal	A quadrilateral with only one set of opposite sides that are parallel	A quadrilateral with two sets of adjacent sides that are equal

Modeled Instruction

EXAMPLE 1

What type of quadrilateral is shown below?

Follow these steps to solve the problem.

Step 1 Determine if any of the sides are equal in length.

Both sets of opposite sides are equal.

Step 2 Determine if any of the sides are parallel or perpendicular.

Both sets of opposite sides are parallel.

SOLUTION: The shape is a parallelogram.

Try It! **Use what you know to solve this problem.**

1 What is the name of this quadrilateral? ______________________

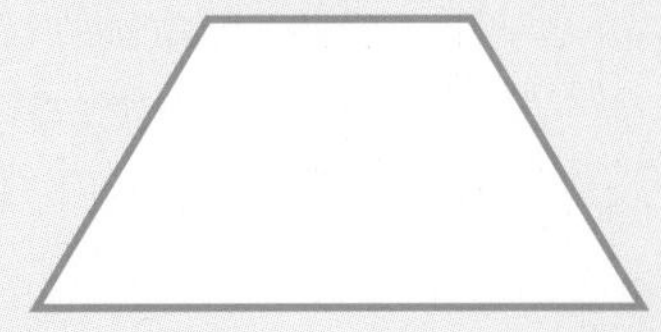

EXAMPLE 2

Circle all of the kites.

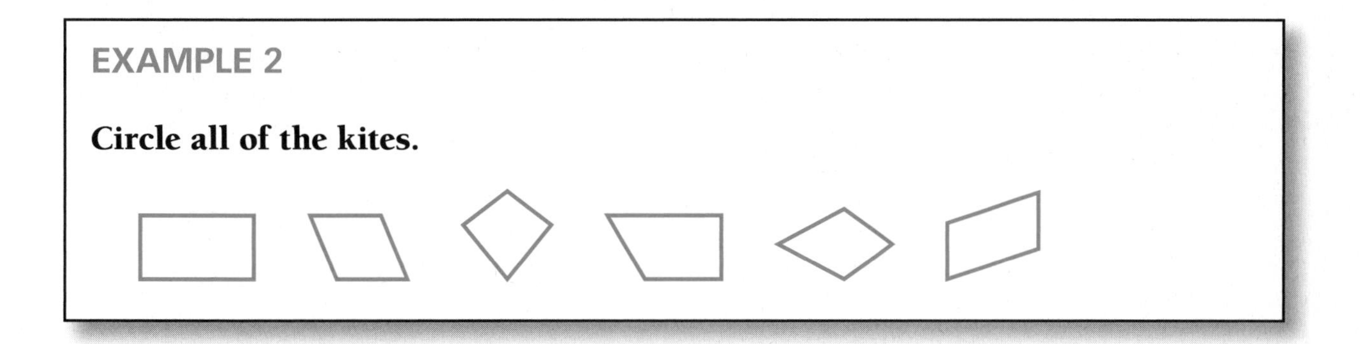

Follow these steps to solve the problem.

Step 1 Remember that a kite has two sets of adjacent sides that are equal.

Step 2 Look at the sides of each quadrilateral.

The first quadrilateral has 2 sets of opposite sides that are equal.
The second quadrilateral has 2 sets of opposite sides that are equal, but it also has 2 sets of adjacent sides that are equal.
The third quadrilateral has 2 sets of adjacent sides that are equal.
The fourth quadrilateral has no sides that are equal.
The fifth quadrilateral has 2 sets of adjacent sides that are equal.
The sixth quadrilateral has 2 sets of opposite sides that are equal.

SOLUTION: The second, third, and fifth quadrilaterals are kites and should be circled.

Try It! **Use what you know to solve this problem.**

1 Circle all of the trapezoids.

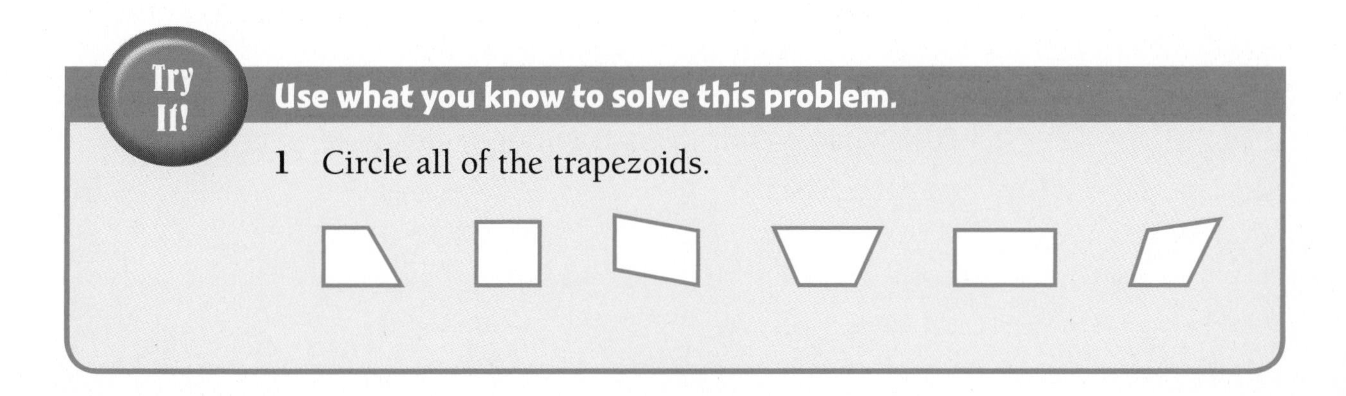

Read the Think About It to understand the problem.
Then solve the problem.

Think About It

Think about what parallel and perpendicular lines look like.

Which quadrilateral has sides that are always parallel and perpendicular?

A rhombus

B rectangle

C trapezoid

D kite

EXPLANATION:

A rectangle always has parallel and perpendicular sides.

CORRECT ANSWER:

Answer choice **B** is correct.

INCORRECT ANSWERS:

Read why the other answer choices are not correct.

A A rhombus has sides that are always parallel but not always perpendicular.

C A trapezoid has one pair of sides that are parallel, but the sides are not always perpendicular.

D A kite has sides that are not parallel or perpendicular.

Guided Practice

Hints

Think about shapes that have sides that are the same length.

Draw a trapezoid and count the number of sides.

Think about the definitions of square and rhombus.

Solve each problem. Use the Hints to help you. Then explain how you found your solution.

1 What is the name of this shape?

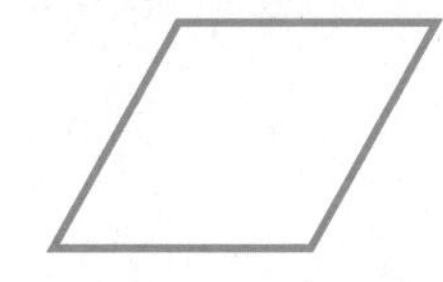

Solution: ______________________________

Explanation: ______________________________

____

2 How many sides does a trapezoid have?

Solution: ______________________________

Explanation: ______________________________

____

3 Jay says the shape below is a square. Jared says it is a rhombus. Who is correct?

Solution: ______________________________

Explanation: ______________________________

____

PAIR SHARE

With your partner, share and discuss your answers and supporting details.

1 Which quadrilateral is a rectangle?

Ⓐ 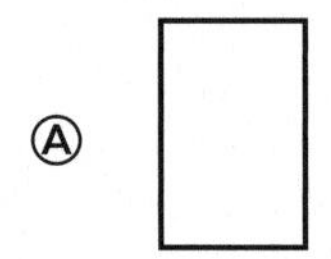

Ⓑ

Ⓒ 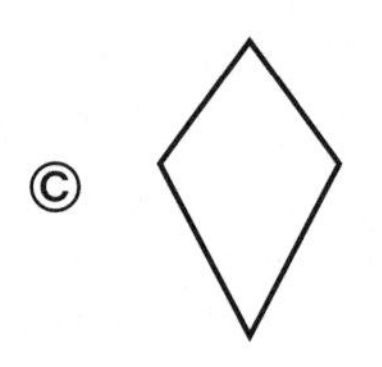

Ⓓ

2 Martin drew the shape below.

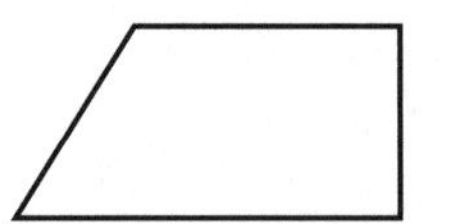

What is the name of this shape?

Ⓕ kite

Ⓖ parallelogram

Ⓗ trapezoid

Ⓘ rhombus

3 Which quadrilaterals **always** have right angles?

Ⓐ trapezoid and rhombus

Ⓑ rectangle and square

Ⓒ square and rhombus

Ⓓ rectangle and parallelogram

4 Which polygon could **only** be called a parallelogram?

Ⓕ 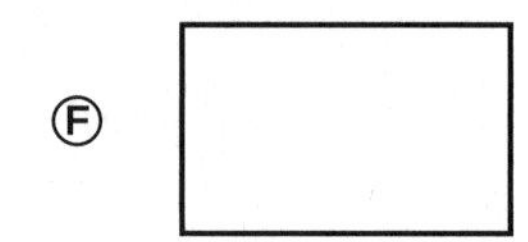

Ⓖ 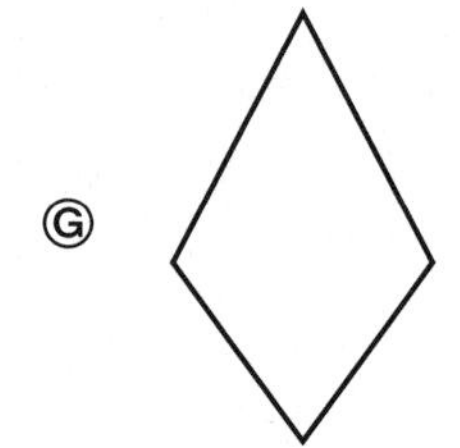

Ⓗ 

Ⓘ 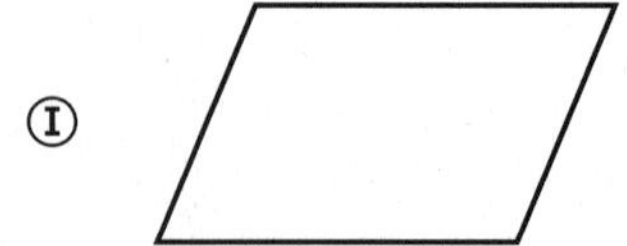

Lesson 10
Other Shapes

NGSSS

MA.3.G.3.1: Describe, analyze, compare and classify two-dimensional shapes using sides and angles—including acute, obtuse, and right angles—and connect these ideas to the definition of shapes.

Introduction

You have already learned about different kinds of triangles and quadrilaterals. But there are many other kinds of polygons, too. In this lesson you will see some shapes you know. You might also see some shapes you do not know.

The table below shows you some different kinds of polygons.

Pentagon	Hexagon	Octagon	Decagon
A polygon with 5 sides and 5 angles.	A polygon with 6 sides and 6 angles.	A polygon with 8 sides and 8 angles.	A polygon with 10 sides and 10 angles.

The shapes in the table above are all **regular polygons**. In a regular polygon, all of the sides are the same length, and the angles are the same size. In an **irregular polygon**, the sides are not all the same length, and the angles may be different sizes. An irregular pentagon, hexagon, octagon, and decagon are shown below.

Modeled Instruction

EXAMPLE 1

What type of polygon is shown below?

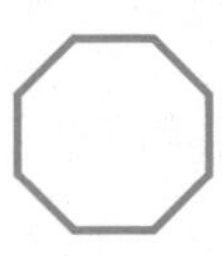

Follow these steps to solve the problem.

Step 1 Count how many sides the polygon has.

The polygon has 8 sides.

Step 2 Find the name of the polygon that has 8 sides.

An octagon has 8 sides.

SOLUTION: The polygon is an octagon.

Try It! **Use what you know to solve these problems.**

1 What type of polygon is shown below? ____________________

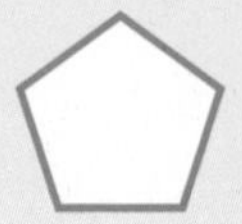

2 What type of polygon is shown below? ____________________

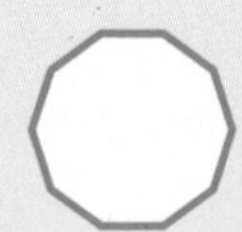

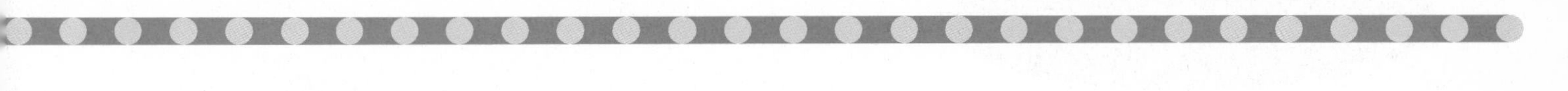

EXAMPLE 2

Circle all of the hexagons.

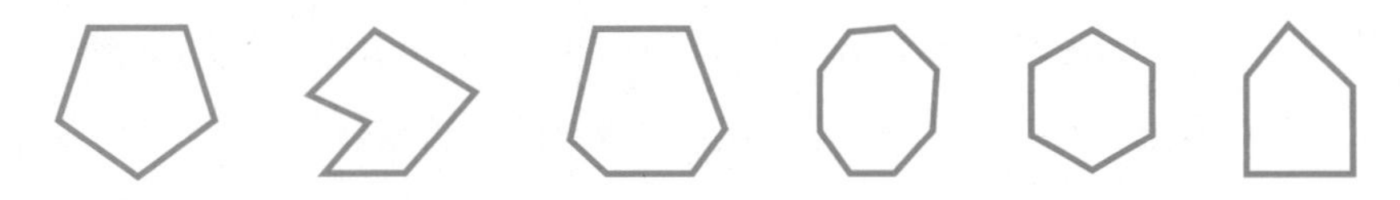

Follow these steps to solve the problem.

Step 1 Remember that a hexagon has 6 sides and 6 angles.

Step 2 Count the sides and angles of each polygon.

The first polygon has 5 sides and angles.
The second polygon has 6 sides and angles.
The third polygon has 6 sides and angles.
The fourth polygon has 8 sides and angles.
The fifth polygon has 6 sides and angles.
The sixth polygon has 5 sides and angles.

SOLUTION: The second, third, and fifth polygons are hexagons and should be circled.

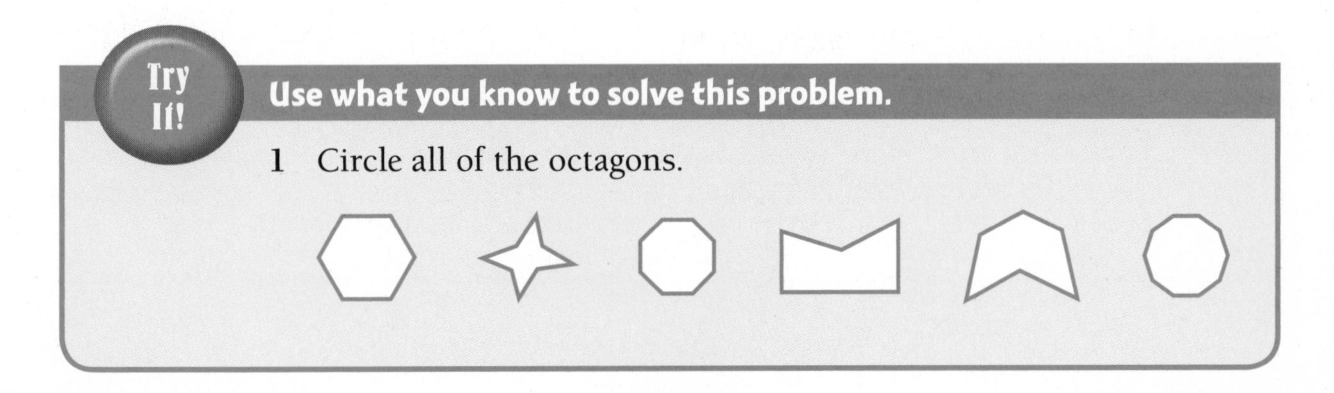

Use what you know to solve this problem.

1 Circle all of the octagons.

Read the Think About It to understand the problem. Then solve the problem.

Think About It

How many sides and angles does each shape have?

Amanda drew a polygon with 5 sides and 5 angles. What type of shape did Amanda draw?

A pentagon

B decagon

C octagon

D hexagon

EXPLANATION:

A pentagon has 5 sides and 5 angles.

CORRECT ANSWER:

Answer choice **A** is correct.

INCORRECT ANSWERS:

Read why the other answer choices are not correct.

B A decagon is not correct because it has 10 sides and 10 angles.

C An octagon is not correct because it has 8 sides and 8 angles.

D A hexagon is not correct because it has 6 sides and 6 angles.

Guided Practice

Hints

An angle is formed when two sides meet.

Think about how many sides a decagon has and how many sides a pentagon has.

Review what regular and irregular polygons are.

Solve each problem. Use the Hints to help you. Then explain how you found your solution.

1 How many angles are in this shape?

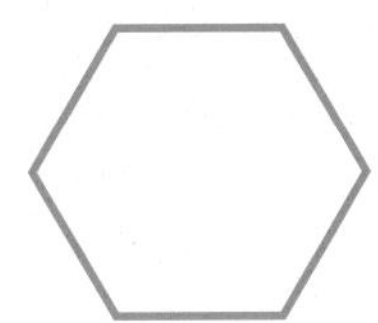

Solution: ______________________________

Explanation: ______________________________

____

2 How many more sides does a decagon have than a pentagon?

Solution: ______________________________

Explanation: ______________________________

____

3 Kate says the shape below is an octagon. Julie says it isn't an octagon because the sides are different lengths. Who is correct?

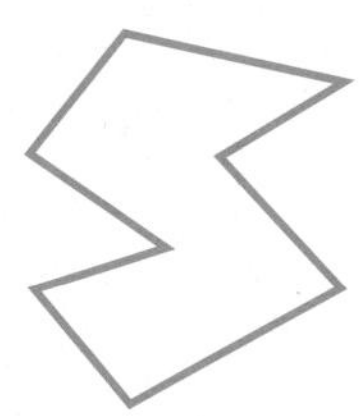

Solution: ______________________________

Explanation: ______________________________

____

PAIR SHARE

With your partner, share and discuss your answers and supporting details.

1 Which polygon has six angles?

Ⓐ 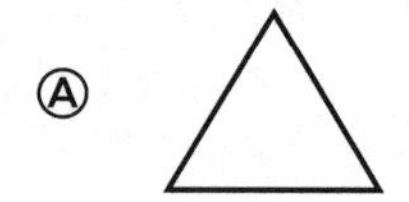

Ⓑ 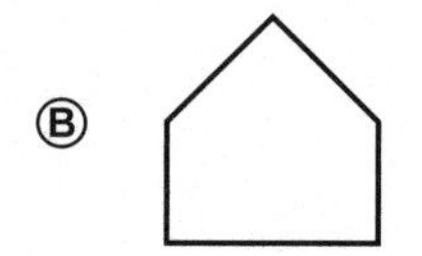

Ⓒ 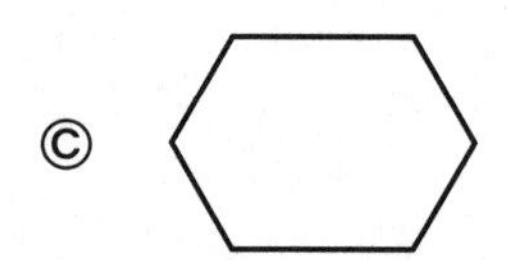

Ⓓ 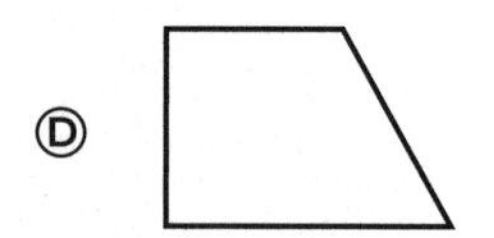

2 Will drew the shape below.

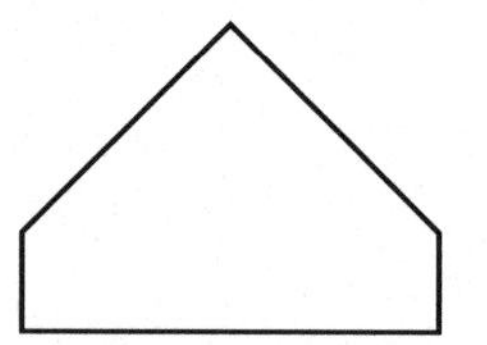

What is the name of this shape?

Ⓕ hexagon

Ⓖ octagon

Ⓗ triangle

Ⓘ pentagon

3 Enrique saw the sign below.

What shape is the sign?

Ⓐ decagon

Ⓑ octagon

Ⓒ pentagon

Ⓓ hexagon

4 Which polygon is a decagon?

Ⓕ 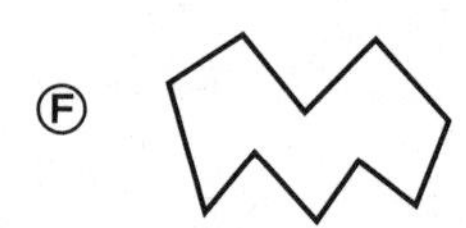

Ⓖ 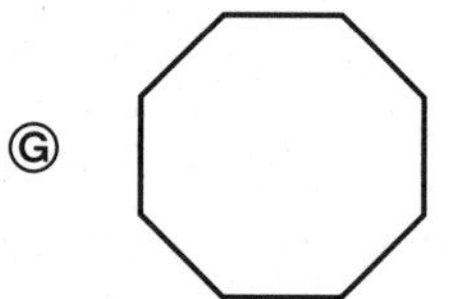

Ⓗ 

Ⓘ 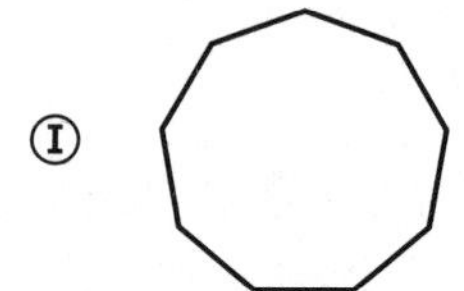

Lesson 11

Composing and Decomposing Polygons

NGSSS

MA.3.G.3.2: Compose, decompose, and transform polygons to make other polygons, include concave and convex polygons with three, four, five, six, eight, or ten sides.

Introduction

In this lesson, you will learn about combining and dividing polygons to make new polygons.

- **You can combine polygons to make another polygon.**

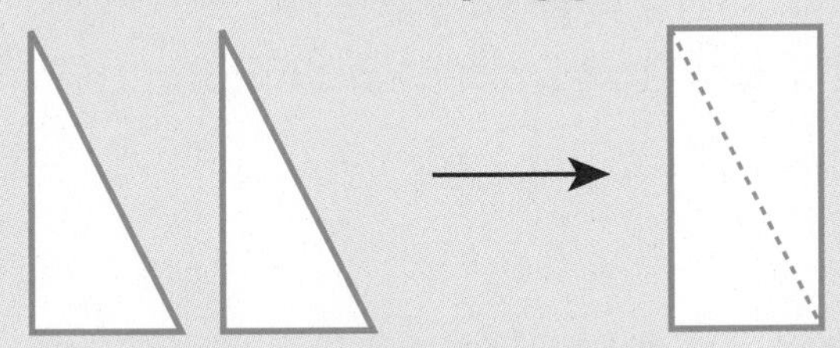

The triangles on the left were combined to make the rectangle on the right. The dotted line shows where the triangles were connected to each other to form the rectangle.

- **You can divide polygons to make other polygons.**

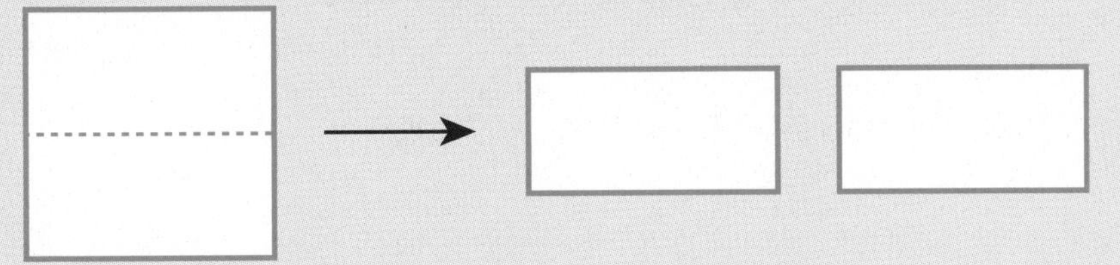

The square on the left was divided to make the rectangles on the right. The dotted line shows where the square was divided to form the rectangles.

EXAMPLE 1

Draw a line on the triangle to divide it into a triangle and a trapezoid.

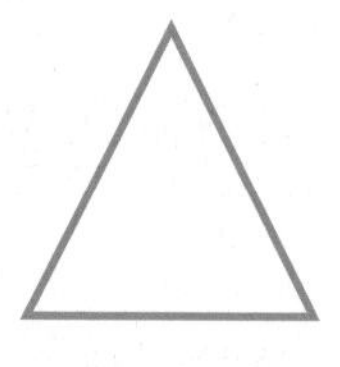

Follow these steps to solve the problem.

Step 1 Review what new polygons you need to form when dividing the triangle.

A triangle has 3 sides.
A trapezoid has 4 sides. One pair of opposite sides is parallel; the other pair of opposite sides is not parallel.

Step 2 Determine where you could draw a line on the triangle to form the new polygons.

A line could be drawn straight across the triangle.

SOLUTION: One possible place to draw the line is shown.

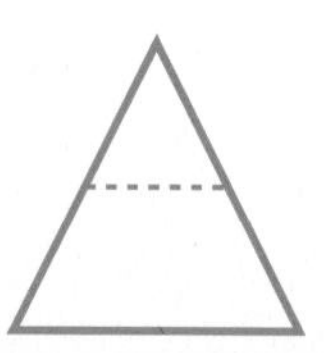

Try It! **Use what you know to solve this problem.**

1 Draw a line on the trapezoid to divide it into a triangle and a parallelogram.

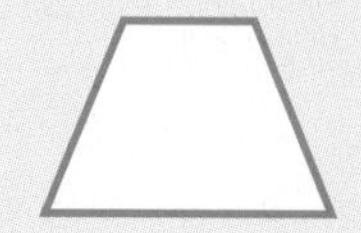

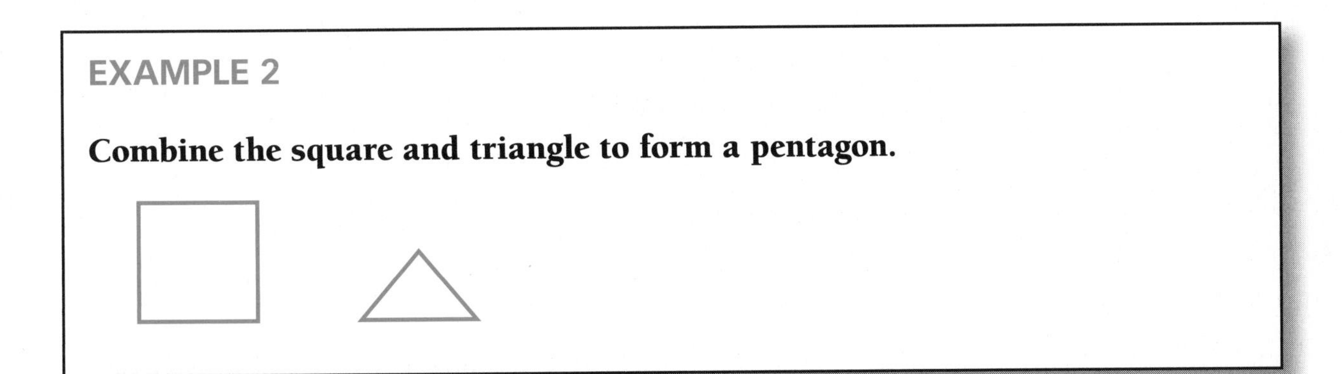

Follow these steps to solve the problem.

Step 1 Review the polygon you need to form.

A pentagon has five sides.

Step 2 Determine where you could combine the square and the triangle to from a pentagon.

The base of the triangle is the same length as the sides of the square, so the base of the triangle could be connected to any side of the square.

SOLUTION: One possible way to combine the square and triangle to form a pentagon is shown below.

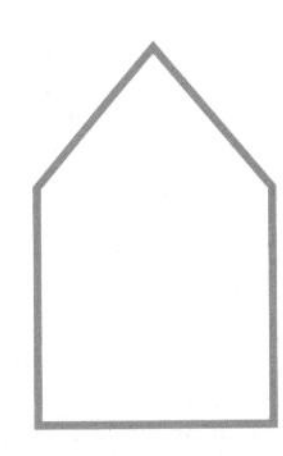

Try It! **Use what you know to solve this problem.**

1 Combine the two trapezoids to form a hexagon.

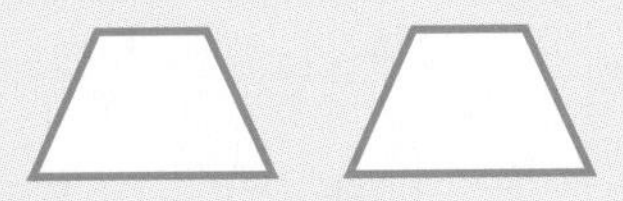

Read the Think About It to solve the problem.
Then solve the problem.

Think About It

Try to draw a line on Josh's figure to divide it into a set of shapes in one of the answer choices.

Josh used two shape stickers to form the figure below.

Which of the following shows the stickers Josh could have used to form the figure, without overlapping?

A

B

C

D

EXPLANATION:

Look at each pair of figures and determine if they could be combined to make Josh's figure.

CORRECT ANSWER:

Answer choice **A** is correct.

INCORRECT ANSWERS:

Read why the other answer choices are not correct.

B A rectangle and a triangle cannot be combined to make the figure.

C A parallelogram and a trapezoid cannot be combined to make the figure.

D Two trapezoids cannot be combined to make the figure.

Hints

Picture how you could combine each pair of shapes. Remember that sometimes shapes can be combined in more than one way.

Think about what triangles and trapezoids can look like.

Be sure to only use two shapes to make the figure.

PAIR SHARE

With your partner, share and discuss your answers and supporting details.

Solve each problem. Use the Hints to help you. Then explain how you found your solution.

1 Which pair of shapes could be combined to form a square?

Solution: ______________________________

Explanation: ______________________________

____

____

2 Draw a line on the pentagon to form a triangle and a trapezoid.

Solution:

Explanation: ______________________________

____

____

3 Jesse had five shape stickers: a small triangle, a large triangle, a square, a rectangle, and a hexagon. Which two stickers could he have combined to make the figure below?

Solution: ______________________________

Explanation: ______________________________

____

____

1 Desmond made the figure below using shape stickers.

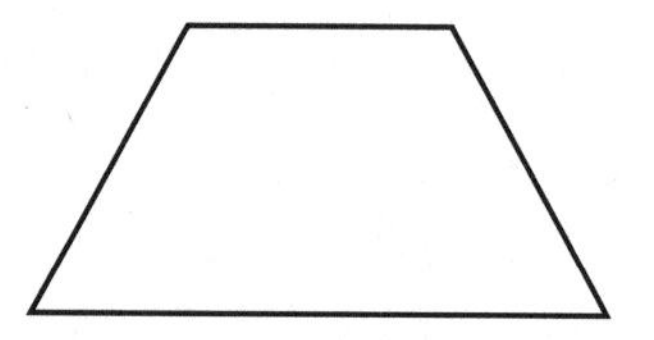

Which two shape stickers could Desmond have combined to make his figure, with no overlapping?

Ⓐ 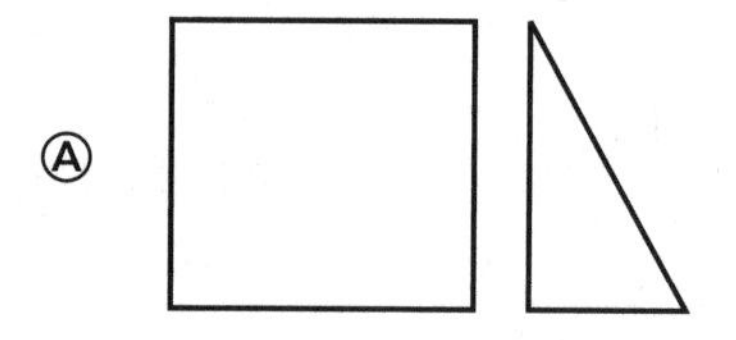

Ⓑ 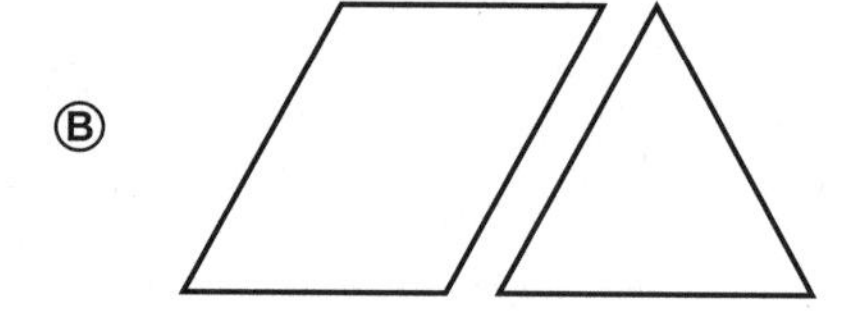

Ⓒ 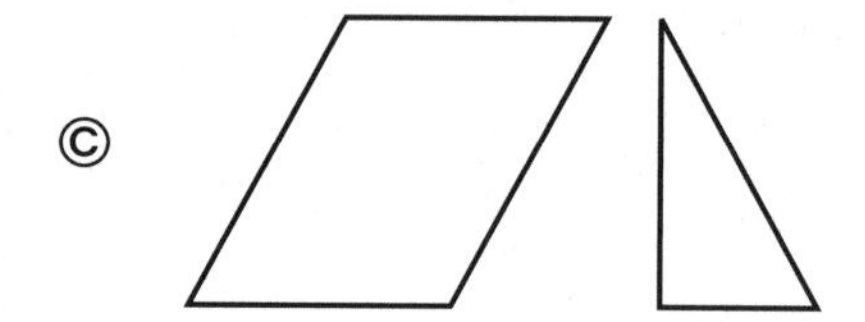

Ⓓ 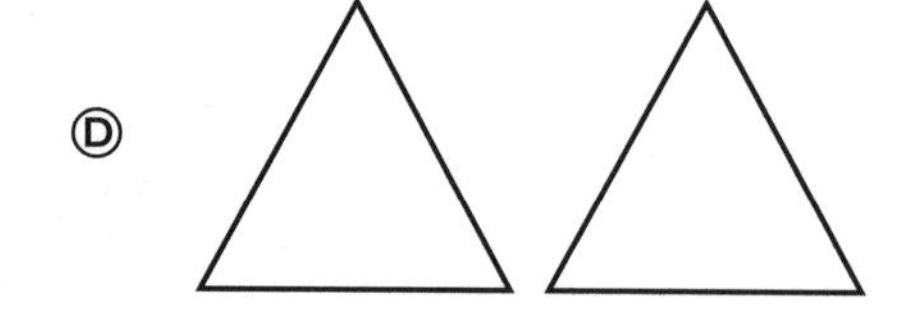

2 Look at the figure below.

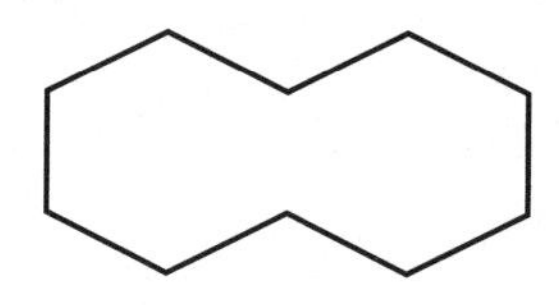

Sam cut the figure apart to form some new polygons. Which set of shapes could Sam have made?

Ⓕ 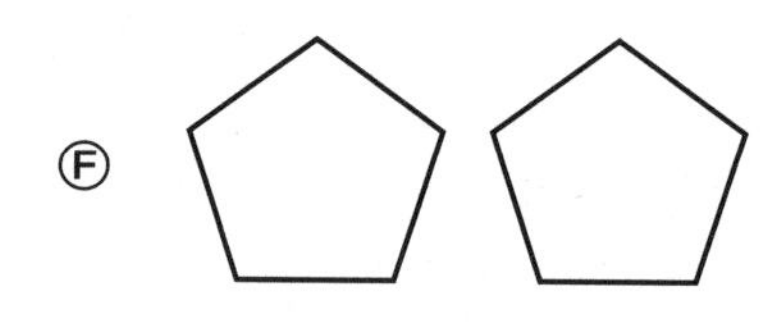

Ⓖ 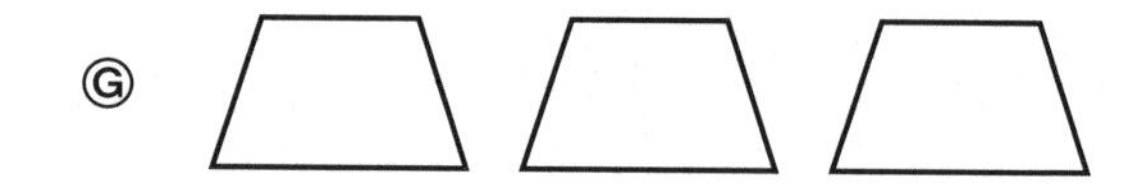

Ⓗ 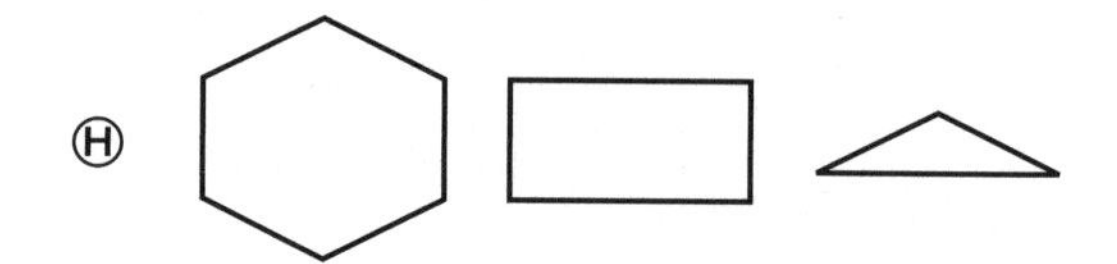

Ⓘ 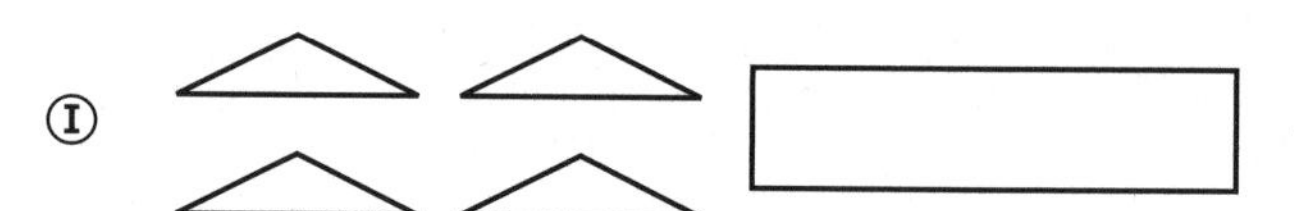

Lesson 12

Congruent Figures and Symmetry

NGSSS

MA.3.G.3.3: Build, draw and analyze two-dimensional shapes from several orientations in order to examine and apply congruence and symmetry.

Introduction

In this lesson, you will learn about congruent figures and symmetry.

Congruent figures are figures that are exactly alike. They are the same shape *and* the same size. Even if one figure is turned, they are still congruent. These are congruent figures.

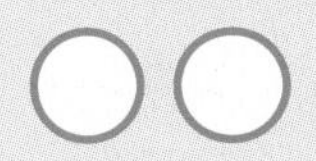  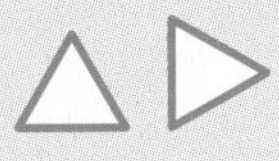

A figure has **symmetry** if you can fold the shape so it has two matching parts. The line it is folded along is a **line of symmetry**. The figures on the left below have symmetry. The figures on the right do not.

 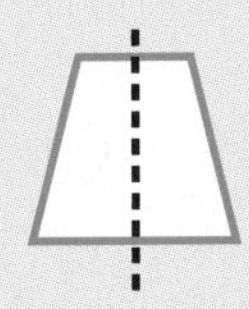 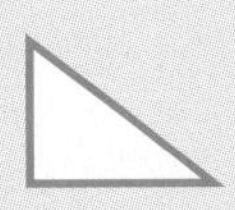 

The two parts of a symmetrical figure match exactly. One side is a reflection (flip) of the other side. If you were to cut the shape apart along the line of symmetry, the two new shapes would be congruent.

EXAMPLE 1

Which pair of figures is congruent? Explain your answer.

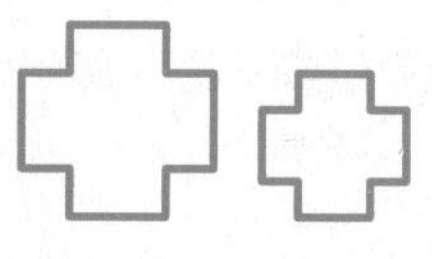

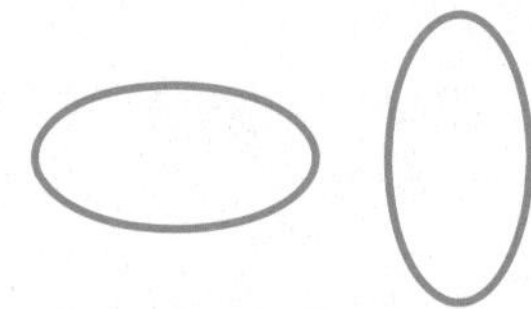

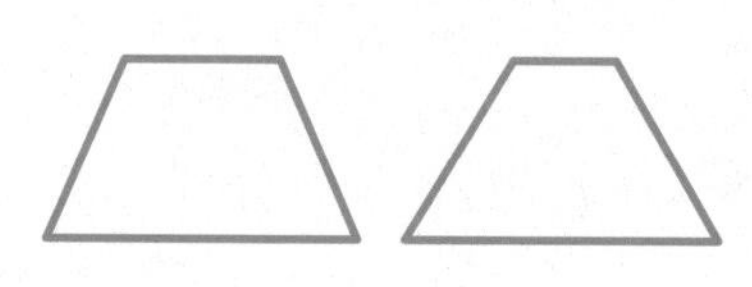

Follow these steps to solve the problem.

Step 1 Look at each pair of figures.

You are looking for the pair that has the same size and shape.

Step 2 First, study the shape of each figure in the pair.

The first figures are the same shape. The ovals are the same shape. The trapezoids are not the same shape.

Step 3 Then, look at the size of each figure in the pair.

The first pair of figures are different sizes. The ovals are the same size, even though one is turned.

SOLUTION: The ovals are the only pair of figures that are congruent. They are the same shape and size.

Use what you know to solve this problem.

1 Which pair of figures is congruent? Explain your answer.

____

____

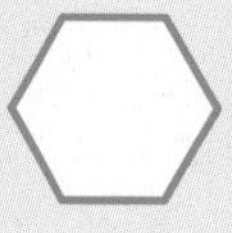

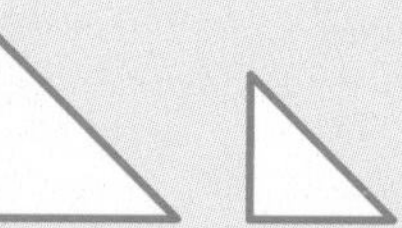

Does the dotted line on the pentagon show a line of symmetry? Explain your answer.

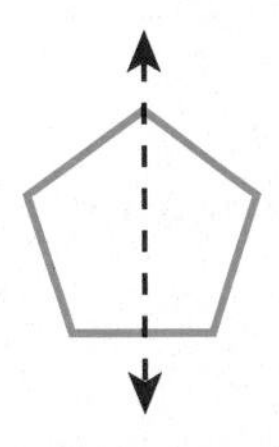

Follow these steps to solve the problem.

Step 1 Think about what the dotted line means. If you fold the figure along the dotted line, the two parts should match exactly.

Step 2 Look at the dotted line going up and down. Decide if this is a line of symmetry. If you fold along this dotted line, the two parts of the pentagon will match exactly. This is a line of symmetry.

SOLUTION: The dotted line is a line of symmetry. It divides the shape into two equal parts.

Try It! **Use what you know to solve this problem.**

1 Does the dotted line on the triangle show a line of symmetry? Explain your answer.

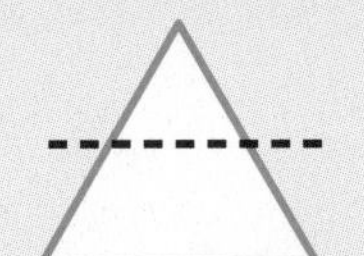

____

____

____

EXAMPLE 3

Draw two lines of symmetry on the shape to the right.

Follow these steps to solve the problem.

Step 1 Find the center of the shape and make a dot with your pencil. Your lines of symmetry will pass through the center of the shape.

Step 2 Think about how you would fold the shape to make the two parts match exactly.

Step 3 One way you can fold the shape is from top to bottom. This means the dotted lines will go across the shape from left to right.

Step 4 The other way to fold the shape is from side to side. This means the dotted lines will go up and down.

SOLUTION:

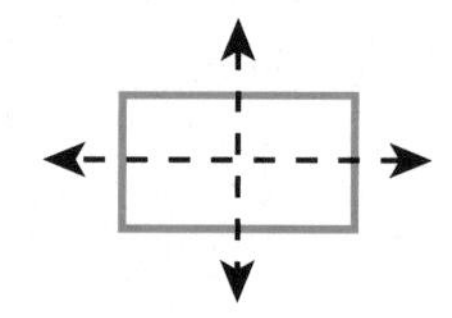

Try It! **Use what you know to solve these problems.**

1 How many lines of symmetry does this shape have? ______________________

2 Does the picture show a line of symmetry? Explain your answer.

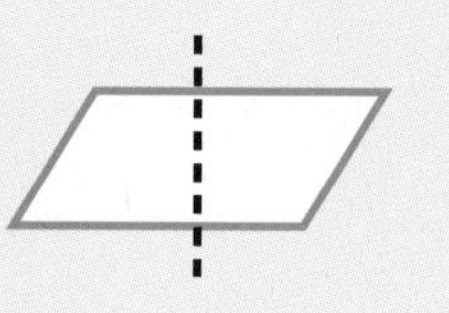

____

____

Read the Think About It to understand the problem. Then solve the problem.

Think About It

You need to find two congruent pieces. What does congruent mean?

Micah was given a piece of paper shaped like a triangle. He cut it into 2 congruent pieces. Which could be the two pieces of paper?

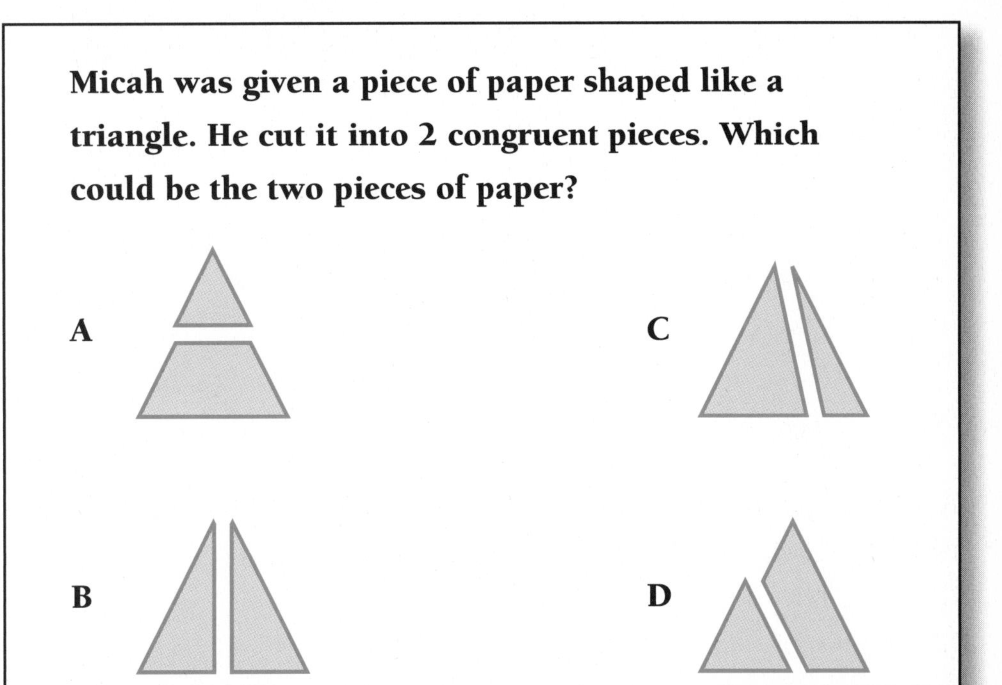

EXPLANATION:

Look for the answer choice that has two pieces that are the same shape and size.

CORRECT ANSWER:

Answer choice **B** is correct.

INCORRECT ANSWERS:

Read why the other answer choices are not correct.

A The two pieces are not the same shape and size.

C The two pieces are not the same shape and size.

D The two pieces are not the same shape and size.

Guided Practice

Hints

Congruent figures can face different directions.

A line of symmetry must cross through the center of the figure.

Review the names of different quadrilaterals.

PAIR SHARE

With your partner, share and discuss your answers and supporting details.

Solve each problem. Use the Hints to help you. Then explain how you found your solution.

1 Tell whether the following figures are congruent or not congruent.

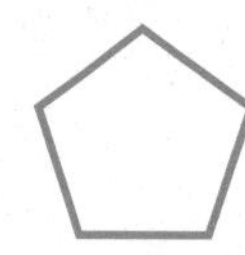
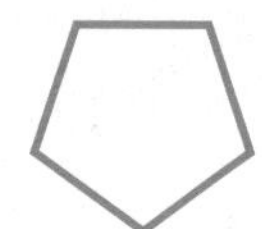

Solution: ______________________________

Explanation: ______________________________

____

2 Does the picture show more than one line of symmetry? Explain your answer.

Solution: ______________________________

Explanation: ______________________________

____

3 What two congruent shapes would be made if the hexagon were cut along the line of symmetry as shown below?

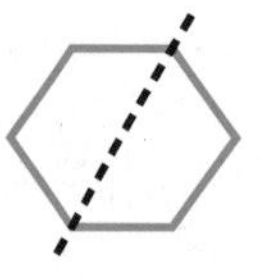

Solution: ______________________________

Explanation: ______________________________

____

1 Which pair of figures is congruent?

Ⓐ

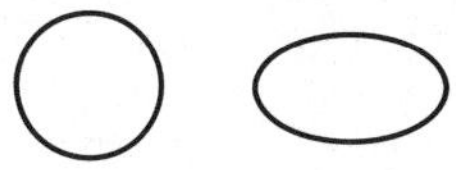

Ⓑ

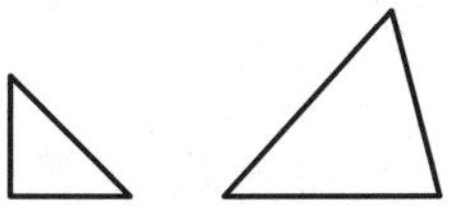

Ⓒ

Ⓓ

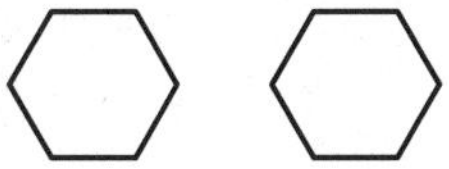

2 Which figure shows a line of symmetry?

Ⓕ

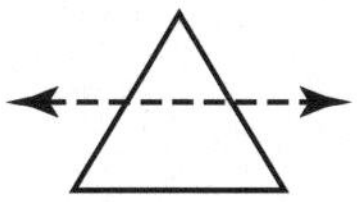

Ⓖ

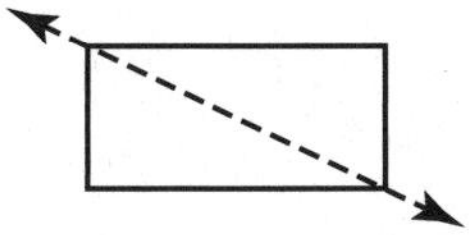

Ⓗ

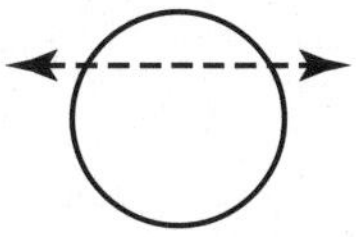

Ⓘ

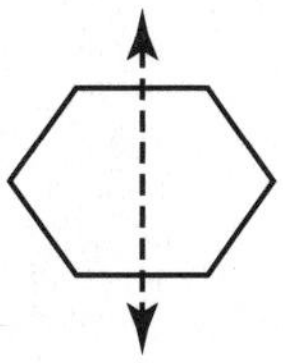

3 Which shape has exactly two lines of symmetry?

Ⓐ 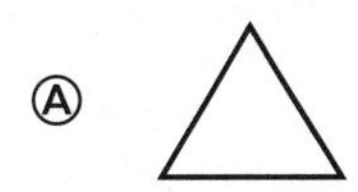

Ⓑ 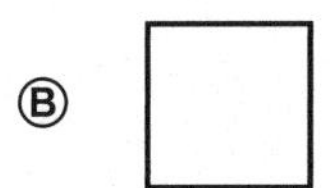

Ⓒ 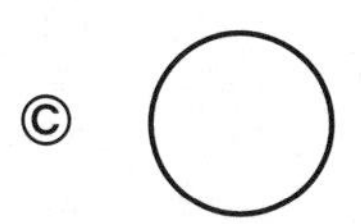

Ⓓ 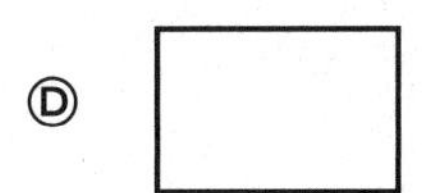

4 Which two congruent shapes would be formed if the figure below were cut along the line of symmetry?

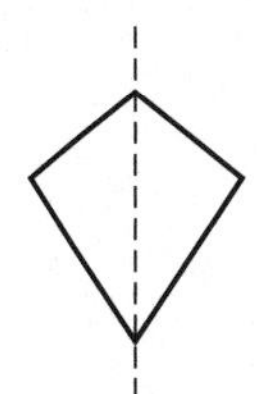

Ⓕ two trapezoids

Ⓖ two triangles

Ⓗ two parallelograms

Ⓘ two kites

5 Which pair of figures does **not** appear to be congruent?

Ⓐ 

Ⓑ

Ⓒ

Ⓓ

6 Which shape shows a correct line of symmetry?

Ⓕ 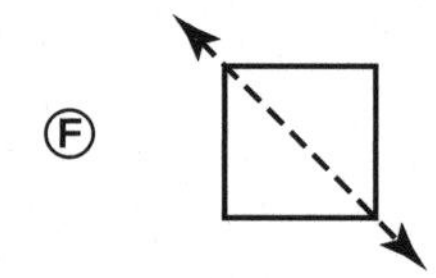

Ⓖ 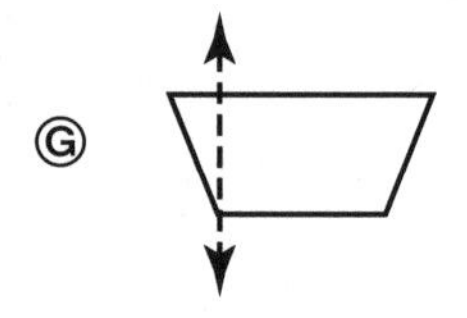

Ⓗ 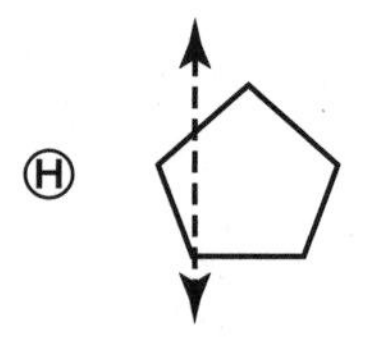

Ⓘ

7 Look at this figure.

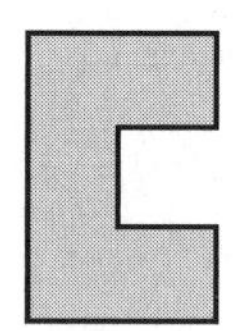

Which figure is congruent to the figure above?

Ⓐ 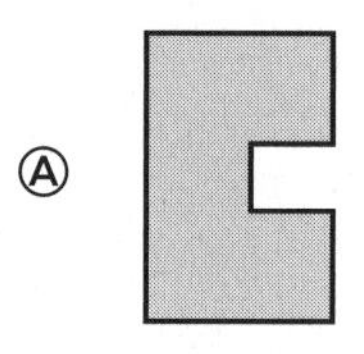

Ⓑ 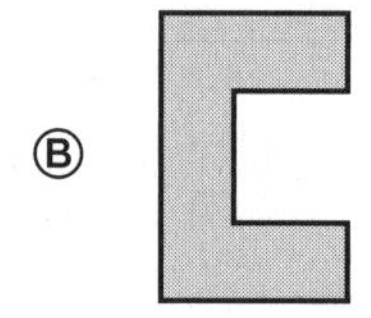

Ⓒ 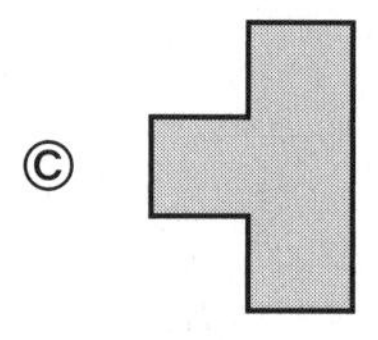

Ⓓ 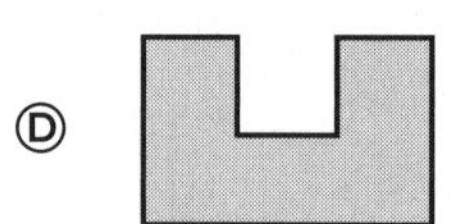

Lesson 13
Patterns

NGSSS

MA.3.A.4.1: Create, analyze, and represent patterns and relationships using words, variables, tables, and graphs.

Introduction

This lesson will show you how to find and continue a pattern. A **pattern** is an ordered set of numbers or shapes that follows a rule. A **rule** describes how to extend a pattern.

Has a Pattern	Does Not Have a Pattern

2, 10, 18, 26, 34, 42	15, 23, 35, 46, 67, 89

- **To find the missing shape in the pattern below:**

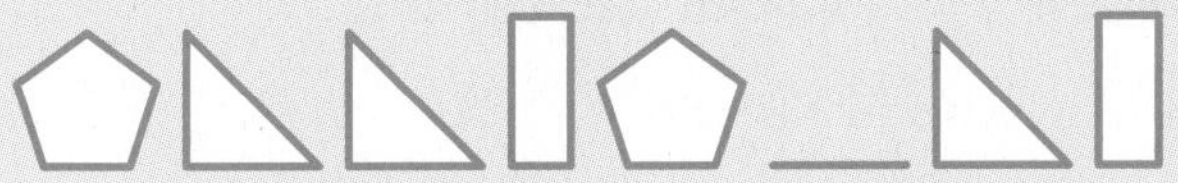

Find the repeating part.	pentagon, triangle, triangle, rectangle
The repeating part is the rule.	Draw a line under the repeating section.
Look at the next section.	pentagon, _____, triangle, rectangle

The missing shape in the pattern is the triangle.

- **To find the next number in the pattern below:**

52, 48, 44, 40, 36, _____

Are the numbers getting larger or smaller?	Each number gets smaller.
Find how the first two numbers change.	From 52 to 48, subtract 4.
Find how the next two numbers change.	From 48 to 44, subtract 4.
Test the rule with each pair of numbers.	The rule is always true.

The next number in the pattern is $36 - 4 = 32$.

EXAMPLE 1

These shapes follow a pattern. Describe the rule.

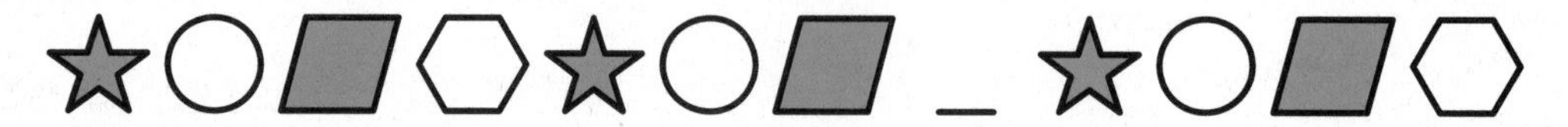

Which shape is missing from the pattern?

Follow these steps to solve the problem.

Step 1 Find the repeating part of the pattern. The repeating part is the rule.

The pattern is shaded star, white circle, shaded parallelogram, white hexagon.

Step 2 Draw a line under the repeating section of the pattern.
Compare this to the section with the missing shape.

There is a shaded star, white circle, and shaded parallelogram.

Step 3 Find the missing shape.

The white hexagon is missing in the second section.
It belongs after the shaded parallelogram.

SOLUTION: The missing shape in the pattern is the white hexagon.

Use what you know to solve this problem.

1 These shapes follow a pattern. Describe the rule. Then find the missing shape. ______________________________

____

EXAMPLE 2

The numbers below follow a pattern. Describe the rule. What are the next two numbers?

15, 21, 27, 33, _____, _____

Follow these steps to solve the problem.

Step 1 Decide if the numbers are getting larger or smaller.

Each number gets larger.

Step 2 Look at the first two numbers in the pattern. Find how they change.

To get to 21 from 15, add 6.

Step 3 Test the rule with each pair of numbers in the pattern.

The rule is true between each pair of numbers.

Step 4 Find the next two numbers.

Add 6 to the last number in the list: $33 + 6 = 39$.
Then add 6 to 39 for the last number in the list: $39 + 6 = 45$.

SOLUTION: The rule is to add 6 to each number. The next two numbers are 39 and 45.

Use what you know to solve this problem.

1 The numbers below follow a pattern. Describe the rule. Then write the missing number in this pattern. ____________________

____

2, 4, _____, 16, 32, 64

Modeled Instruction

EXAMPLE 3

Tyrone drew the pattern below. Describe the rule. How many boxes will be in the fifth figure?

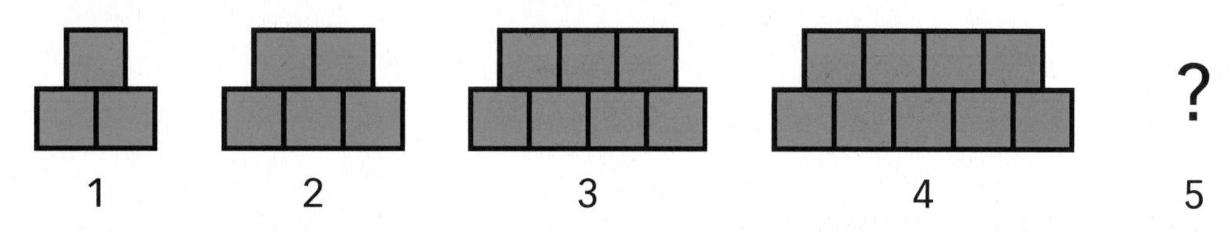

Follow these steps to solve the problem.

Step 1 Decide if the number of boxes is getting larger or smaller.

The number of boxes is getting larger.

Step 2 Look at the first two figures in the pattern. Find how they change.

To get from the first figure to the second figure, add 2 boxes (1 to each row).

Step 3 Test the rule with each pair of figures in the pattern.

The rule is true between each pair of figures.

Step 4 Find the number of boxes in the next figure.

Add 2 to the number of boxes in the last figure: $9 + 2 = 11$.

SOLUTION: The rule is to add 2 boxes each time. The fifth figure will have 11 boxes.

Try It! **Use what you know to solve this problem.**

1 These dots follow a pattern. Describe the rule. Then find the total number of dots in the missing figure. ______________________

____

● ● ●
● ●
●

______

● ● ● ● ●
● ● ● ●
● ● ●

● ● ● ● ● ●
● ● ● ● ●
● ● ● ●

Read the Think About It to understand the problem. Then solve the problem.

Think About It

A function table shows the pattern between two sets of numbers. What is the relationship between the numbers in the *x* column and the numbers in the *y* column?

What number is missing in the function table?

x	*y*
1	5
2	10
3	
4	20

A 11

B 15

C 20

D 25

EXPLANATION:

To find the number in the *y* column, multiply the number in the *x* column by 5.

CORRECT ANSWER:

Answer choice **B** is correct.

INCORRECT ANSWERS:

Read why the other answer choices are not correct.

A 11 is not correct because it does not follow the rule of $x \times 5$.

C 20 is not correct because it does not follow the rule of $x \times 5$.

D 25 is not correct because it does not follow the rule of $x \times 5$.

Guided Practice

Hints

Look at the list. Decide whether the numbers are getting larger or smaller. What operation could you use for the rule?

Sometimes saying the pattern out loud helps you find the repeating part.

When you find a rule that works for the first two numbers, check that it works for each pair in the list.

PAIR SHARE

With your partner, share and discuss your answers and supporting details.

Solve each problem. Use the Hints to help you. Then explain how you found your solution.

1 The numbers below follow a pattern.

41, 44, 47, 50, ____, ____

Which numbers come next in this pattern?

Solution: ______________________________

Explanation: ______________________________

____

2 These shapes follow a pattern.

  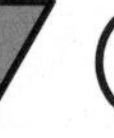   ___ 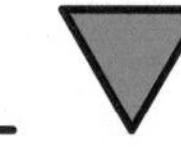   

Which shape is missing from the pattern?

Solution: ______________________________

Explanation: ______________________________

____

3 The table shows the list of numbers three students wrote.

Student	List
Aaron	5, 10, 20, 35, 60
Brian	72, 67, 62, 51, 46
Luis	48, 41, 34, 27, 20

Which student wrote a list that is a pattern?

Solution: ______________________________

Explanation: ______________________________

____

FL Math Practice

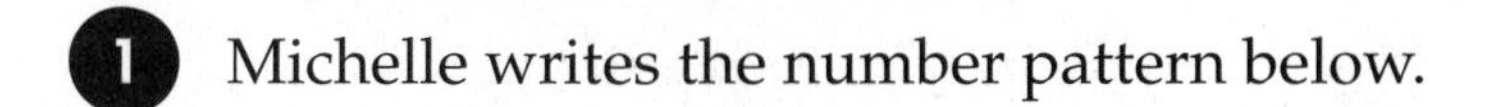

1 Michelle writes the number pattern below.

67, 59, 51, 43, 35, __?__

How would Michelle find the next number in the pattern?

Ⓐ divide 35 by 8

Ⓑ multiply 35 by 8

Ⓒ add 8 to 35

Ⓓ subtract 8 from 35

2 Sonia drew the pattern below.

What are the next two shapes in Sonia's pattern?

Ⓕ

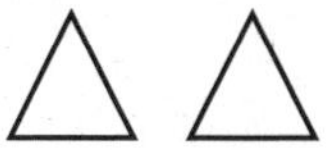

Ⓖ

Ⓗ

Ⓘ

3 The table below shows the number of minutes it takes Jeff to read different numbers of pages in his book.

READING RATE

Pages	Minutes
1	3
2	6
3	9
4	12
5	?

If the pattern in the table continues, how many minutes will it take Jeff to read 5 pages?

Ⓐ 13

Ⓑ 15

Ⓒ 16

Ⓓ 18

4 Look at the number pattern below.

5, 11, 17, 23, __?__, 35

What is the missing number in the pattern?

Ⓕ 25

Ⓖ 28

Ⓗ 29

Ⓘ 30

5 What is the missing number in the function table below?

x	y
3	9
5	15
8	24
9	

Ⓐ 30

Ⓑ 27

Ⓒ 25

Ⓓ 21

Lesson 14
Length

NGSSS

MA.3.G.5.2: Measure objects using fractional parts of linear units such as $\frac{1}{2}$, $\frac{1}{4}$, and $\frac{1}{10}$.

Introduction

Length is the distance from one point to another point. A **unit** is a basic amount used to measure. Some units of length are listed in the tables below.

Customary Unit	Example
Inch	width of a quarter

Metric Unit	Example
Millimeter	thickness of a penny
Centimeter	width of a fingernail

Rulers are used to measure length. Most rulers divide each inch into fractional parts, which you can use to measure $\frac{1}{4}$, $\frac{1}{2}$, and $\frac{3}{4}$ of an inch.

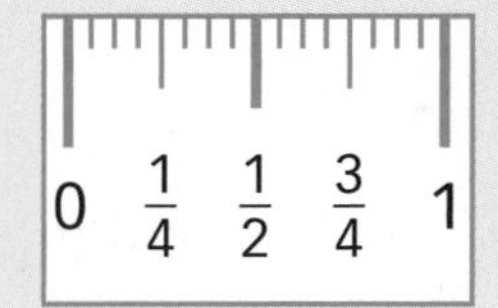

Each centimeter is divided into 10 millimeters.

- **To find the length of the key to the nearest centimeter:**

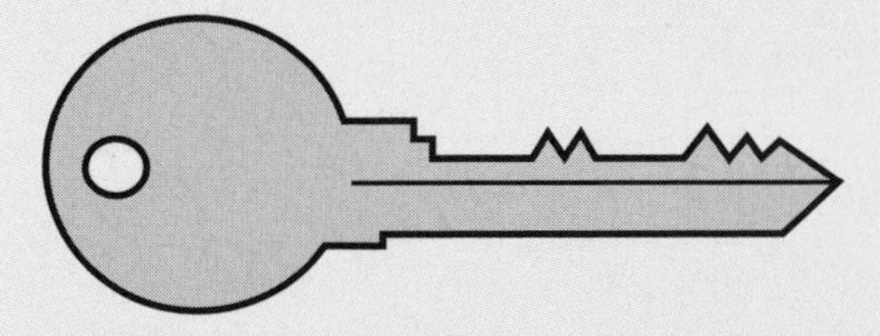

Line up the left edge (the 0 mark) of your centimeter ruler with the left edge of the key. Then follow the key to its farthest point on the right. Look down at the ruler and find the mark that is closest to the right edge of the key.

The key ends closest to the 6. The key is about 6 cm in length.

EXAMPLE 1

Look at the rectangle below. Use a ruler to measure side *FG* to the nearest half inch. About how long is side *FG*?

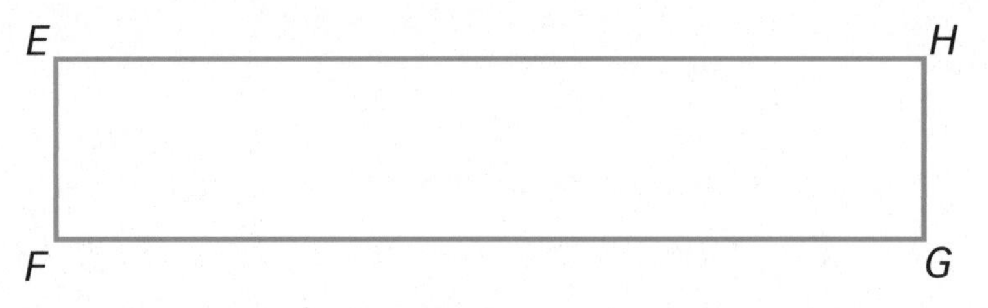

Follow these steps to solve the problem.

Step 1 Make sure you are using the correct ruler. The ruler should show inches. On an inch ruler, the distance between each whole number is about the diameter of a quarter.

Step 2 Follow along the length of side *FG*. Line up the first mark on the ruler (the 0 mark) with point *F*. Follow the side of the rectangle to point *G*.

Step 3 Find the length to the nearest half inch. Point *G* is exactly halfway between the 3-inch mark and the 4-inch mark.

SOLUTION: Side *FG* is about $3\frac{1}{2}$ inches in length.

Try It! **Use what you know to solve this problem.**

1 Use a ruler to measure the length of the pencil below to the nearest half inch. What is the length of the pencil? __________

EXAMPLE 2

Use a ruler to measure the straw below to the nearest millimeter.

Follow these steps to solve the problem.

Step 1 Make sure you are using the correct ruler. The ruler should show centimeters. Each centimeter is divided into 10 parts. Each line represents 1 millimeter.

Step 2 Line up the first mark on the ruler (the 0 mark) with the left end of the straw. Follow the straw to the right end.

Step 3 Find the length to the nearest millimeter. The straw ends 5 millimeters after the 7.

SOLUTION: The straw is 7 centimeters, 5 millimeters long. Since there are 10 millimeters in each centimeter, you could also say the straw is 75 millimeters long.

Try It!

Use what you know to solve this problem.

1 Use a ruler to measure the length of the popsicle stick below to the nearest millimeter. What is the length of the popsicle stick?

____

Guided Instruction

Read the Think About It to understand the problem. Then solve the problem.

Think About It

Where do you need to line up the first mark on the ruler?

Mr. Yu is using a piece of chalk like the one shown below.

What is the exact length, in inches, of the chalk?

A $1\frac{1}{4}$ inches

B $1\frac{1}{2}$ inches

C $1\frac{3}{4}$ inches

D 2 inches

EXPLANATION:

Line up the first mark on the ruler with the left side of the chalk. Look for the mark where the right side of the chalk ends.

CORRECT ANSWER:

Answer choice **C** is correct.

INCORRECT ANSWERS:

Read why the other choices are not correct.

A $1\frac{1}{4}$ inches is shorter than the chalk.

B $1\frac{1}{2}$ inches is shorter than the chalk.

D 2 inches is longer than the chalk.

Guided Practice

Hints

Be sure to use the right ruler. Use the examples from the beginning of the lesson to check which ruler you are using.

The nearest half inch might be at a half-inch mark or at a whole-inch mark.

How many millimeters are in a centimeter?

Solve each problem. Use the Hints to help you. Then explain how you found your solution.

1 Use a ruler to measure the length of the butterfly below to the nearest centimeter. About how long is the butterfly?

Solution: ______________________________

Explanation: ______________________________

____

2 How long is the crayon to the nearest half inch?

CRAYON

Solution: ______________________________

Explanation: ______________________________

____

3 How long is the piece of yarn to the nearest millimeter?

Solution: ______________________________

Explanation: ______________________________

____

PAIR SHARE

With your partner, share and discuss your answers and supporting details.

1 Jesse has a paper clip like the one shown below.

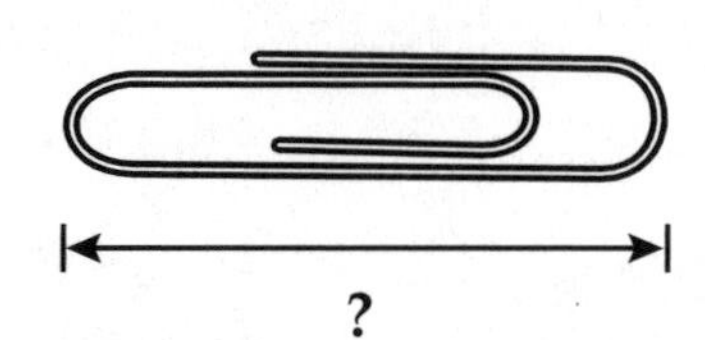

Using a ruler, what is the exact length, in centimeters, of the paper clip?

Ⓐ 4 cm

Ⓑ 3 cm

Ⓒ 2 cm

Ⓓ 1 cm

2 Maddy found a shell like the one shown below.

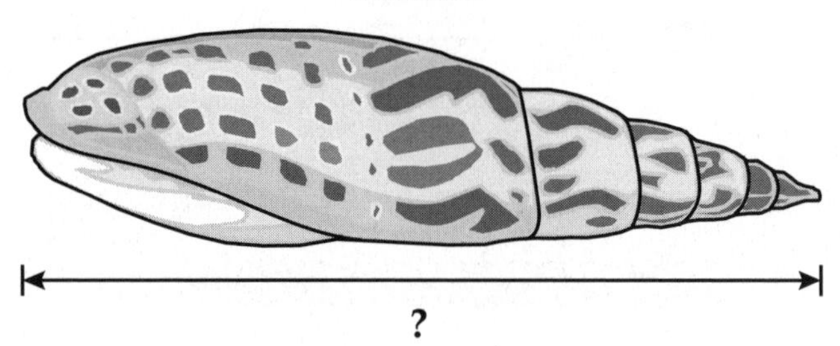

Using a ruler, what is the exact length, in inches, of the shell?

Ⓕ 3 inches

Ⓖ $3\frac{1}{4}$ inches

Ⓗ $3\frac{1}{2}$ inches

Ⓘ $3\frac{3}{4}$ inches

3 Mason plays golf with a ball like the one shown below.

GOLF BALL

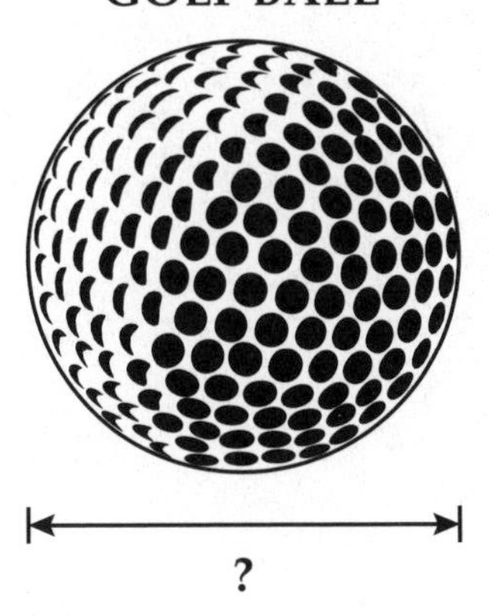

?

Using a ruler, what is the exact length, in inches, of the ball?

Ⓐ 1 inch

Ⓑ $1\frac{1}{2}$ inches

Ⓒ 2 inches

Ⓓ $2\frac{1}{2}$ inches

4 Look at the stick of gum shown below.

STICK OF GUM

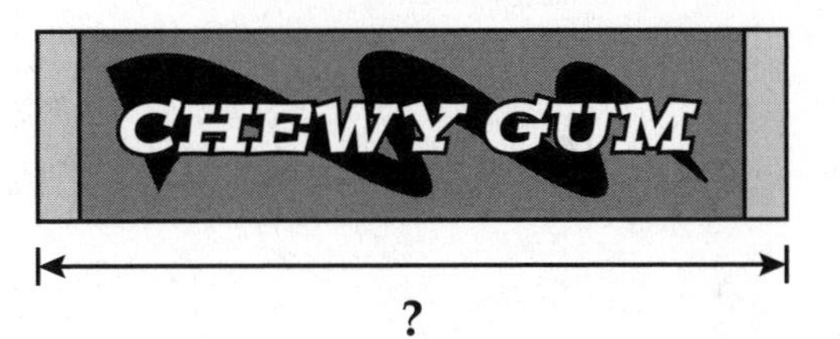

?

Using a ruler, what is the exact length, in millimeters, of the stick of gum?

Ⓕ 6 mm

Ⓖ 7 mm

Ⓗ 63 mm

Ⓘ 65 mm

5 David ate his cereal with a spoon like the one below.

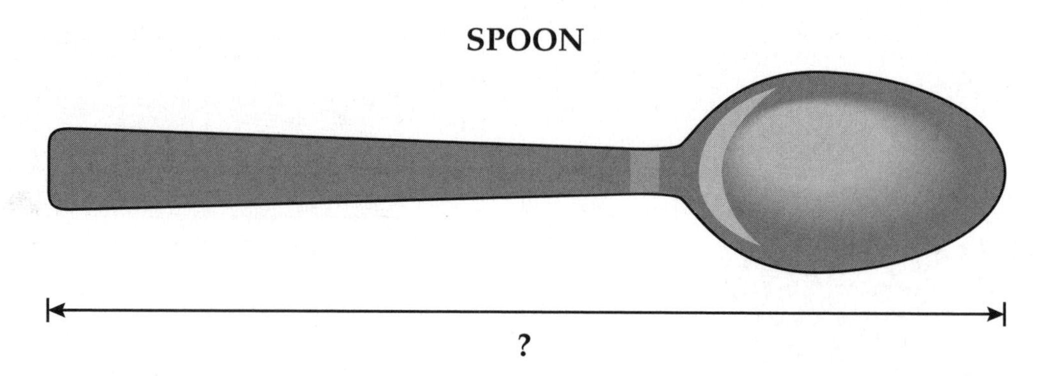

Using a ruler, what is the exact length, in inches, of the spoon?

Ⓐ 5 inches

Ⓑ $4\frac{3}{4}$ inches

Ⓒ $4\frac{1}{2}$ inches

Ⓓ $4\frac{1}{4}$ inches

6 Look at the piece of licorice shown below.

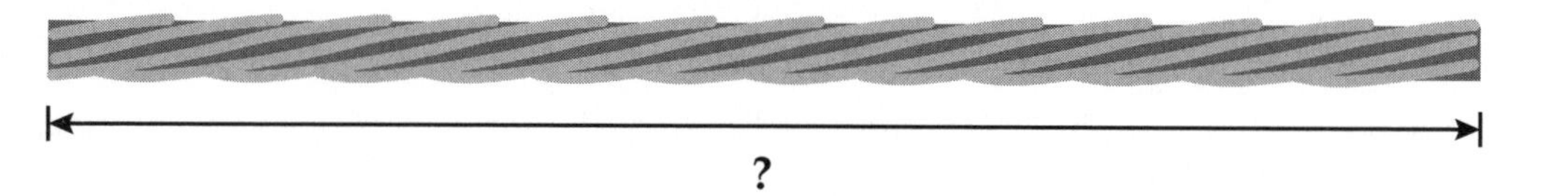

Using a ruler, what is the exact length, in centimeters, of the licorice?

Ⓕ 135 cm

Ⓖ 130 cm

Ⓗ 14 cm

Ⓘ 13 cm

Lesson 15
Perimeter

NGSSS

MA.3.G.5.1: Select appropriate units, strategies, and tools to solve problems involving perimeter.

Introduction

In this lesson, you will find the perimeter of a shape. **Perimeter** is the distance around an object. To find the perimeter of any shape, add the lengths of all the sides together.

9 ft 9 ft

12 ft

9 ft + 9 ft + 12 ft = 30 ft

The perimeter of the triangle is 30 ft.

- **To find the perimeter of the figure below:**

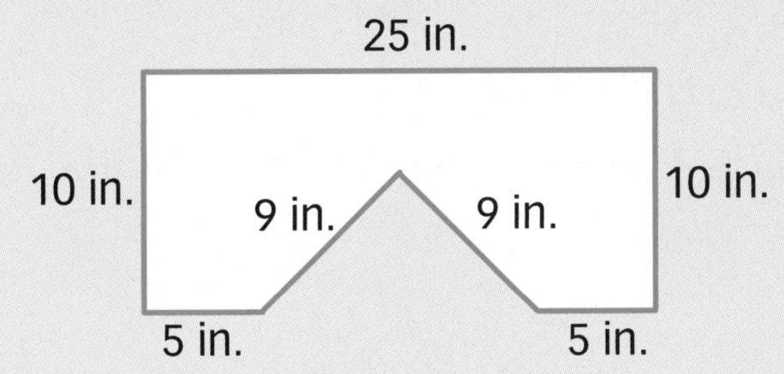

Step	Example
Start at one corner of the figure.	Choose the left side.
Write the length of a side.	10 in.
Trace along the outline of the figure.	Write the length of each side.
Write an addition sentence.	10 + 5 + 9 + 9 + 5 + 10 + 25.
Count the number of sides in the figure and the measurements in the addition sentence.	There are 7 sides in the figure and 7 measurements in the addition sentence.
Find the sum of the lengths.	10 + 5 + 9 + 9 + 5 + 10 + 25 = 73

The perimeter of the figure is 73 inches.

Modeled Instruction

EXAMPLE 1

What is the perimeter of the rectangle?

21 m
32 m

Follow these steps to solve the problem.

Step 1 Find the missing side lengths. In a rectangle, the opposite sides have the same measure.

The side opposite 32 m is 32 m. The side opposite 21 m is 21 m.

Step 2 Trace along the outline of the figure. Write an addition sentence.

21 + 32 + 21 + 32

Step 3 Check that you have all of the sides listed.

There are 4 sides in the figure. There are 4 measurements in the addition sentence.

Step 4 Find the sum of the side lengths.

21 + 32 + 21 + 32 = 106

SOLUTION: The perimeter of the rectangle is 106 m.

Try It! **Use what you know to solve these problems.**

1 What is the perimeter of the triangle?

____

3 cm
5 cm
4 cm

2 What is the perimeter of a square with sides 16 yards long?

____

EXAMPLE 2

Use a ruler to measure the perimeter of the figure to the nearest centimeter.

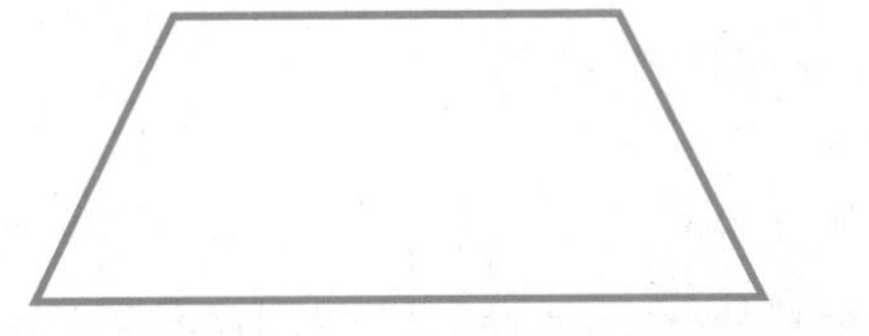

Follow these steps to solve the problem.

Step 1 Measure the length of each side with a centimeter ruler.

Place the ruler along each side.

Line up the 0 on the ruler with the left corner of each side.

Step 2 Label each side length on the figure.

Step 3 Start at one corner. Trace along the outline of the figure.

Write the length of each side in an addition sentence: $2 + 3 + 2 + 5$.

Step 4 Check that you have all of the sides in your addition sentence.

There are 4 sides in the figure.

There are 4 measurements in the addition sentence.

Step 5 Find the sum of the side lengths: $2 + 3 + 2 + 5 = 12$.

SOLUTION: The perimeter of this figure is 12 cm.

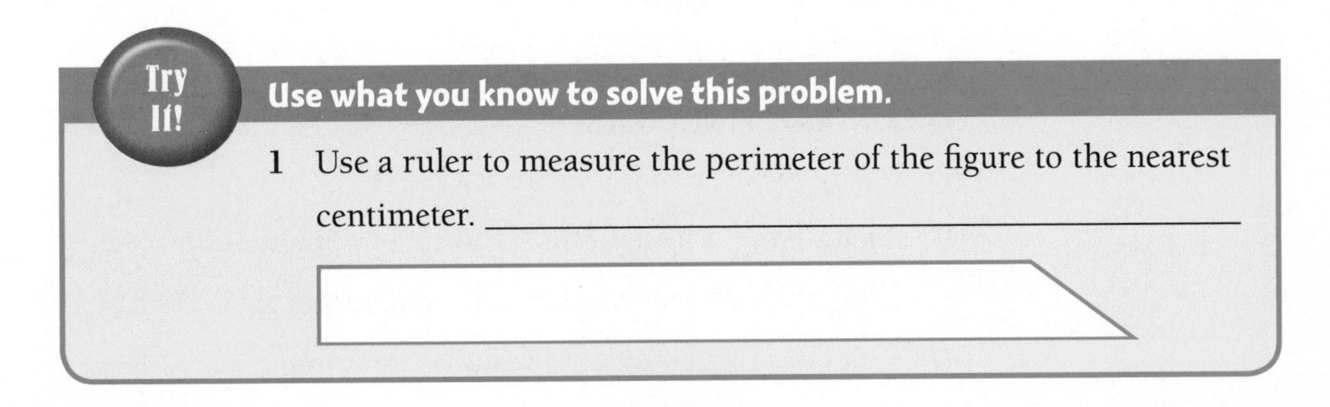

Try It!

Use what you know to solve this problem.

1 Use a ruler to measure the perimeter of the figure to the nearest centimeter. ______________________

Guided Instruction

Read the Think About It to understand the problem. Then solve the problem.

Think About It

How many numbers do you need to add together to find the perimeter?

The rug in Kara's bedroom has a perimeter of 36 feet, as shown below.

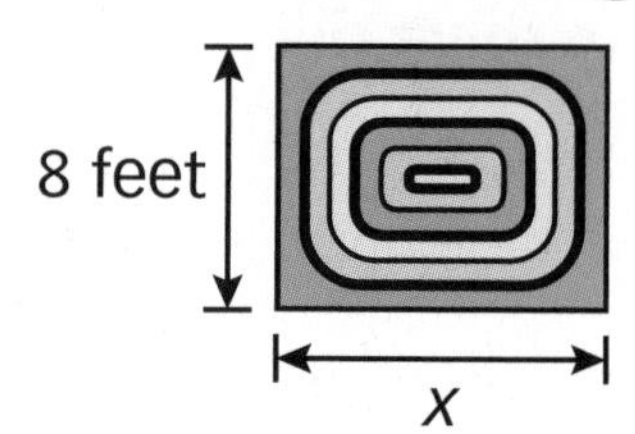

If the width of the rug is 8 feet, what is the length?

A 10 feet

B 12 feet

C 20 feet

D 28 feet

EXPLANATION:

To find the perimeter, you need to add 8 + 8 + length + length. Check each answer choice to see which one will result in a perimeter of 36.

CORRECT ANSWER:

Answer choice **A** is correct.

INCORRECT ANSWERS:

Read why the other choices are not correct.

B A length of 12 feet would result in a perimeter of 40 feet.

C A length of 20 feet would result in a perimeter of 56 feet.

D A length of 28 feet would result in a perimeter of 72 feet.

Hints

Use what you know about rectangles to find each missing side length.

Be sure to measure each side using millimeters. Label the sides as you measure.

Count the number of sides in the figure. You should have that many numbers to add in your addition sentence.

Solve each problem. Use the Hints to help you. Then explain how you found your solution.

1 What is the perimeter of the rectangle?

8 yd
19 yd

Solution: ______________________________

Explanation: ______________________________

2 Joe got the sticker below on one of his math papers. Use a ruler to measure the perimeter of the sticker to the nearest millimeter.

Solution: ______________________________

Explanation: ______________________________

3 Find the perimeter of the figure.

16 ft
9 ft
16 ft
12 ft
9 ft

Solution: ______________________________

Explanation: ______________________________

With your partner, share and discuss your answers and supporting details.

1. Jill wants to build a sandbox that has a perimeter of 24 meters.

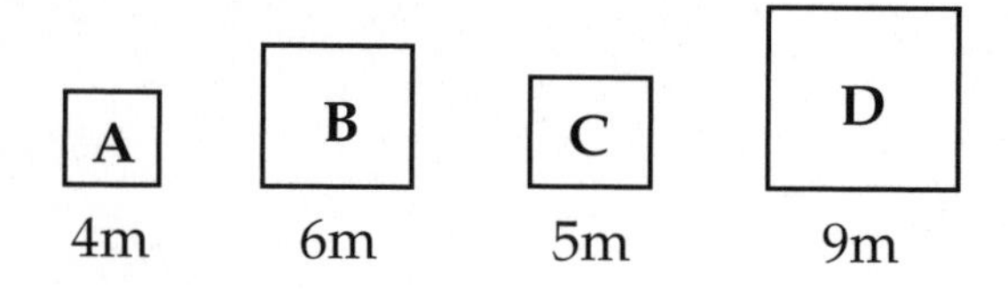

Which square could represent a sandbox with a perimeter of 24 m?

Ⓐ A

Ⓑ B

Ⓒ C

Ⓓ D

2. Lisa's living room is shaped like the figure below.

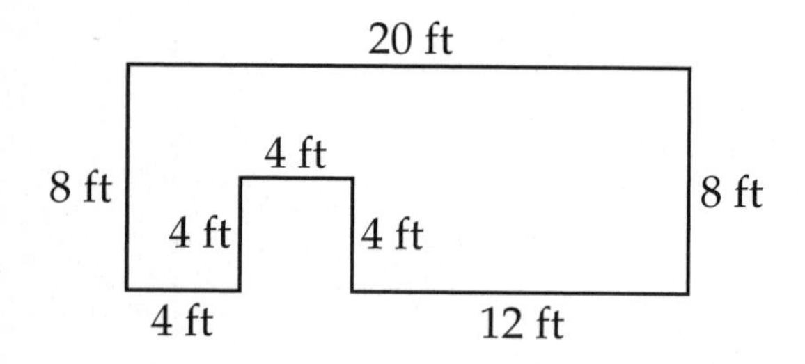

What is the perimeter of Lisa's living room?

Ⓕ 56 ft

Ⓖ 60 ft

Ⓗ 64 ft

Ⓘ 160 ft

3. Jenna's kitchen table has a perimeter of 16 feet, as shown below.

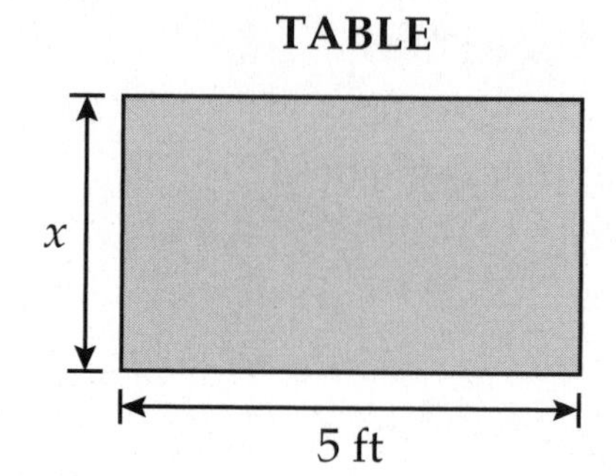

If the length of the table is 5 feet, what is the width?

Ⓐ 11 feet

Ⓑ 9 feet

Ⓒ 5 feet

Ⓓ 3 feet

4. Marc drew the shape below.

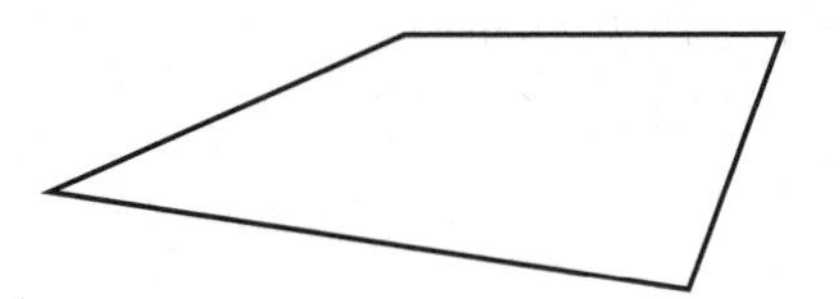

Use your ruler to measure the sides of Marc's shape. What is the perimeter of the shape, to the nearest centimeter?

Ⓕ 4 cm

Ⓖ 6 cm

Ⓗ 11 cm

Ⓘ 14 cm

Lesson 16
Time

NGSSS

MA.3.G.5.3: Tell time to the nearest minute and to the nearest quarter hour, and determine the amount of time elapsed.

Introduction

Time tells you how long it takes something to happen. Time can be measured in seconds, minutes, hours, days, weeks, months, or years. Clocks and calendars are used to measure time.

Digital clocks tell the time by showing the numbers. The hours are before the : symbol. The minutes are after the : symbol. The digital clock to the right shows the time is 3:15.

Analog clocks show the time using an hour hand and a minute hand. The short hand points to the hour. The long hand points to the minute. The numbers on the clock (1–12) tell the hours. To find the minutes, look at the numbers and the small marks between the numbers. Each number is 5 minutes apart. The "1" shows 5 minutes, the "2" shows 10 minutes, the "3" shows 15 minutes, and so on. The analog clock above shows 3:15.

To find **elapsed time**, you count the number of hours and minutes from the starting time to the ending time.

- **Find the elapsed time from 1:00 to 3:30.**

Count the number of full hours. 1:00 until 2:00 and 2:00 to 3:00	2 hours
Count the number of minutes. 3:00 until 3:30.	30 minutes

So, the elapsed time between 1:00 and 3:30 is 2 hours, 30 minutes.

EXAMPLE 1

What time is shown on the clock?

Follow these steps to solve the problem.

Step 1 Find the hour hand on the clock. The hour hand is the shorter hand.

The hour hand is barely past the 3.
This means the time is in the 3:00 hour.

Step 2 Find the minute hand. The minute hand is the longer hand.

The minute hand is 3 marks past the 2.
Remember that each number stands for 5 minutes.
Start at the 12 and count by 5s until you get to the 2. The 1 is 5 minutes past the hour, and the 2 is 10 minutes past the hour.
Then add 3 more minutes for the 3 marks past the 2. That makes it 13 minutes past the hour.

Step 3 Write the time.

Write the hour first. Then write the minutes after the : symbol.

SOLUTION: The clock shows 3:13.

Use what you know to solve this problem.

1 What time is shown on the clock?

____

EXAMPLE 2

Ellie started working on her homework at the time shown on the clock. If she finished at 5:00, how long did it take Ellie to do her homework?

Follow these steps to solve the problem.

Step 1 Find the time Ellie started her homework.

The hour hand is past the 4 and the minute hand is on the 5, so Ellie started her homework at 4:25.

Step 2 Count the number of full hours between 4:25 and 5:00.

One full hour after 4:25 would be 5:25, so the elapsed time is less than one hour.

Step 3 Count the number of minutes.

The minute hand is on the 5. At 5:00, the minute hand will be on the 12. Put your finger on the 5. Move around the clock counting by 5s until you get to the 12 to find the number of minutes.

SOLUTION: It took Ellie 35 minutes to do her homework.

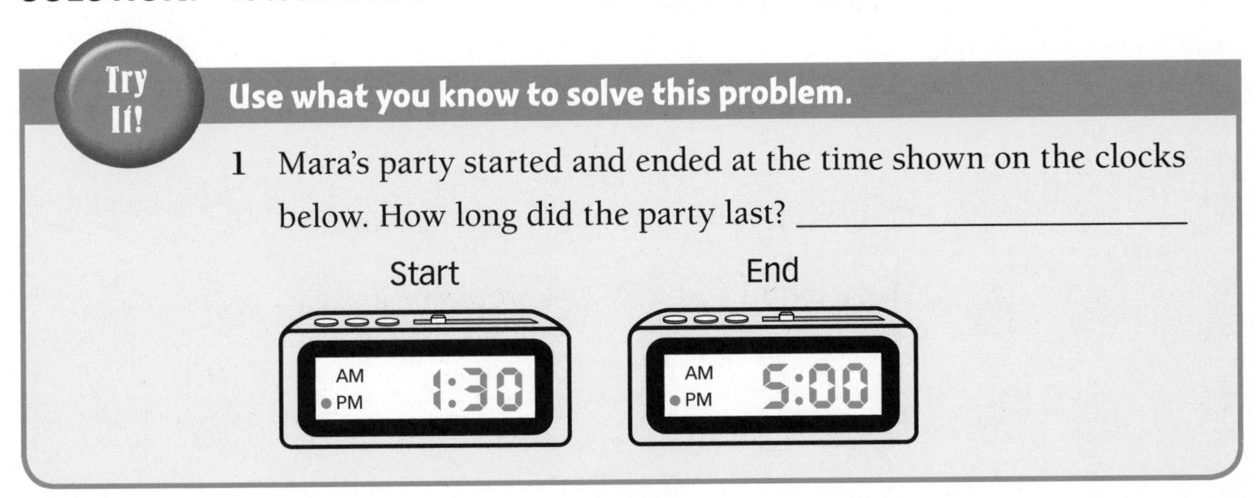

Try It! **Use what you know to solve this problem.**

1 Mara's party started and ended at the time shown on the clocks below. How long did the party last? ______________

Read the Think About It to understand the problem. Then solve the problem.

Think About It

What are the names of the months in order? How many months is it from May to October?

Josie started saving money for a new bike on May 1. She bought a bike on October 1. How many months did it take for Josie to save the money for her bike?

A 4

B 5

C 6

D 10

EXPLANATION:

Start with May. Say the months in order until October. Count 1 each time you say a month. June would be 1 month, July would be 2 months, and so on.

CORRECT ANSWER:

Answer choice **B** is correct.

INCORRECT ANSWERS:

Read why the other choices are not correct.

A 4 months from May 1 would be September 1.

C 6 months from May 1 would be November 1.

D 10 months from May 1 would be March 1 of the next year.

Guided Practice

Hints

Look at the hour hand and then the minute hand to find the time. The hour hand is the shorter hand.

Count the number of hours first. Then count the number of minutes.

Remember, there are 7 days in 1 week.

PAIR SHARE

With your partner, share and discuss your answers and supporting details.

Solve each problem. Use the Hints to help you. Then explain how you found your solution.

1 Rochelle has a piano lesson at the time shown on the clock. What time is her piano lesson?

Solution: ______________________________

Explanation: ______________________________

2 A movie started and ended at the times shown on the clocks below. How long was the movie?

Start

End

Solution: ______________________________

Explanation: ______________________________

3 Sarah's birthday is on February 7. Jane's birthday is on February 28. How many weeks is it between the two birthdays?

FEBRUARY

Su	M	T	W	Th	F	Sa
1	2	3	4	5	6	7
8	9	10	11	12	13	14
15	16	17	18	19	20	21
22	23	24	25	26	27	28

Solution: ______________________________

Explanation: ______________________________

1 Laura has to be at work at the time shown on the clock below.

At what time does Laura have to be at work?

Ⓐ 1:07

Ⓑ 1:35

Ⓒ 7:05

Ⓓ 7:07

2 Jeff starts school at the time shown below.

School ends at 3:10 P.M. How long is Jeff at school each day?

Ⓕ 5 hours

Ⓖ 6 hours

Ⓗ 7 hours

Ⓘ 8 hours

4 Lucy's little sister was born in 2005. Her little brother was born in 2008. How many years was it between the births of Lucy's sister and brother?

Ⓐ 3

Ⓑ 4

Ⓒ 5

Ⓓ 8

4 Manny's tuba lesson starts at the time shown below.

If the lesson ends at 3:15, how long is Manny's tuba lesson?

Ⓕ 15 minutes

Ⓖ 30 minutes

Ⓗ 35 minutes

Ⓘ 45 minutes

Lesson 17

Comparing, Ordering, and Representing Numbers

NGSSS

MA.3.A.6.1: Represent, compute, estimate, and solve problems using numbers through hundred thousands

Introduction

This lesson will show you how to compare and order whole numbers. You will also learn about different representations of numbers.

When you compare two numbers, you decide which is larger or smaller. Symbols like greater than (>), less than (<), equal to (=), and not equal to (≠) can be used to compare two numbers.

Place value tells how much each digit in a number is worth. Start with the largest place value to compare numbers. Then move to the right.

thousands	hundreds	tens	ones
2	4	7	3
2	6	8	5

- **To compare the numbers in the chart:**

Start with the largest place value.	Both numbers have a 2 in the thousands place.
Look at the next larger place value.	The digits are different.
Look for the smallest digit.	$4 < 6$.

So, 2,473 is less than 2,685. This is also written as $2{,}473 < 2{,}685$.

- **Numbers can be represented in different ways.**

The number 2,473 from the chart can be thought of as 2 thousands, 4 hundreds, 7 tens, and 3 ones. It can also be thought of as 24 hundreds and 73 ones or as 2 thousands, 47 tens and 3 ones. There are many different ways to represent any number you are given.

Modeled Instruction

EXAMPLE 1

Name three ways to represent the number 753.

Follow these steps to solve the problem.

Step 1 One of the easiest ways to represent a number is to use the place values of each digit. 7 is in the hundreds place, so use 7 hundreds. 5 is in the tens place, so use 5 tens. 3 is in the ones place, so use 3 ones.

Step 2 Find another way to represent the number. Start with 7 hundreds, 5 tens, and 3 ones. Since there are 10 tens in 1 hundred, you could trade 1 hundred for 10 tens. This would give you 6 hundreds, 15 tens, and 3 ones.

Step 3 Find another way to represent the number. Start with 7 hundreds, 5 tens, and 3 ones. Since there are 10 ones in 1 ten, you could trade 5 tens for 50 ones. This would give you 7 hundreds and 53 ones.

SOLUTION: You can represent 753 with 7 hundreds, 5 tens, and 3 ones; 6 hundreds, 15 tens, and 3 ones; or 7 hundreds and 53 ones.

Try It! **Use what you know to solve this problem.**

1 Name three ways to represent the number 3,892.

___

___

___

EXAMPLE 2

Which number is greater?

6,372 **6,319**

Follow these steps to solve the problem.

Step 1 Line up the numbers by place value.

6,372
6,319

Step 2 Start with the largest place value. Both numbers have a 6 in the thousands place. Look at the next largest place value. Both numbers have a 3 in the hundreds place. Move to the right and compare. The digits in the tens place are different.

Step 3 Compare the digits that are different by using a symbol. 7 is greater than 1, so $7 > 1$. The number with 7 in the tens place is greater than the number with 1 in the tens place.

Step 4 6,372 is greater than 6,319. Use a symbol to compare the numbers.

SOLUTION: $6{,}372 > 6{,}319$

Use what you know to solve these problems.

1 Which number is greater: 228,051 or 228,150? ______________

2 Which number is greater: 79,467 or 89,463? ______________

3 Use a symbol to compare 103,521 and 103,521. ______________

____

Read the Think About It to understand the problem.
Then solve the problem.

Think About It

Look at the thousands place of each number in the answer choices. Can you narrow down your choices?

Which list shows the numbers from least to greatest?

A 43,408; 43,480; 44,038; 48,340

B 48,340; 44,038; 43,480; 43,408

C 43,408; 44,038; 43,480; 48,340

D 43,480; 43,408; 44,038; 48,340

EXPLANATION:

Look at the numbers in the first list. They all have 4 in the ten-thousands place. Look at the thousands place. 8 is greater than 4, so 48,340 is greater than 44,038. 4 is greater than 3, so 44,038 is greater than 43,408 and 43,480. Two numbers have 3 thousands. The digits in the hundreds place are the same. Compare the digits in the tens place. 0 is less than 8, so 43,408 is less than 43,480.

CORRECT ANSWER:

Answer choice **A** is correct.

INCORRECT ANSWERS:

Read why the other answer choices are not correct.

B is not correct because the numbers are listed from greatest to least.

C is not correct because 44,038 is greater than 43,480.

D is not correct because 43,480 is greater than 43,408.

Guided Practice

Hints

Start with the largest place value. Compare and move to the right.

Think about what could be traded for 1 hundred or 1 thousand.

Order the scores first. Then write the names in the same order.

Solve each problem. Use the Hints to help you. Then explain how you found your solution.

1 Is this sentence true?

$9{,}738 < 9{,}684$

Solution: ______________________________

Explanation: ______________________________

____

____

2 Collin used 4 thousands, 7 hundreds, and 3 tens to represent the number 4,730. What is another way to represent 4,730?

Solution: ______________________________

Explanation: ______________________________

____

____

3 The table below shows the video game scores of four players.

Player	Gianna	Isaac	Jack	Neva
Score	8,075	7,892	8,040	9,798

List the players in order from greatest to least scores.

Solution: ______________________________

Explanation: ______________________________

____

____

PAIR SHARE

With your partner, share and discuss your answers and supporting details.

FL Math Practice

1 Which list shows the numbers in order from **least** to **greatest**?

Ⓐ 8,490; 8,094; 4,980; 948

Ⓑ 4,980; 8,094; 8,490; 948

Ⓒ 948; 4,980; 8,490; 8,094

Ⓓ 948; 4,980; 8,094; 8,490

2 In this list, which is the **least** number?

401,325   401,523   401,235   401,352

Ⓕ 401,352

Ⓖ 401,325

Ⓗ 401,235

Ⓘ 401,523

3 Which correctly compares the numbers?

Ⓐ $2{,}915 > 2{,}519$

Ⓑ $2{,}915 < 2{,}519$

Ⓒ $2{,}519 = 2{,}915$

Ⓓ $2{,}519 > 2{,}915$

4 Which shows one way to represent the number 1,075?

Ⓕ 1 hundred, 7 tens, 5 ones

Ⓖ 1 thousand, 7 hundreds, 5 ones

Ⓗ 10 hundreds, 7 tens, 5 ones

Ⓘ 1 thousand, 75 tens

5 This table shows the amount of money donated by four teams.

Team	Dollars Donated
Comets	17,368
Cowboys	15,942
Rangers	16,790
Stars	15,807

Which compares the amount of money the Rangers donated to the amount the Comets donated?

Ⓐ $17{,}368 < 15{,}942$

Ⓑ $16{,}790 < 17{,}368$

Ⓒ $16{,}790 > 15{,}807$

Ⓓ $15{,}942 < 16{,}790$

Lesson 18

Estimation

NGSSS

MA.3.A.6.1: Represent, compute, estimate, and solve problems using numbers through hundred thousands.

Introduction

When you **estimate**, you find a number close to the exact amount. This makes it easier to do the math in your head. You can also use estimation to check your answers. Your estimated answer will give you a hint about whether your answer is right or wrong. Below are three different ways to estimate sums.

- **To estimate the sum of 136 and 263:**

Step	Result
Round the first number to the nearest hundred.	136 rounds to 100.
Round the second number to the nearest hundred.	263 rounds to 300.
Find the sum of the rounded numbers.	100 + 300 = 400.

The sum of 136 and 263 is about 400.

- **To estimate the sum of 23 and 78:**

Step	Result
Think of numbers that are close to the original numbers that are easy to add in your head.	23 is close to 25. 78 is close to 75
Find the sum of the compatible numbers.	25 + 75 = 100.

The sum of 23 and 78 is about 100.

- **To estimate the sum of 320, 295, 311, and 273:**

Step	Result
Check to see if all numbers in the group are close to the same number.	320, 295, 311, and 273 are all close to 300.
Add 300 four times.	300 + 300 + 300 + 300 = 1,200

The sum of 320, 295, 311, and 273 is about 1,200.

Modeled Instruction

EXAMPLE 1

A store sold 6,767 frozen pizzas last year and 8,230 this year. About how many more pizzas were sold this year than last year?

Follow these steps to solve the problem.

Step 1 The problem uses the word *about* in the question. It does not ask for an exact answer, so you can estimate. Since it asks *how many more*, it is a subtraction problem.

Step 2 To estimate, first round each number to the nearest thousand.

6,767 rounds up to 7,000.
8,230 rounds down to 8,000.

Step 3 Set up the subtraction problem using the rounded numbers. Subtract the rounded number of pizzas sold last year (7,000) from the rounded number of pizzas sold this year (8,000).

8,000 − 7,000

SOLUTION: The store sold about 1,000 more pizzas this year than last year.

Try It! **Use what you know to solve these problems.**

1 Ted has 690 pennies. Kari has 532 pennies. About how many more pennies does Ted have than Kari? ____________________

2 Nevin is trying to solve the problem 44 + 59 + 27. Estimate the answer to his problem. ______________________________

EXAMPLE 2

Trevor scored 33,075 points on a pinball game. Nicole scored 65,050 points. Estimate the difference between the two scores.

Follow these steps to solve the problem.

Step 1 The problem uses the word *estimate*, so you do not have to find an exact answer. Since it asks for the difference, it is a subtraction problem.

Step 2 To estimate, think of numbers close to the original numbers that are easy to subtract in your head.

Change 33,075 to 35,000.
Change 65,050 to 65,000.

Step 3 Set up the subtraction problem using the compatible numbers. Subtract the new number for Trevor's score (35,000) from the new number for Nicole's score (65,000).

65,000 − 35,000

SOLUTION: The difference between the two scores is about 30,000.

Try It! **Use what you know to solve these problems.**

1 The population of Port St. Lucie is 154,353. The population of Hialeah is 210,542. About how many people live in the two cities combined? ____________________

2 Becca is trying to solve the problem 957 − 62. Estimate the answer to her problem. ____________________

Read the Think About It to understand the problem. Then solve the problem.

Think About It

What number are all three numbers in the problem close to?

On Sunday, 36,883 people visited the Florida State Fair. There were 31,576 visitors on Monday and 27,325 on Tuesday. About how many people were at the fair on the 3 days combined?

A 30,000

B 60,000

C 90,000

D 120,000

EXPLANATION:

All three numbers are near 30,000, so add 30,000 three times.

CORRECT ANSWER:

Answer choice **C** is correct.

INCORRECT ANSWERS:

Read why the other choices are not correct.

A 30,000 is only an estimate of one of the days.

B 60,000 is 30,000 added twice.

D 120,000 is 30,000 added four times.

Guided Practice

Hints

This problem is asking for the best way to estimate, not for the actual answer.

Which digit should you look at when you want to round to the nearest hundred?

What does the word *estimate* tell you about how to solve the problem?

Solve each problem. Use the Hints to help you. Then explain how you found your solution.

1 What is the best way to estimate the answer to the following problem?

$456 + 562 + 488 + 523 = ?$

Solution: ______________________________

Explanation: ______________________________

____

2 Fairmeadows Elementary School has 423 students. Crossroads Elementary School has 371 students. About how many students are there all together?

Solution: ______________________________

Explanation: ______________________________

____

3 Harry's dad is buying a new car. The first one he looked at was priced at $24,550. The second one was priced at $19,325. Estimate the difference between the prices of the two cars.

Solution: ______________________________

Explanation: ______________________________

____

PAIR SHARE

With your partner, share and discuss your answers and supporting details.

1. Pablo went to the zoo. He spent 24 minutes watching the monkeys, 19 minutes watching the tigers, 17 minutes watching the dolphins, and 29 minutes watching the giraffes. Which is the **best estimate** for the total number of minutes Pablo spent watching these animals?

   Ⓐ 40 minutes

   Ⓑ 60 minutes

   Ⓒ 80 minutes

   Ⓓ 100 minutes

2. A grocery store sold 3,423 watermelons and 4,090 cantaloupes this year. Which is the **best estimate** for the number of watermelons and cantaloupes combined?

   Ⓕ 7,000

   Ⓖ 8,000

   Ⓗ 9,000

   Ⓘ 10,000

3. A restaurant served 274 people on Monday, 342 people on Tuesday, and 450 people on Wednesday. Estimate the total number of people the restaurant served on those three days.

   Ⓐ 800

   Ⓑ 900

   Ⓒ 1,000

   Ⓓ 1,100

4. Gary's Granola Factory produced 34,684 granola bars last week and 72,328 granola bars this week. Which is the **best estimate** for how many more granola bars they produced this week than last week?

   Ⓕ 110,000

   Ⓖ 100,000

   Ⓗ 40,000

   Ⓘ 30,000

Lesson 19
Problem Solving

NGSSS

MA.3.A.6.2: Solve non-routine problems by making a table, chart, or list and searching for patterns.

Introduction

In this lesson, you will practice solving problems. There are some problems where you cannot use number sentences to help you figure out the answer. You can use tables, charts, or lists to help you organize information to solve the problem. Other times you can look for a pattern to find the answer.

- **Addi, Tucker, and Zoie are going to stand in a line. How many different ways can they line up?**

Make a table to show the different possibilities.

1st	2nd	3rd
Addi	Tucker	Zoie
Addi	Zoie	Tucker
Tucker	Addi	Zoie
Tucker	Zoie	Addi
Zoie	Tucker	Addi
Zoie	Addi	Tucker

There are 6 different ways the 3 children could stand in a line. Notice there are 2 different times that Addi is first in line, 2 different times that Tucker is first in line, and 2 different times that Zoie is first in line.

EXAMPLE 1

Lianna can choose one kind of ice cream: chocolate or vanilla. She can choose one topping to put on it: fudge, caramel, or marshmallow. How many possible combinations of ice cream and topping are there?

Follow these steps to solve the problem.

Step 1 Make a list of all the possible combinations with chocolate ice cream.

chocolate with fudge
chocolate with caramel
chocolate with marshmallow

Step 2 Make a list of all the possible combinations with vanilla ice cream.

vanilla with fudge
vanilla with caramel
vanilla with marshmallow

Step 3 Count the total number of combinations.

SOLUTION: There are 6 possible combinations of ice cream and topping.

Try It! **Use what you know to solve this problem.**

1 Morgan is choosing her outfit for school today. She can pick either a pink or yellow shirt. She can pick a blue or gray skirt. She can also pick a pair of white or brown shoes. How many possible combinations of 1 shirt, 1 skirt, and 1 pair of shoes does Morgan have to choose from? ____________________

EXAMPLE 2

Mark, Emily, and Abby are each wearing a different color shirt: blue, green, and red. Neither of the girls is wearing blue. Abby is not wearing green. What color shirt is each child wearing? Use the table to help you find the answer.

	Blue	Green	Red
Mark			
Emily			
Abby			

Follow these steps to solve the problem.

Step 1 Read the first statement about the shirts: Neither of the girls is wearing blue. In the blue column in the chart, write "no" next to Emily and Abby. Since Mark is the only one left in the blue column, write "yes" next to his name for blue and "no" for green and red.

Step 2 Read the next statement: Abby is not wearing green. In the green column on the chart, write "no" next to Abby. Since Abby has a no for both blue and green, write "yes" in the red column next to Abby.

Step 3 Since Abby is wearing red, put "no" in the red column for Emily. The only spot left for Emily is green, so write "yes" in the green column.

SOLUTION: Mark is wearing blue, Emily is wearing green, and Abby is wearing red.

Try It! **Use what you know to solve this problem.**

1 Jeff, Ella, and Tim each like a different sport: tennis, baseball, and soccer. Tim's sport uses a racket. Ella's sport does not use a bat. What sport is each child's favorite? Use the table to help you.

	T	B	S
Jeff			
Ella			
Tim			

____

Read the Think About It to understand the problem. Then solve the problem.

Think About It

What is the pattern in the table? Look at the change in the number of dollars between Day 1 and Day 2, and then between Day 2 and Day 3. Then examine the change between Days 3 and 4, and between 4 and 5. Do they have something in common?

The table below shows how many dollar bills Victor has in his wallet each day one week.

Day	1	2	3	4	5	6	7
Dollars	3	2	5	4	7	6	9

If the pattern continues, how many dollars will Victor have on Day 8?

A 8

B 10

C 11

D 12

EXPLANATION:

Find the pattern. 3 dollars are added one day and 1 dollar is taken away the next day. Keep following the pattern up to Day 8.

CORRECT ANSWER:

Answer choice **A** is correct.

EXPLANATION:

Read why the other answer choices are not correct.

B 10 is not correct because it is 1 more than 9, not 1 less.

C 11 is not correct because it is 2 more than 9, not 1 less.

D 12 is not correct because it is 3 more than 9, not 1 less.

Hints

Make a list of all the possible combinations. You can use abbreviations (like T for turkey and H for ham) to make writing the list easier.

Count the total number of cards that have been drawn as you go. After the first two turns, 3 cards have been drawn. After the third turn, 6 cards have been drawn.

PAIR SHARE

With your partner, share and discuss your answers and supporting details.

Solve each problem. Use the Hints to help you. Then explain how you found your answer.

1 The lists below show the sandwich, fruit, and drink choices that Britney has for lunch.

Sandwich: turkey, ham, cheese
Fruit: apple, orange
Drink: milk, juice

Britney can choose 1 kind of sandwich, 1 piece of fruit, and 1 drink. How many possible combinations does Britney have to choose from for lunch?

Solution: ______________________________

Explanation: ______________________________

____

____

2 Eva, Caroline, and Justin have a stack of 15 cards. They will take turns drawing cards, each time drawing 1 more card than was just drawn. Eva will start by drawing 1, then Caroline will draw 2, Justin will draw 3, Eva will draw 4, and so on. Who will draw the last card in the stack?

Solution: ______________________________

Explanation: ______________________________

____

____

1 Paul, Rosa, and Ben are each in charge of a different chore: wash dishes, empty the garbage, or fold laundry. Rosa does not have to wash dishes. Neither of the boys fold the laundry. Ben empties the garbage. Which table below correctly shows which child does each chore?

Ⓐ

	Dishes	Garbage	Laundry
Paul	no	yes	no
Rosa	no	no	yes
Ben	yes	no	no

Ⓑ

	Dishes	Garbage	Laundry
Paul	no	no	yes
Rosa	yes	no	no
Ben	no	yes	no

Ⓒ

	Dishes	Garbage	Laundry
Paul	no	yes	no
Rosa	no	no	yes
Ben	no	yes	no

Ⓓ

	Dishes	Garbage	Laundry
Paul	yes	no	no
Rosa	no	no	yes
Ben	no	yes	no

2 The table below shows the art classes and sports classes that Hannah can choose this school year.

Art Classes	Sports Classes
Painting	Tennis
Drawing	Basketball
Pottery	Swimming

Hannah will choose 1 art class and 1 sports class. How many possible combinations of 1 art class and 1 sports class does Hannah have to choose from?

Ⓕ 6

Ⓖ 8

Ⓗ 9

Ⓘ 12

3 Jess, Kai, Zara, and Tate are running a race. How many different possibilities are there for the order they will finish?

Ⓐ 4

Ⓑ 8

Ⓒ 12

Ⓓ 24

4 Olivia made a table to show how many books she read each week for 8 weeks.

Week	Number of Books
1	1
2	2
3	1
4	2
5	1
6	2
7	1
8	2

If the pattern continues, how many total books will Olivia have read after 10 weeks?

Ⓕ 15

Ⓖ 12

Ⓗ 9

Ⓘ 2

Lesson 20

Frequency Tables

NGSSS

MA.3.S.7.1: Construct and analyze frequency tables, bar graphs, pictographs, and line plots from data, including data collected through observations, surveys, and experiments.

Introduction

A **frequency table** is one way to organize and show information. Suppose you asked ten people, "What is your favorite color?" A frequency table could help you organize the data. **Data** are important pieces of information. In this case, the answers given by the 10 people are the data.

The frequency table below shows the favorite colors of 10 people.

Color	Tally	Number
Red	||	2
Blue	卌	5
Green	||	2
Yellow	|	1

The first column is Color. It lists the answers given by the 10 people. There could have been more or fewer colors, depending on the answers. If all 10 people had chosen red as their favorite color, red would have been the only color listed in the Color column.

The second column is Tally. It shows a tally mark (|) for each time that answer was given. Each tally mark stands for 1. A group of 5 tally marks looks like this: 卌. Tallies make it easy to write down answers as they are given.

The Number column tells you the total number of tally marks in each row.

The frequency table above shows that 2 people chose red, 5 people chose blue, 2 people chose green, and 1 person chose yellow as their favorite color.

Modeled Instruction

EXAMPLE 1

This table shows the number of different kinds of pets students in Miss Marsh's class have.

Pet	Tally	Number
Dog	~~||||~~ |||	
Cat	~~||||~~ ||	
Fish	||||	

What should the missing numbers be?

Follow these steps to solve the problem.

Step 1 Count the tally marks in the first row.

The group of 4 straight tallies with a diagonal line through it stands for 5 tallies. There are 3 tally marks next to the set of 5.

5 tallies + 3 tallies = 8 tallies. There are 8 total tallies in the Dog row.

Step 2 Count the tallies in the second and third rows.

There are 7 tally marks for Cat.

There are 4 tally marks for Fish.

SOLUTION: The missing numbers are 8 for Dog, 7 for Cat, and 4 for Fish.

Use what you know to solve this problem.

1 How many lizards were counted in the table below? ___________

Reptile	Tally	Number
Snake	|||	3
Lizard	~~||||~~	

EXAMPLE 2

This table shows the number of each type of fruit that was sold at a fruit stand on Saturday.

Fruit	Tally	Number
Apples	HHH II	
Oranges	IIII	
Pears	II	

How many more apples were sold than pears?

Follow these steps to solve the problem.

Step 1 Find the number of apples sold on Saturday.

There are 7 tallies. Put a 7 in the Number column.

Step 2 Find the number of pears sold on Saturday.

There are 2 tallies. Put a 2 in the Number column.

Step 3 Subtract the number of pears sold from the number of apples sold. The difference will tell you how many more apples than pears were sold.

$7 - 2 = 5$

SOLUTION: The fruit stand sold 5 more apples than pears on Saturday.

Try It! **Use what you know to solve this problem.**

1 How many blue and red marbles were counted in all? __________

Marble Color	Tally	Number
Blue	HHH IIII	
Red	HHH I	

Read the Think About It to understand the problem. Then solve the problem.

Think About It

Look at the Number column to see how many of Amelia's friends chose cheese.

Amelia asked 10 friends what kind of pizza they like. Their responses are shown in the frequency table.

Kind of Pizza	Tally	Number
Cheese		5
Pepperoni	II	2
Sausage	III	3

Which set of tally marks would complete the table?

A II

B III

C ~~IIII~~

D ~~IIII~~ I

EXPLANATION:

The Cheese row is missing tally marks. 5 students chose cheese, so pick the answer choice that shows 5 tally marks.

CORRECT ANSWER:

Answer choice **C** is correct.

INCORRECT ANSWERS:

Read why the other answer choices are not correct.

A This answer choice shows 2 tally marks, not 5.

B This answer choice shows 3 tally marks, not 5.

D This answer choice shows 6 tally marks, not 5.

Guided Practice

Hints

Remember that the diagonal tally marks show a group of 5 tallies.

"How many more" means this is a subtraction problem. Look at the table to find the numbers you need to use.

PAIR SHARE

With your partner, share and discuss your answers and supporting details.

Solve each problem. Use the Hints to help you. Then explain how you found your solution.

1 What is the missing number in the frequency table?

Size	Tally	Number
Small	卌	5
Medium	卌 卌	
Large	卌 III	8

Solution: ______________________________

Explanation: ______________________________

____

2 The frequency table shows the number of pairs of each type of shoe Mindy has. How many more pairs of sandals does she have than tennis shoes?

Type of Shoes	Tally	Number
Dress Shoes	卌 I	
Sandals	卌 IIII	
Slippers	II	
Tennis Shoes	III	

Solution: ______________________________

Explanation: ______________________________

____

1 Stephen recorded the number of each type of cookie that students picked at lunch one day. Below is his list.

chocolate chip, peanut butter, chocolate chip, sugar, peanut butter, sugar, chocolate chip, chocolate chip, chocolate chip, sugar, chocolate chip, peanut butter, peanut butter, sugar, chocolate chip, chocolate chip, chocolate chip, sugar, chocolate chip, peanut butter, sugar, peanut butter

Which frequency table correctly displays the data?

Ⓐ

Cookie	Tally	Number
Chocolate Chip	~~||||~~ ~~||||~~	10
Peanut Butter	~~||||~~	5
Sugar	~~||||~~	5

Ⓑ

Cookie	Tally	Number
Chocolate Chip	~~||||~~ ~~||||~~	10
Peanut Butter	~~||||~~		6
Sugar	~~||||~~		6

Ⓒ

Cookie	Tally	Number
Chocolate Chip	~~||||~~ ~~||||~~	10
Peanut Butter	~~||||~~	5
Sugar	~~||||~~		6

Ⓓ

Cookie	Tally	Number
Chocolate Chip	~~||||~~		6
Peanut Butter	~~||||~~ ~~||||~~	10
Sugar	~~||||~~		6

2 Raymond recorded the eye color of each student in his class. Below is his list and the frequency table he made.

brown, blue, blue, green, brown, brown, green, brown, blue, blue, brown, green, green, blue, brown, green, brown, brown, blue, blue, blue, brown, green, blue

Eye color	Tally	Number
Brown		
Green	卌	5
Blue	卌 II	7

Which set of tally marks would complete the table?

Ⓕ 卌 III

Ⓖ 卌 II

Ⓗ 卌

Ⓘ 卌 IIII

3 The table shows the favorite subjects of the students in Brook's class.

Subject	Tally	Number
Math	𝍸 III	8
Reading	𝍸 II	7
Science	𝍸 III	8
Social Studies	𝍸	5

Which two subjects were chosen by the same number of students?

Ⓐ math and reading

Ⓑ math and science

Ⓒ science and social studies

Ⓓ reading and social studies

Lesson 21
Pictographs

NGSSS

MA.3.S.7.1: Construct and analyze frequency tables, bar graphs, pictographs, and line plots from data, including data collected through observations, surveys, and experiments.

Introduction

A **pictograph** uses a picture to stand for a number or type of data. The **key** shows the number each picture stands for.

Look at the pictograph below.

How Students Get to School

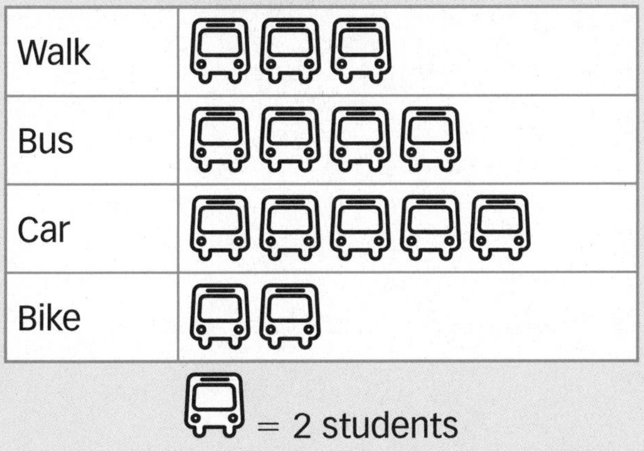

Walk	
Bus	
Car	
Bike	

= 2 students

- **To find the number of students who walk to school:**

Read the key. The key shows that each stands for 2 students. This means for every in the pictograph, you multiply by 2.

The different ways to get to school are listed on the left side. Find the row labeled "Walk." Count the number of pictures in that row. There are 3 pictures. Each picture stands for 2 students, so multiply 2 by 3.
$2 \times 3 = 6$.

There are 6 students who walk to school.

EXAMPLE 1

This pictograph shows the number of different kinds of books in Mr. Modena's classroom.

How many mystery books are there?

Kinds of Books

Fantasy	📖📖
Adventure	📖📖📖📖
Mystery	📖📖📖½

📖 = 2 books

Follow these steps to solve the problem.

Step 1 Figure out what the picture stands for by looking at the key.

The key shows that each picture of a book stands for 2 books.

Step 2 Find the row that shows the number of mystery books.

There are $3\frac{1}{2}$ book pictures in the Mystery row.

Step 3 Each of the 3 pictures of a whole book stands for 2 books.

$3 \times 2 = 6$ books

The picture of $\frac{1}{2}$ book stands for 1 book.

$6 + 1 = 7$. So, there are 7 mysteries.

SOLUTION: There are 7 mystery books in Mr. Modena's classroom.

Try It! **Use what you know to solve this problem.**

1 How many kids play the drums? ______________________

Instruments Played

Instrument	Number of Kids
Drums	♫♫
Flute	♫♫♫

♫ = 1 kid

EXAMPLE 2

This pictograph shows the number of boys and girls in Mrs. Lee's class.

How many more boys are there than girls?

Mrs. Lee's Class

Students	Number of Students
Boys	☺ ☺ ☺
Girls	☺ ☺

☺ = 5 students

Follow these steps to solve the problem.

Step 1 Find the number of boys in Mrs. Lee's class.

Each face stands for 5 students. There are 3 faces in the Boys row. $5 \times 3 = 15$. There are 15 boys in Mrs. Lee's class.

Step 2 Find the number of girls in Mrs. Lee's class.

There are 2 faces in the Girls row. $5 \times 2 = 10$. There are 10 girls in Mrs. Lee's class.

Step 3 Subtract the number of girls from the number of boys.

$15 - 10 = 5$

SOLUTION: There are 5 more boys than girls in Mrs. Lee's class.

Try It! **Use what you know to solve this problem.**

1 How many ice cream cones were sold altogether? ______________

Ice Cream Flavors

Flavor	Number of Cones Sold
Chocolate	🍦 🍦 🍦 🍦 🍦
Vanilla	🍦 🍦

🍦 = 5 cones

Guided Instruction

Read the Think About It to understand the problem. The solve the problem.

Think About It

Find the month that is missing data in the pictograph. Look at the key. How many bikes does each ⊛ represent?

Bill's Bike Shop sold 30 bikes in April, 40 bikes in May, 20 bikes in June, and 30 bikes in July.

Bikes Sold

Months	Number of Bikes
April	⊛⊛⊛
May	⊛⊛⊛⊛
June	⊛⊛
July	

⊛ = 10 bikes

Which of the following would complete the pictograph?

A ⊛⊛⊛

B ⊛⊛

C ⊛⊛⊛⊛

D ⊛⊛⊛⊛⊛⊛

EXPLANATION:

There were 30 bikes sold in July. Look at the key. Each ⊛ represents 10 bikes, so there should be 3 ⊛ in the blank space.

CORRECT ANSWER:

Answer choice **A** is correct.

CORRECT ANSWER:

Read why the other answer choices are not correct.

B This represents 20 bikes, not 30.

C This represents 40 bikes, not 30.

D This represents 60 bikes, not 30.

Guided Practice

Hints

Be sure to put your answers in the correct column in the table.

Remember to use the key when you look at pictographs.

PAIR SHARE

With your partner, share and discuss your answers and supporting details.

Solve each problem. Use the Hints to help you. Then explain how you found your solution.

1 The pictograph shows how students in a third-grade class voted for their favorite colors. Draw a table that matches the graph.

Favorite Colors

Red	✎ ✎ ✎
Blue	✎ ✎ ✎ ✎ ✎ ✎
Green	✎ ✎ ✎ ✎
Yellow	✎ ✎

✎ = 2 votes

Solution:

Color	Red	Blue	Green	Yellow
Votes				

Explanation: ____

____

2 During a road trip, two brothers recorded the colors of cars they saw. The pictograph below shows their results. How many total cars did they see during the road trip?

Car Colors

Red	🚗 🚗 🚗 🚗 🚗 🚗
Silver	🚗 🚗 🚗 🚗 🚗 🚗 🚗 🚗
Black	🚗 🚗 🚗 🚗 🚗 🚗

🚗 = 10 cars

Solution: ____

Explanation: ____

____

The pictograph below shows how students voted for their favorite subject. Use the graph to answer questions 1 and 2.

FAVORITE SUBJECTS

Subject	Votes
Science	📚 📚 📚 📚 📚 📚 📚
Math	📚 📚 📚 📚 📚 📚 📚 📚
Reading	📚 📚 📚 📚 📚 📚
History	📚 📚 📚 📚 📚

KEY
📚 = 5 students

1 Which two subjects were each the favorite of at least 35 students?

Ⓐ Science and Reading

Ⓑ Reading and History

Ⓒ Science and Math

Ⓓ Math and History

2 According to the graph, how many more students like math than history?

Ⓕ 3

Ⓖ 5

Ⓗ 10

Ⓘ 15

3 Katy likes to watch birds. The pictograph below shows how many of each type of bird she saw last weekend.

BIRDS SEEN

Bird	Number Seen
Bluebird	
Purple martin	
Wren	

KEY
= 2 birds

How many bluebirds and purple martins did Katy see altogether?

Ⓐ 3

Ⓑ 4

Ⓒ 8

Ⓓ 10

4 Austin recorded the number of each type of hit he had during his last baseball season in the table below.

AUSTIN'S HITS

Type of Hit	Number of Hits
Single	50
Double	30
Triple	10
Home Run	20

Which pictograph correctly displays Austin's data?

AUSTIN'S HITS

Type of Hit	Number of Hits
Single	/ / / / /
Double	/ / /
Triple	/
Home Run	/ /

Ⓕ

AUSTIN'S HITS

Type of Hit	Number of Hits
Single	/ / / /
Double	/ / /
Triple	/
Home Run	/ /

Ⓗ

AUSTIN'S HITS

Type of Hit	Number of Hits
Single	/ / /
Double	/ / / / /
Triple	/
Home Run	/ /

Ⓖ

AUSTIN'S HITS

Type of Hit	Number of Hits
Single	/ / / / /
Double	/ / /
Triple	/ /
Home Run	/ /

Ⓘ

KEY	/ = 10 hits

Lesson 22
Bar Graphs

NGSSS

MA.3.S.7.1: Construct and analyze frequency tables, bar graphs, pictographs, and line plots from data, including data collected through observations, surveys, and experiments.

Introduction

A **bar graph** uses bars to show data and compare information. Usually, the bottom of a bar graph shows different categories of one topic. The side of a bar graph usually tells you what is being measured. The **scale** shows the units used on a bar graph. Bar graphs can go up and down or from side to side.

The bar graph to the right shows the favorite drinks of students in Mr. Hansen's class. The bottom of the bar graph shows different kinds of drinks. The side of the bar graph shows the number of students who prefer the different drinks.

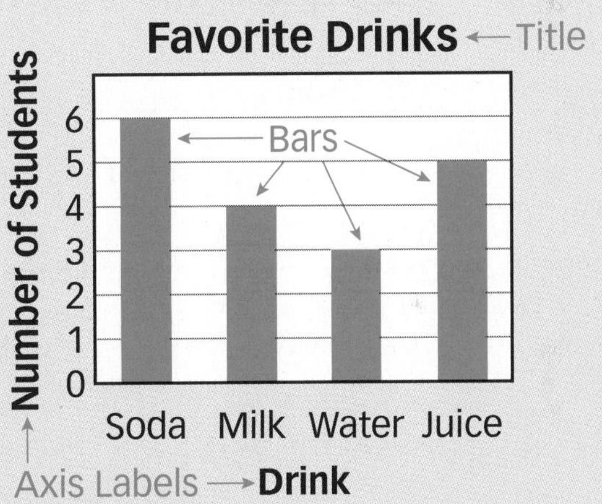

Bar Graph Part	What It Tells You
Title	This graph is about favorite drinks.
Axis Labels	The **vertical axis** shows the number of students. The **horizontal axis** shows the kinds of drinks.
Scales	The number of students goes up to 6 by 1s. The drinks are soda, milk, water, and juice.
Height of the Bars	There were 6 votes for Soda, 4 votes for Milk, 3 votes for Water, and 5 votes for Juice.

Modeled Instruction

EXAMPLE 1

This bar graph shows what Ms. Rosco's students eat for breakfast. Which food did 7 students eat?

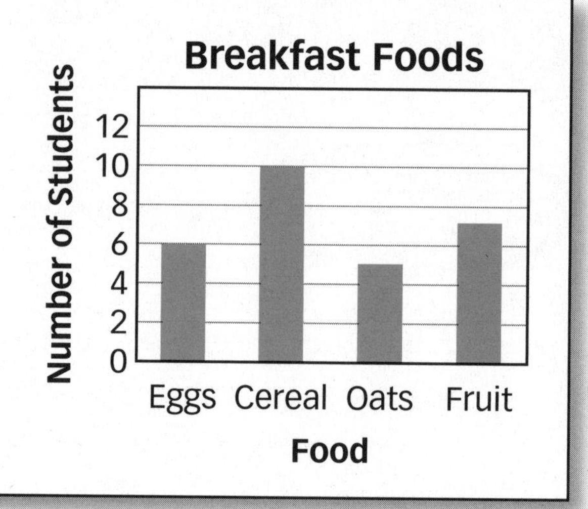

Follow these steps to solve the problem.

Step 1 Look at the scale on the left side of the graph.

The scale shows that the lines count by 2s.

Step 2 Find where 7 is on the scale.

7 is halfway between 6 and 8.

Step 3 Look at the heights of the bars until you see the one that goes up to 7.

Step 4 Read the category label at the bottom of the bar that goes to 7.

It is the bar for Fruit.

SOLUTION: 7 students ate fruit for breakfast.

Use what you know to solve these problems.

1 According to the graph above, how many students eat cereal for breakfast? ______________________

2 Which breakfast food do the fewest number of students eat?

____

EXAMPLE 2

This bar graph shows the number of students in Mrs. Brown's class who play different sports.

How many more students play basketball than baseball?

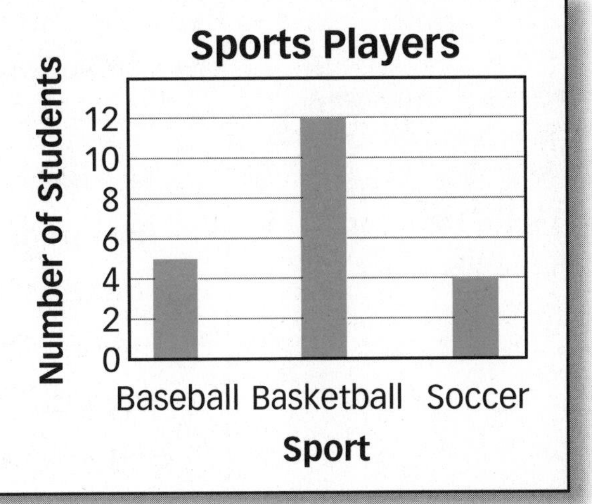

Follow these steps to solve the problem.

Step 1 Find the number of students who play basketball.

Look at the bar for basketball and read the height of the bar from the scale on the left. There are 12 students who play basketball.

Step 2 Find the number of students who play baseball.

Look at the height of the bar for baseball. There are 5 students who play baseball.

Step 3 Subtract the number of baseball players from the number of basketball players.

$12 - 5 = 7$

SOLUTION: There are 7 more basketball players than baseball players.

Try It! **Use what you know to solve these problems.**

1 According to the graph above, how many students play baseball and soccer? ______________________

2 How many more students play baseball than soccer? __________

Guided Instruction

Read the Think About It to understand the problem. Then solve the problem.

Think About It

Look at the height of each bar in the graph. Which bar lines up with the 40?

The bar graph shows the number of cakes sold each week at a bakery. During which week did the bakery sell 40 cakes?

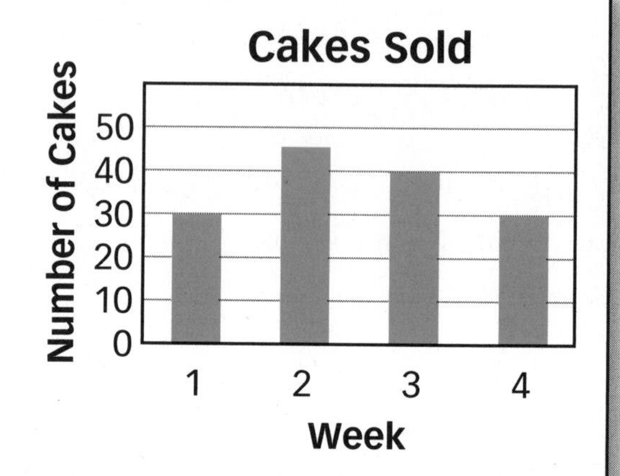

A Week 1

B Week 2

C Week 3

D Week 4

EXPLANATION:

Look for the number 40 on the scale on the side of the graph. Follow the line across until you come to a bar that stops at the line. Look to see what week that bar represents.

CORRECT ANSWER:

Answer choice **C** is correct.

INCORRECT ANSWERS:

Read why the other answer choices are not correct.

A Week 1 is not correct because there were 30 cakes sold.

B Week 2 is not correct because there were 45 cakes sold.

D Week 4 is not correct because there were 30 cakes sold.

Solve each problem. Use the Hints to help you.
Then explain how you found your solution.

Hints

"How many more" means this is a subtraction problem. Use the scale and the bars to find the numbers you need to subtract.

1 Todd asked 20 people where they like to go for fun. How many more people prefer to visit the beach than a museum?

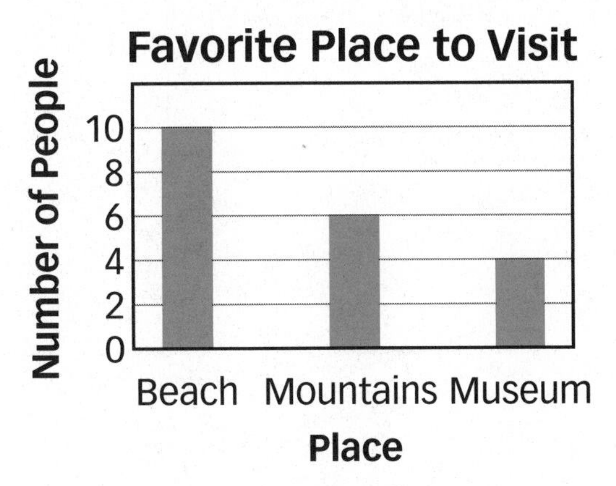

Solution: ______________________________

Explanation: ______________________________

Hints

Use the scale on the left to read the height of each bar.

2 Jan and her friends counted the number of books they read. Which girl read more than 4 books but fewer than 7?

Books

Number of Books: 0 1 2 3 4 5 6 7

Jan Amy Jo Liz

Girl

Solution: ______________________________

Explanation: ______________________________

PAIR SHARE

With your partner, share and discuss your answers and supporting details.

1 The bar graph below shows the number of each type of flower Shonda has in her garden.

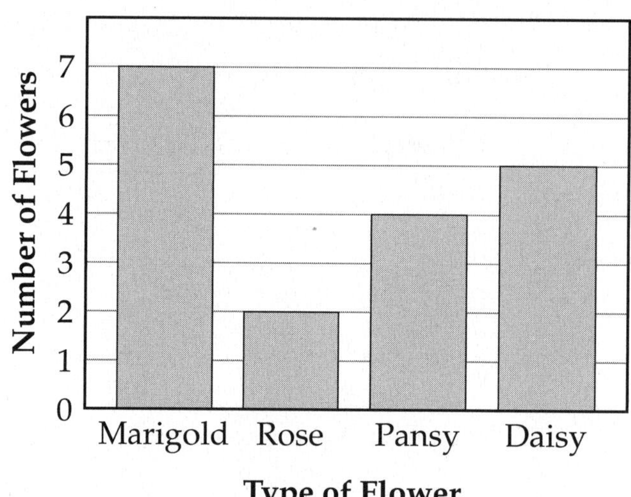

What is the total number of flowers in Shonda's garden?

Ⓐ 7

Ⓑ 9

Ⓒ 18

Ⓓ 19

2 Gina recorded the number of days last month that she wore different colors of shirts. Her results are shown in the following bar graph.

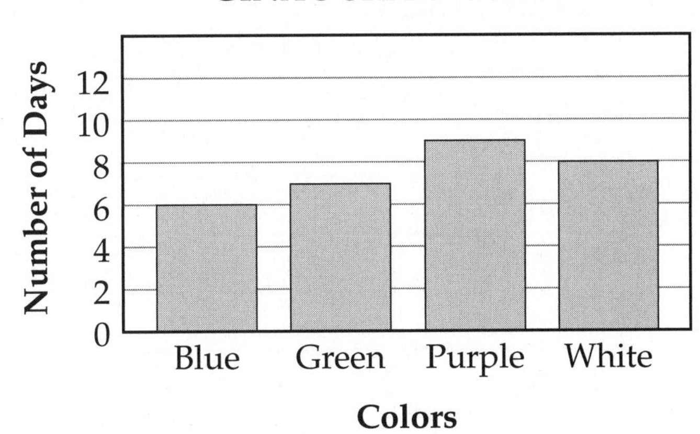

How many days did Gina wear a blue shirt or a green shirt?

Ⓕ 6

Ⓖ 7

Ⓗ 12

Ⓘ 13

3 Jason recorded the number of nights his family ate different foods for dinner in the last two weeks. His results are shown in the table below.

JASON'S DINNERS

Food	Number of Nights
Pizza	4
Tacos	2
Steak	3
Chicken	5

Which bar graph correctly displays Jason's data?

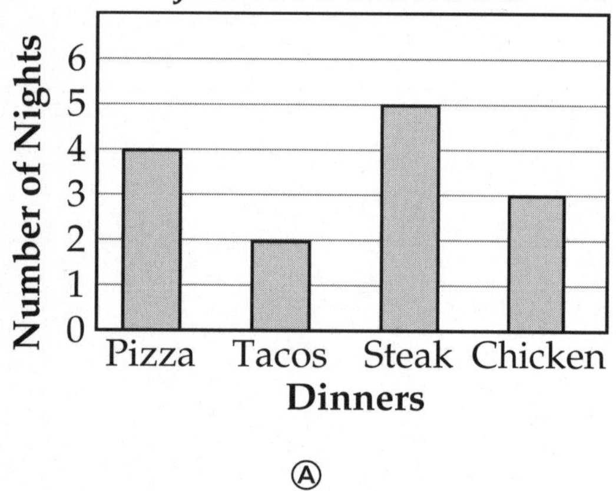

Ⓐ

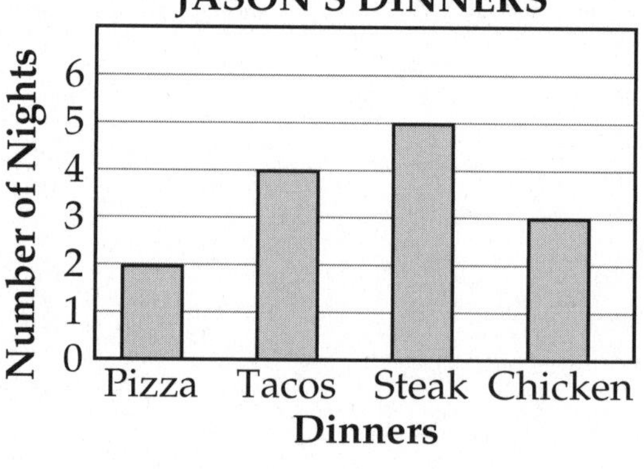

Ⓒ

Ⓑ

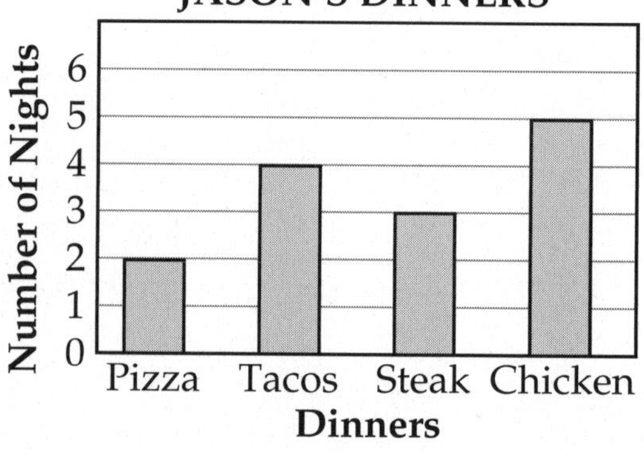

Ⓓ

Lesson 23
Line Plots

NGSSS

MA.3.S.7.1: Construct and analyze frequency tables, bar graphs, pictographs, and line plots from data, including data collected through observations, surveys, and experiments.

Introduction

A **line plot** uses Xs or other marks to show data. Line plots usually show data that involves numbers. The numbers are shown on a number line, and Xs are stacked above the number line to show how many times each data value occurs.

Look at the line plot below.

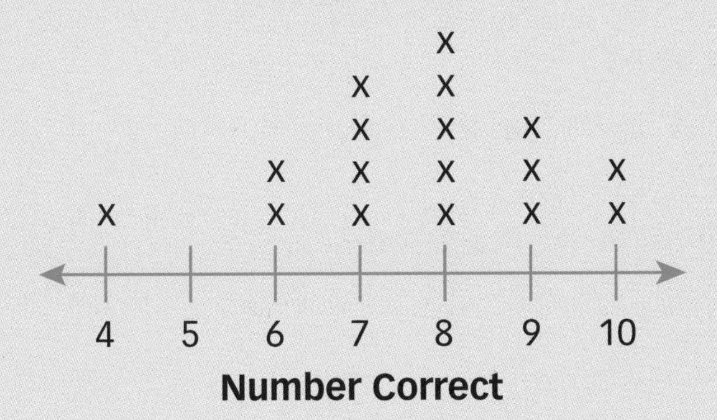

The title of the line plot tells that the line plot is about math quiz scores. The scale of the number line goes from 4 to 10. The label below the scale tells that the numbers represent the number correct on the quiz. Each X represents one student's score.

The line plot above shows that 1 student had a quiz score of 4, 2 students had a score of 6, 4 students scored 7, 5 students scored 8, 3 students scored 9, and 2 students had a score of 10. There were no students with a score of 5.

EXAMPLE 1

Jeremy asked 10 of his friends how many times they had been to the beach in the last month. The line plot shows his results. How many of Jeremy's friends went to the beach 4 times?

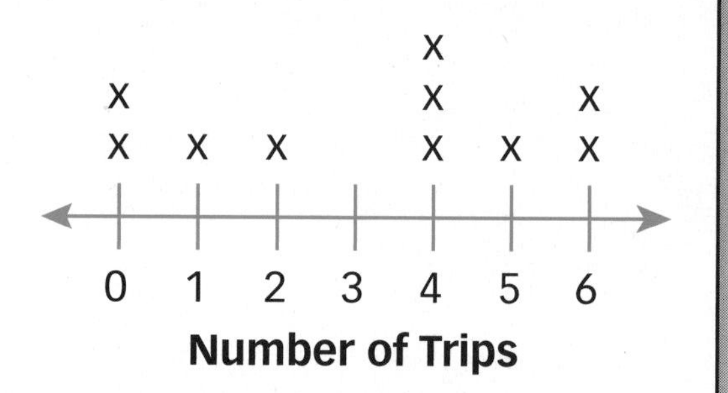

Follow these steps to solve the problem.

Step 1 Find the 4 on the number line.

The 4 is between 3 and 5.

Step 2 Count the number of Xs above the 4.

There are 3 Xs above the 4 on the number line.

SOLUTION: 3 of Jeremy's friends went to the beach 4 times.

Try It! **Use what you know to solve these problems.**

1 According to the line plot above, how many of Jeremy's friends went to the beach 2 times? ____________________

2 How many of Jeremy's friends went to the beach 6 times? ______

3 How many of Jeremy's friends went to the beach 3 times? ______

EXAMPLE 2

The line plot shows the number of goals members of a soccer team have scored so far this season. How many players scored 4 or more goals?

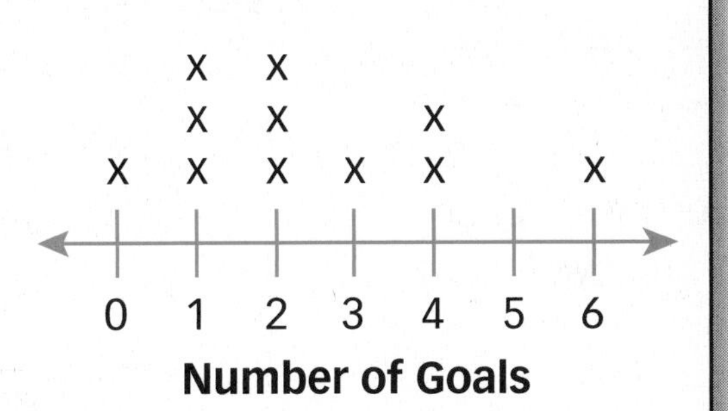

Follow these steps to solve the problem.

Step 1 Determine what data you need to find.

The question asks how many players scored 4 or more goals. So, you need to look at the data for 4, 5, and 6 goals.

Step 2 Count the number of Xs above 4, 5, and 6.

There are 2 Xs above the 4, 0 Xs above 5, and 1 X above 6.

Step 3 Add the number of Xs you counted.

$2 + 0 + 1 = 3$

SOLUTION: 3 players scored 4 or more goals.

Try It! **Use what you know to solve these problems.**

1 According to the line plot above, how many players have scored fewer than 4 goals? ____________

2 How many players have scored either 1 or 2 goals? ____________

3 How many players have scored more than 2 goals? ____________

Read the Think About It to understand the problem. Then solve the problem.

Think About It

How many times did the spinner land on each number?

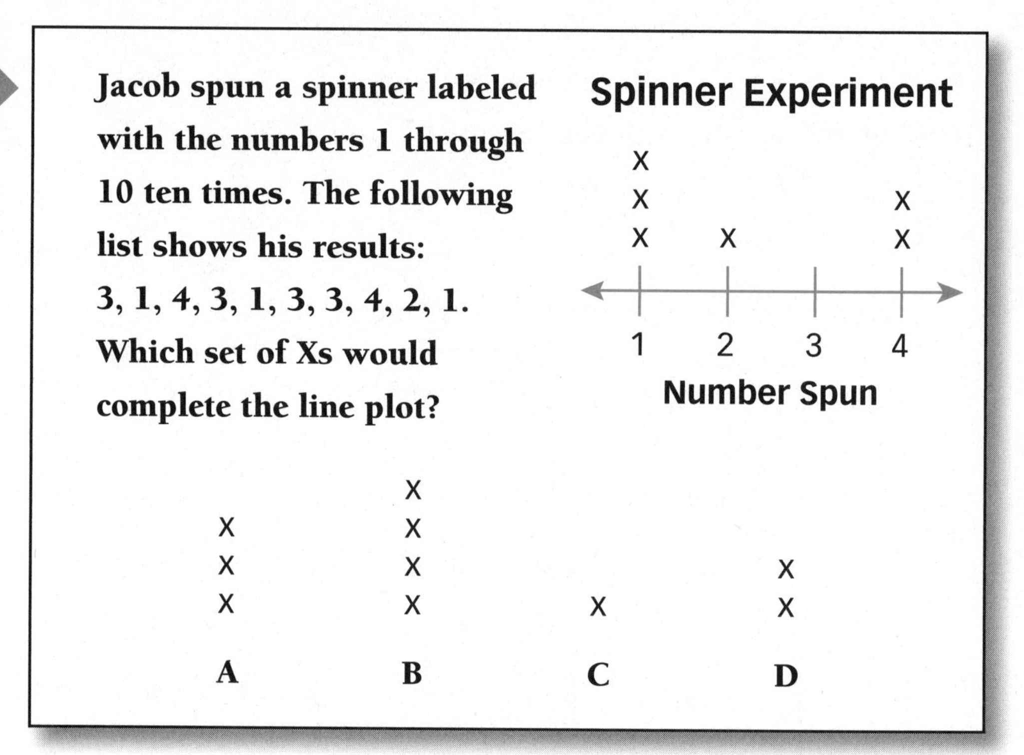

EXPLANATION:

Since the space above 3 is blank, count the number of times Jacob spun a 3. That is how many Xs are needed to complete the line plot.

CORRECT ANSWER:

Answer choice **B** is correct.

INCORRECT ANSWERS:

Read why the other answer choices are not correct.

A This is not correct because 3 was spun more than 3 times.

C This is not correct because 3 was spun more than 1 time.

D This is not correct because 3 was spun more than 2 times.

Guided Practice

Hints

Remember that there may be some numbers on a line plot that do not have any Xs above them. What does this mean?

Find an X that could represent Carrie. What numbers do you need to look at to find the number of students taller than her?

PAIR SHARE

With your partner, share and discuss your answers and supporting details.

Solve each problem. Use the Hints to help you. Then explain how you found your solution.

1 John recorded the number of pages in each chapter of the book he is reading. His data is shown in the line plot below. How many chapters are exactly 16 pages long?

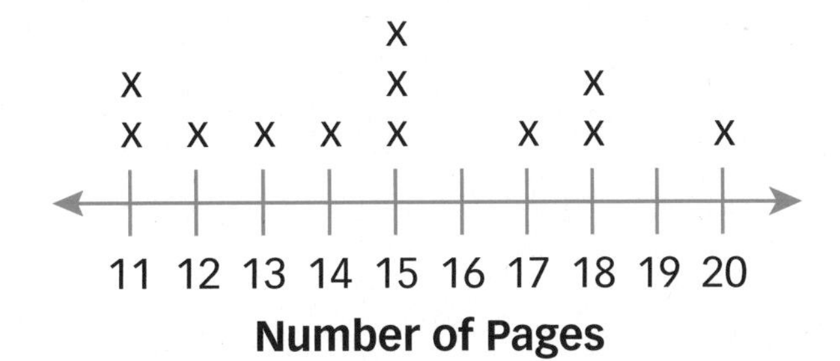

Solution: ____________________

Explanation: ____________________

____

2 Carrie recorded the height of each student in her class in the line plot below. Carrie is 48 inches tall. How many students are taller than Carrie?

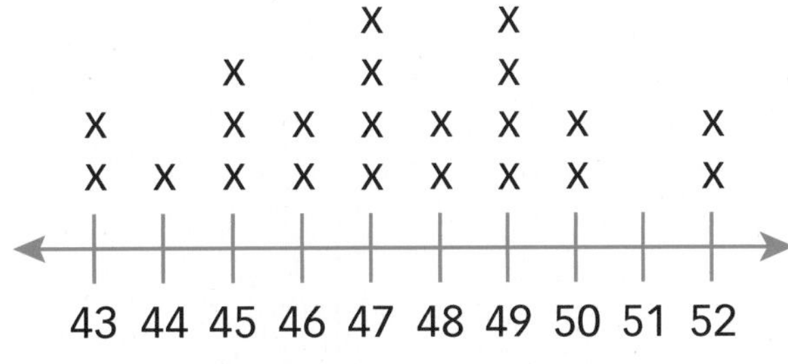

Solution: ____________________

Explanation: ____________________

____

1 John exercises each day by running laps around the track. Each day for the last two weeks he has recorded how many laps he ran: 13, 11, 10, 12, 14, 13, 15, 10, 12, 15, 13, 10, 13, 11. He made the line plot below to show his data.

JOHN'S EXERCISE

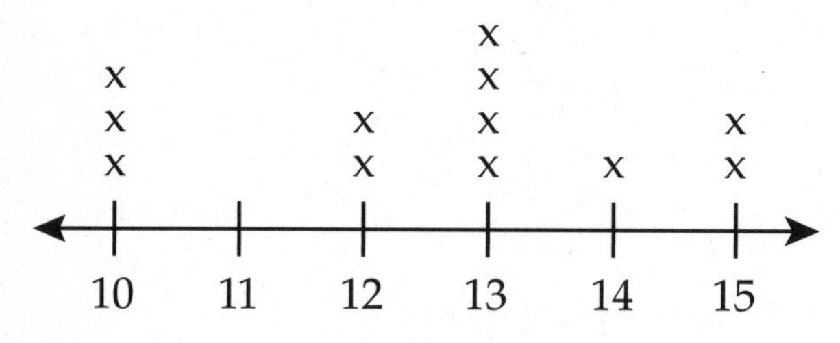

Number of Laps

Which set of Xs should be used to complete the line plot?

Ⓐ x
x

Ⓑ x
x
x
x

Ⓒ x
x
x

Ⓓ x

2 Maria recorded the ages of all the children who live on her street. She made the line plot below to show her data.

AGE OF NEIGHBORS

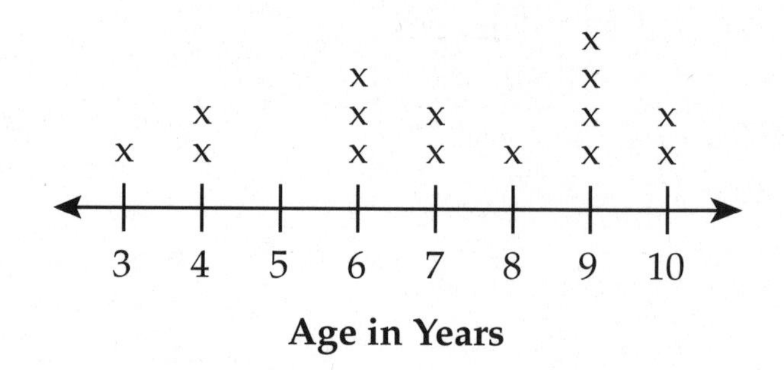

Maria is 8 years old. How many of the children are older than Maria?

Ⓕ 1

Ⓖ 4

Ⓗ 6

Ⓘ 7

Post Test

1 Tyler's nametag is the same size and shape as the parallelogram below. What is the perimeter of Tyler's nametag?

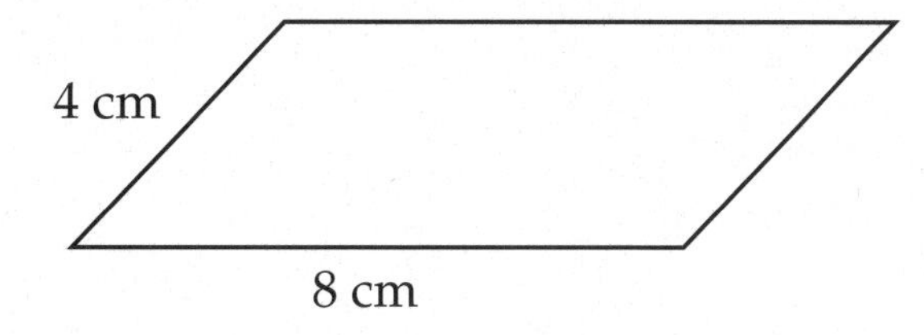

Ⓐ 12 centimeters

Ⓑ 16 centimeters

Ⓒ 24 centimeters

Ⓓ 32 centimeters

2 What equivalent fractions are shown by the shaded parts of this model?

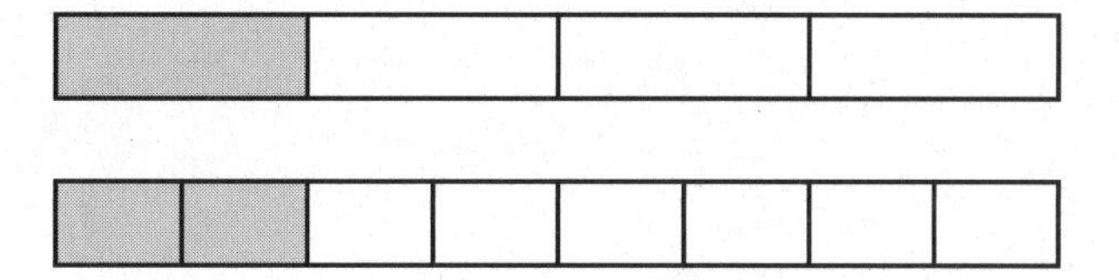

Ⓕ $\frac{3}{4} = \frac{6}{8}$

Ⓖ $\frac{3}{4} = \frac{3}{8}$

Ⓗ $\frac{1}{4} = \frac{4}{8}$

Ⓘ $\frac{1}{4} = \frac{2}{8}$

Go On

3 The Change-a-Lot watch comes with 4 different bands. It also has pop-on covers in 4 different colors. How many combinations of band and cover are possible?

Ⓐ 16

Ⓑ 12

Ⓒ 8

Ⓓ 7

4 In which pair are the figures the same size and shape?

Ⓕ 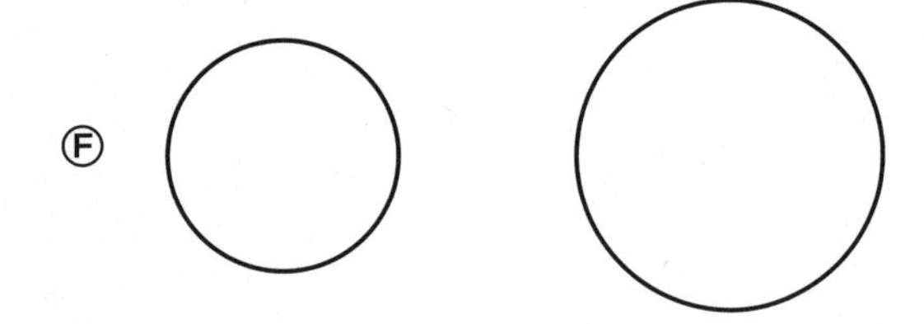

Ⓖ 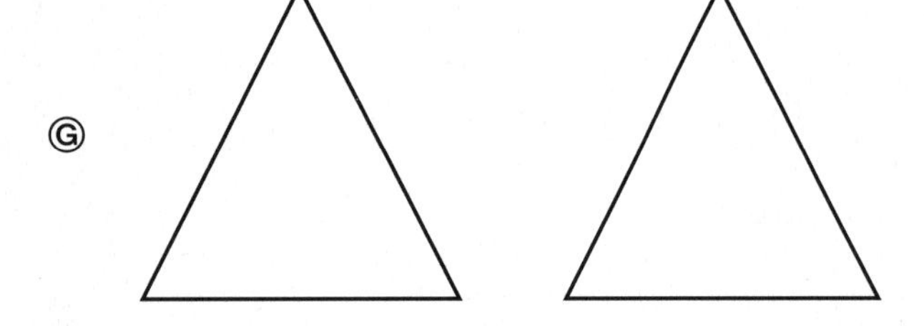

Ⓗ 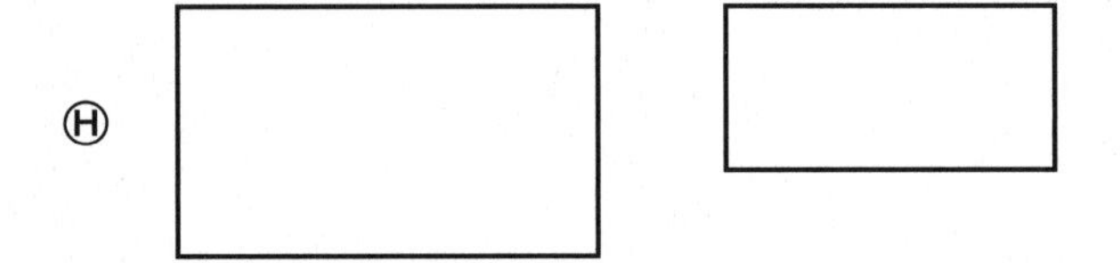

Ⓘ 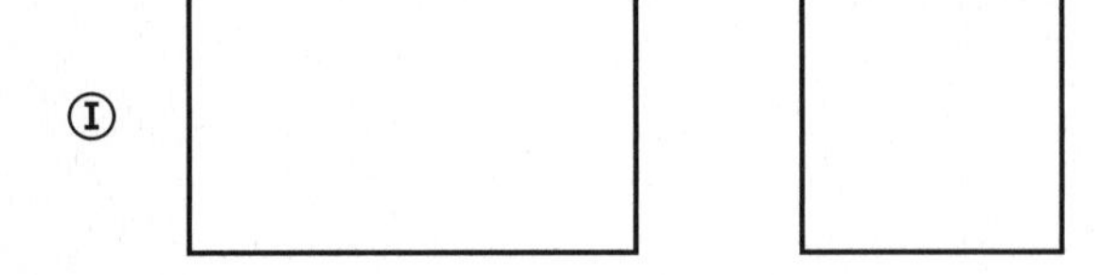

Go On

5 On which of these figures is it possible to draw a line of symmetry?

Ⓒ

Ⓑ

Ⓓ

6 Study the design to figure out the pattern of growth.

☆☆☆ ☆	☆☆☆☆☆☆ ☆☆☆	☆☆☆☆☆☆☆☆☆ ☆☆☆☆☆
A	B	C

How many stars will be in design D?

Ⓕ 7

Ⓖ 12

Ⓗ 15

Ⓘ 19

Go On

7 What mixed number does the model show?

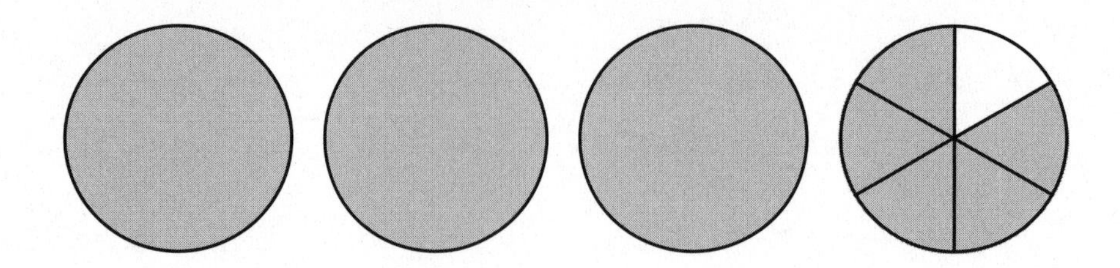

Ⓐ $2\frac{4}{5}$

Ⓑ $2\frac{5}{6}$

Ⓒ $3\frac{4}{5}$

Ⓓ $3\frac{5}{6}$

8 Which quadrilateral could have only 2 right angles?

Ⓕ trapezoid

Ⓖ square

Ⓗ parallelogram

Ⓘ rectangle

Go On

If Carter draws a line from point A to point C on the figure below, what two shapes will be formed?

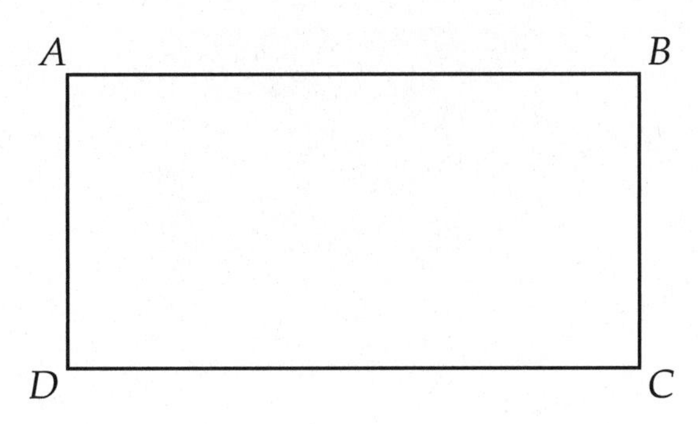

Ⓐ 2 triangles

Ⓑ 1 triangle and 1 trapezoid

Ⓒ 2 squares

Ⓓ 1 rectangle and 1 square

10 Callie did this multiplication problem.

$\square \times 3 = 27$

Which problem could she do to check her answer?

Ⓕ $3 \times 27 = \square$

Ⓖ $30 \div 3 = \square$

Ⓗ $27 \div 3 = \square$

Ⓘ $3 \times 24 = \square$

Go On

11 Li An plans to put a ribbon border around her bulletin board, which is shown below.

How much ribbon does Li An need?

Ⓐ 46 inches

Ⓑ 72 inches

Ⓒ 82 inches

Ⓓ 92 inches

12 Jean wrote an addition sentence to find the answer to 4×8. What sentence did she write?

Ⓕ $4 + 4 + 4 + 4 = 16$

Ⓖ $4 + 4 + 4 + 4 + 4 + 4 = 24$

Ⓗ $8 + 8 + 8 + 8 = 32$

Ⓘ $8 + 4 = 12$

Go On

13 This clock shows the time that Lenny gets on the school bus.

This clock shows the time that Lenny gets to school.

How long does it take Lenny to get to school?

Ⓐ 20 minutes

Ⓑ 30 minutes

Ⓒ 40 minutes

Ⓓ 1 hour

Go On

14 Students at the Elmwood School have to do summer reading. They can choose any 2 books from a list of 4. How many different combinations of 2 books are possible?

Ⓕ 4

Ⓖ 6

Ⓗ 8

Ⓘ 12

15 The graph below shows what students are wearing on their feet today. How many more students are wearing sneakers than sandals?

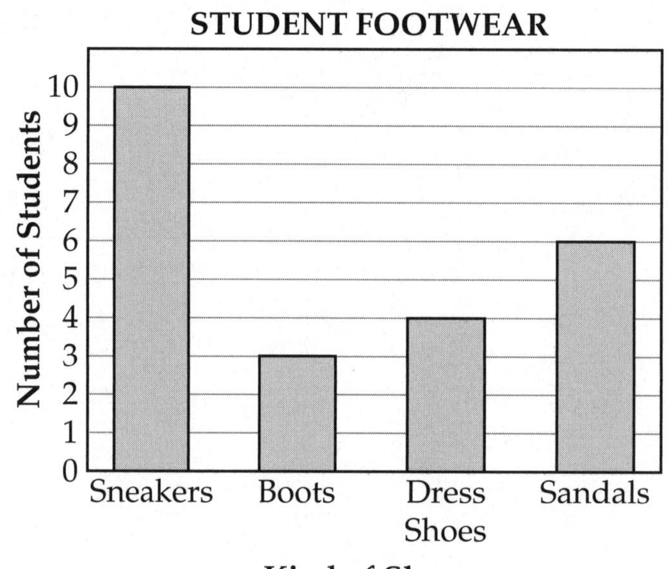

Ⓐ 10

Ⓑ 6

Ⓒ 4

Ⓓ 3

Go On

16 Study the model.

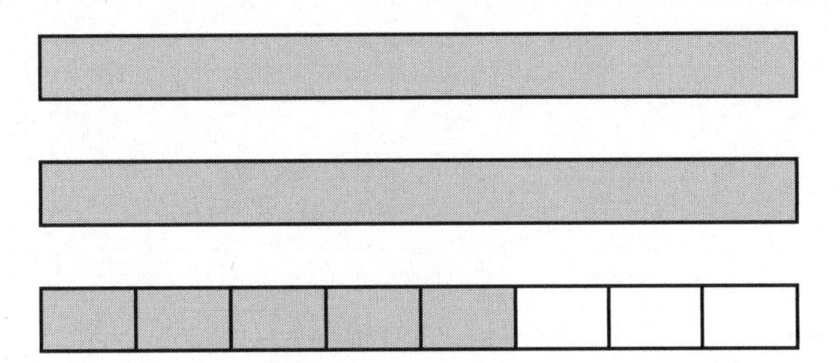

Which model shows the same mixed number?

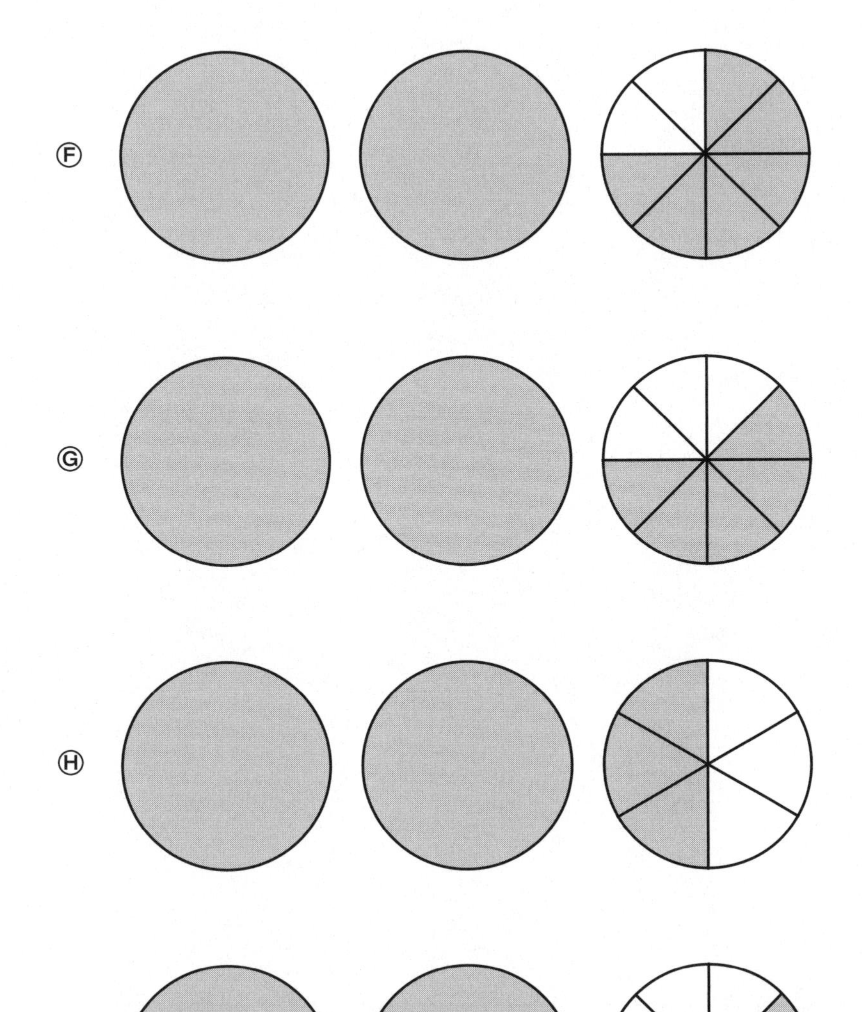

17 Which expression is the same as $(7 + 9) \times 4$?

Ⓐ $(4 \times 7) + (4 \times 9)$

Ⓑ $(4 + 7) \times (4 + 9)$

Ⓒ $7 + (9 \times 4)$

Ⓓ $9 + (7 \times 4)$

18 What do these figures have in common?

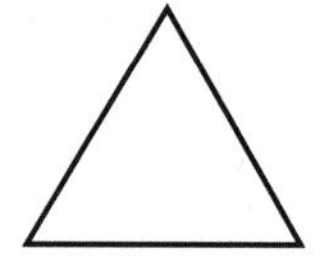

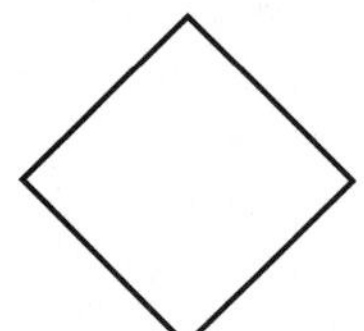

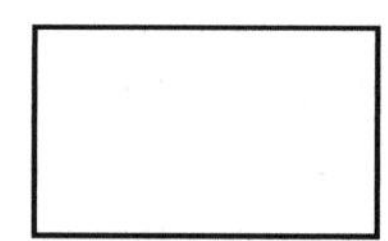

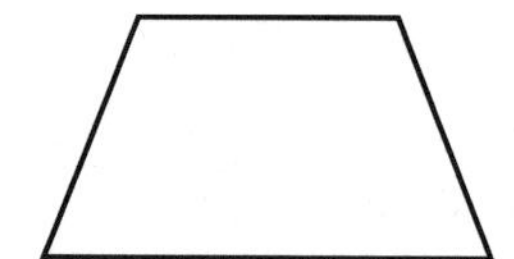

Ⓕ They are all quadrilaterals.

Ⓖ They are all polygons.

Ⓗ They are all parallelograms.

Ⓘ They are all solid figures.

Go On

19 Fairview Farm sells baskets of pears. Terry bought 30 pears. There were 6 pears in each basket. How many baskets of pears did Terry buy?

Ⓐ 5

Ⓑ 10

Ⓒ 24

Ⓓ 36

20 A grocer filled bags with oranges. He used 8 oranges to fill 1 bag and 16 oranges to fill 2 bags. If he continued this pattern, how many oranges did he use to fill 5 bags?

Bags	1	2	3	4	5
Oranges	8	16	24		

Ⓕ 64

Ⓖ 48

Ⓗ 40

Ⓘ 32

Go On

21 Which fraction is the **greatest**?

Ⓐ $\frac{3}{5}$

Ⓑ $\frac{3}{10}$

Ⓒ $\frac{3}{8}$

Ⓓ $\frac{3}{16}$

22 Use your ruler to answer this question. Ms. Hamm, the gym teacher, thinks that the ball that Suri kicked is out of bounds. The line below shows how far out of bounds the ball is. How far out of bounds is the ball?

OUT OF BOUNDS

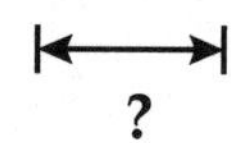

Ⓕ $2\frac{1}{2}$ inches

Ⓖ $1\frac{1}{2}$ inches

Ⓗ 1 inch

Ⓘ $\frac{1}{2}$ inch

Go On

23 Tyrone has a striped beach towel. The stripes start at one end of the towel with a pattern of blue, green, yellow, orange, blue, green, yellow, orange, and so on. There are a total of 22 stripes on the towel. What color stripe is at the other end of the towel?

Ⓐ blue

Ⓑ green

Ⓒ yellow

Ⓓ orange

24 The tally chart shows the number of goals that four soccer players have scored. How many more goals has Cole scored than Lori?

Player	Number of Goals
Cole	𝍸 𝍸
Ho	𝍸 III
Emma	𝍸 𝍸 II
Lori	𝍸 II

Ⓕ 2

Ⓖ 3

Ⓗ 4

Ⓘ 10

25 Jessie bought a camera for $59.21. Then she spent $9.35 on a camera case. **About** how much did Jessie spend altogether?

Ⓐ $60.00

Ⓑ $64.00

Ⓒ $68.00

Ⓓ $72.00

26 What multiplication fact is shown by this array?

```
* * * *
* * * *
* * * *
* * * *
* * * *
```

Ⓕ $4 + 5 = 9$

Ⓖ $5 \times 3 = 15$

Ⓗ $3 + 5 = 8$

Ⓘ $5 \times 4 = 20$

Go On

27 The shaded part of each group of eggs represents a fraction.

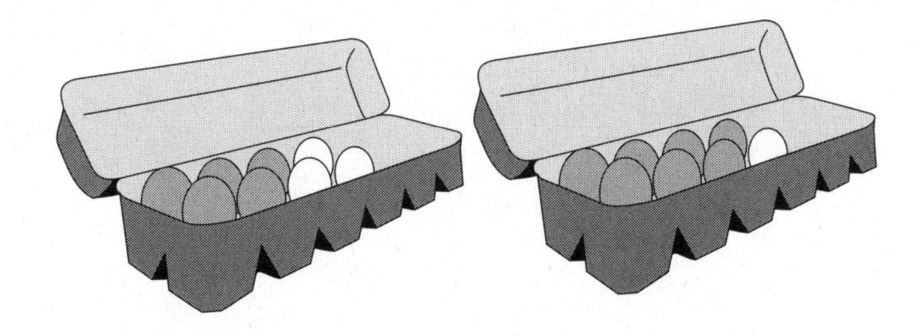

Which correctly compares the values of the fractions?

Ⓐ $\frac{3}{5} < \frac{1}{7}$

Ⓑ $\frac{5}{8} < \frac{7}{8}$

Ⓒ $\frac{5}{8} > \frac{7}{8}$

Ⓓ $\frac{7}{8} = \frac{5}{8}$

28 What kind of triangle has only 2 equal sides?

Ⓕ isosceles triangle

Ⓖ right triangle

Ⓗ equilateral triangle

Ⓘ both an isosceles and an equilateral triangle

Go On

29 Sid baked 4 trays of cookies. Each tray had an equal number of cookies. Sid baked 36 cookies in all. Which number sentence can be used to find the number of cookies on each tray?

Ⓐ $4 + 36 = \square$

Ⓑ $9 \times 4 = \square$

Ⓒ $36 - 4 = \square$

Ⓓ $36 \div 4 = \square$

30 Which figure has a line of symmetry?

Ⓕ 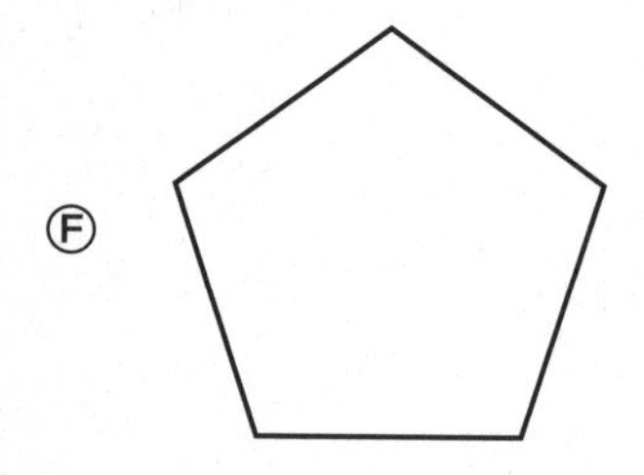

Ⓖ 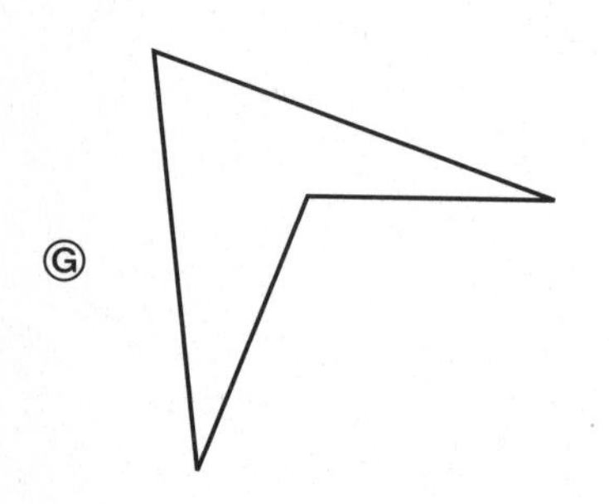

Ⓗ 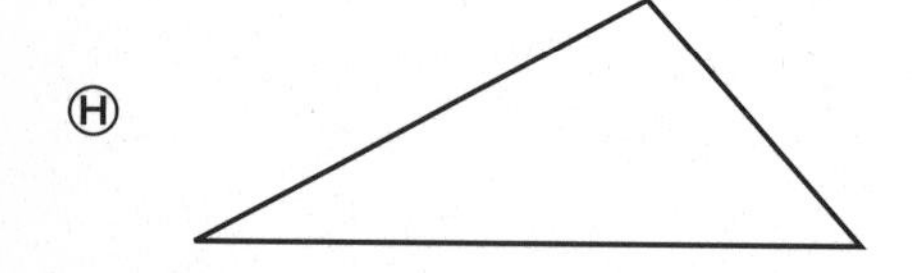

Ⓘ 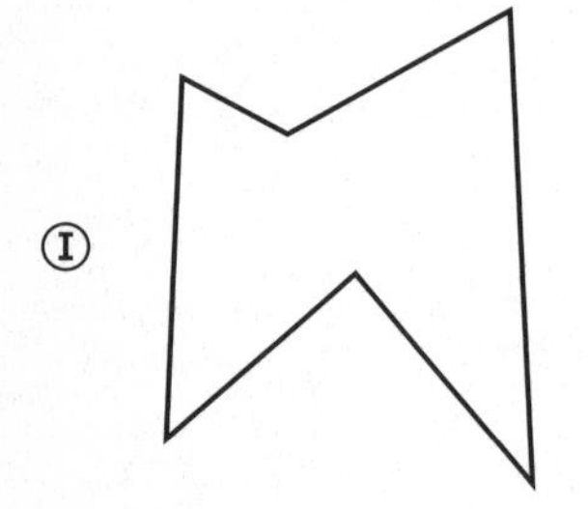

Go On

31 Mrs. Murphy must be home by 5:30 to meet her son. She leaves work at 4:00.

She drives for 35 minutes and stops at the store. She spends 20 minutes in the store. After that, she drives 25 more minutes to her house. Will Mrs. Murphy be on time to meet her son?

Ⓐ Yes, she will arrive home exactly on time.

Ⓑ Yes, she will arrive home 10 minutes early.

Ⓒ No, she will arrive home 10 minutes late.

Ⓓ No, she will arrive home 20 minutes late.

32 Last year, 131,875 people entered a radio station's contest. This year, 253,118 people entered the contest. How many more people entered the contest this year than last year?

Ⓕ 121,243

Ⓖ 122,343

Ⓗ 221,243

Ⓘ 384,993

Go On

33 The chart below shows the different colors, shapes, and sizes of balloons that are sold at Balloon Bazaar.

Color	Shape	Size
red blue yellow	round heart	small large

How many combinations of color, shape, and size are possible?

Ⓐ 7

Ⓑ 8

Ⓒ 12

Ⓓ 18

34 What number is missing in the pattern below?

28, 22, ____, 10, 4

Ⓕ 16

Ⓖ 18

Ⓗ 20

Ⓘ 34

Go On

35 The students in Kylie's class voted for their favorite season. Here are the results:

Spring: 5 Summer: 8 Fall: 3 Winter: 7

Which bar graph shows the correct number of votes for each season?

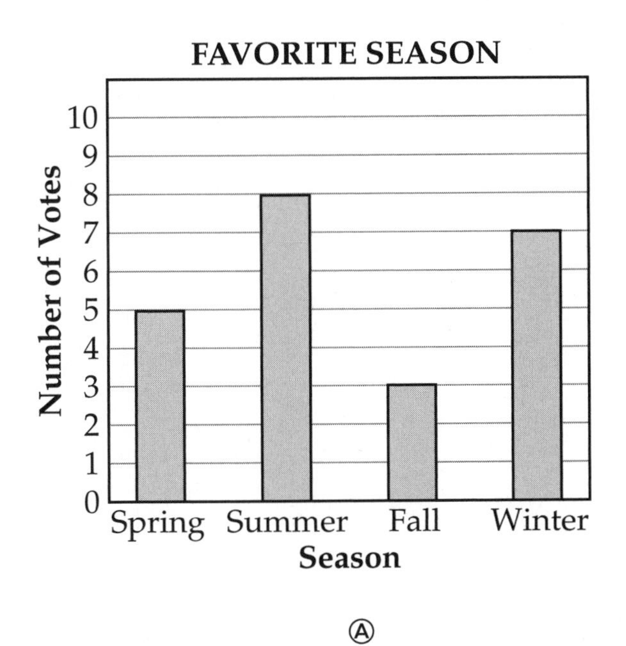

Ⓐ

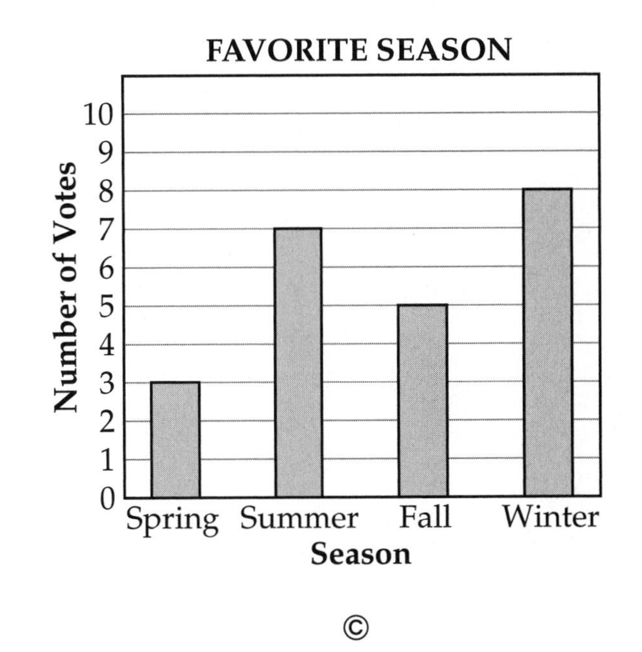

Ⓒ

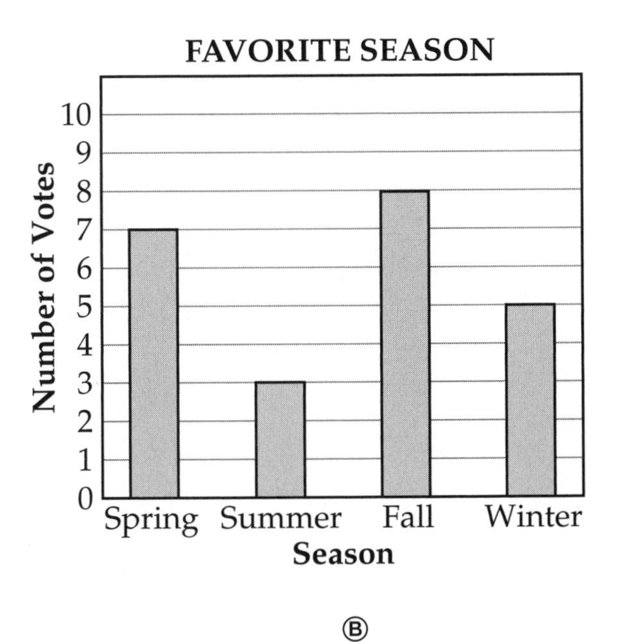

Ⓑ

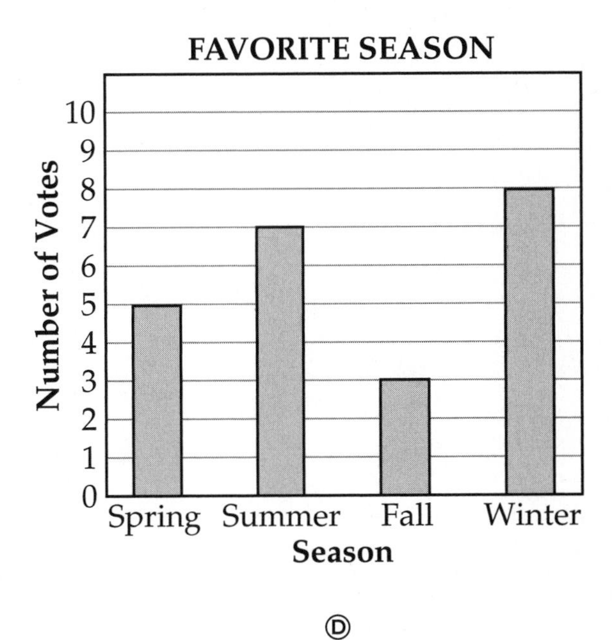

Ⓓ

Go On

36 The circle below shows $\frac{3}{4}$ shaded.

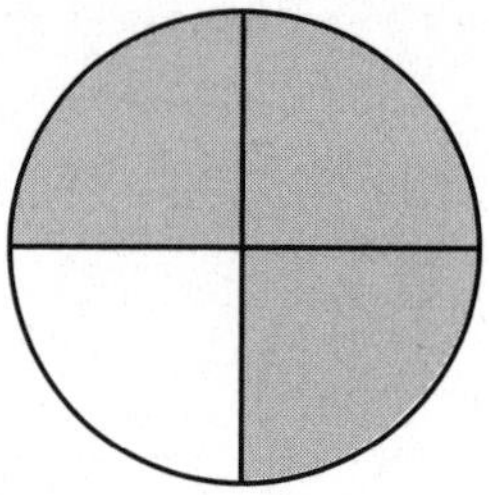

Which circle shows a shaded part equal to $\frac{3}{4}$?

Ⓕ 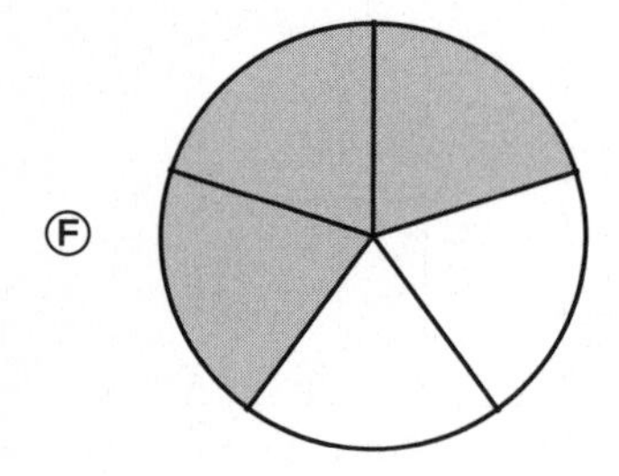

Ⓖ 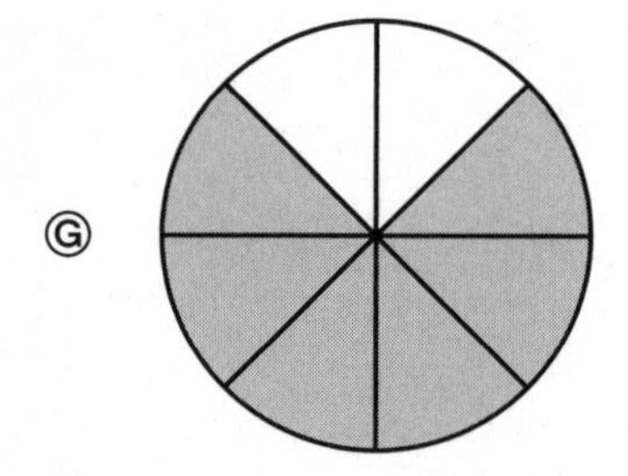

Ⓗ 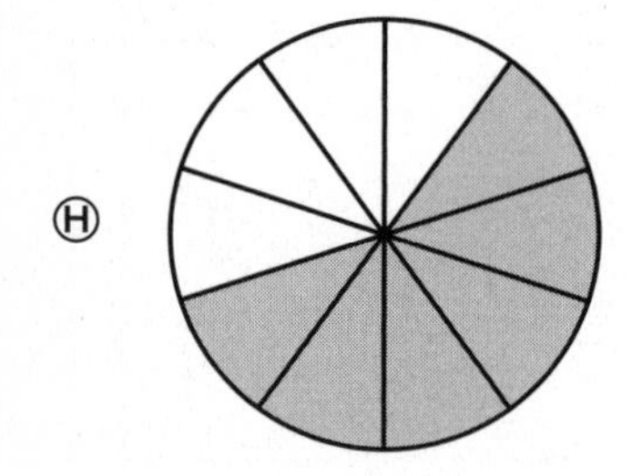

Ⓘ 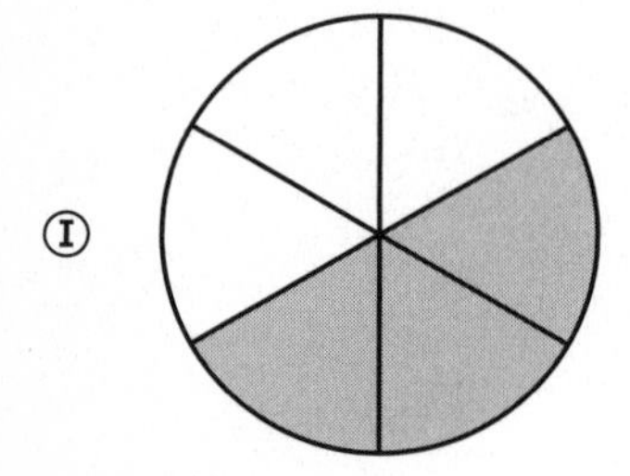

Go On

37 Samantha cut out two shapes, as shown below.

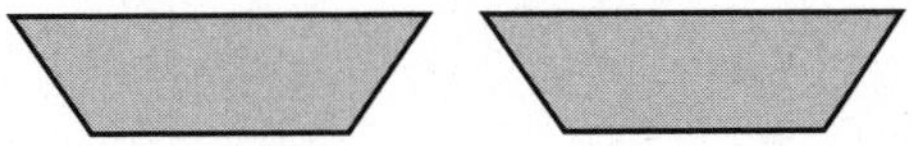

Which of the following shapes could Samantha make if she combined the two shapes, without overlapping?

Ⓐ

Ⓑ

Ⓒ

Ⓓ

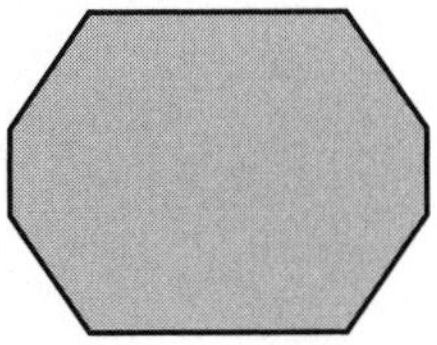

Go On

38 $19 \times 0 =$

Ⓕ 0

Ⓖ 1

Ⓗ 9

Ⓘ 19

39 Sarah practiced her dance routine five days last week. The bar graph below shows how many minutes she practiced each day.

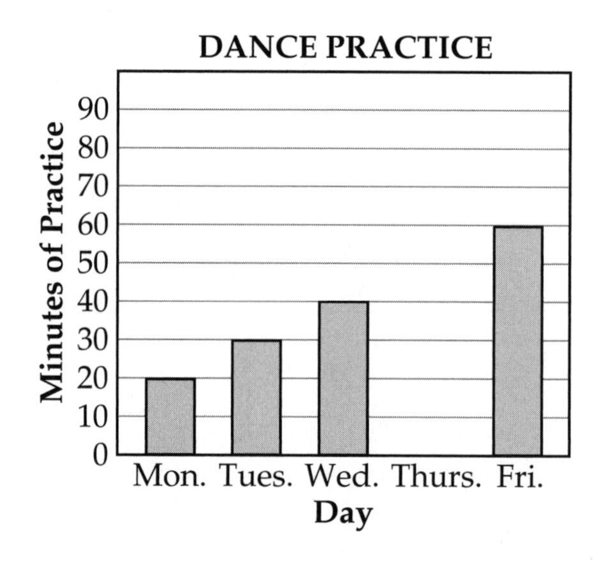

If the number of minutes Sarah practiced each day followed a pattern, how many minutes did she practice on Thursday?

Ⓐ 40

Ⓑ 45

Ⓒ 50

Ⓓ 55

Go On

The line plot shows the results of rolling a number cube with the numbers 1 through 6 on its faces.

NUMBER CUBE RESULTS

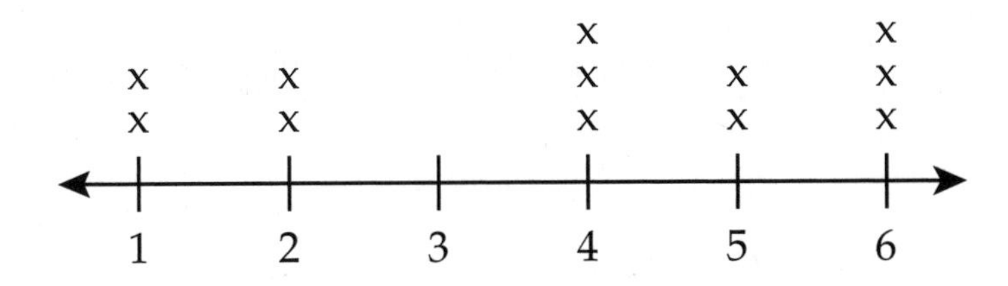

Number Rolled

Which tally chart matches the data in the line plot?

Ⓕ

1	2	3	4	5	6
III	II	I	III	II	II

Ⓖ

1	2	3	4	5	6
II	II		III	II	III

Ⓗ

1	2	3	4	5	6
III	III	I	IIII	III	IIII

Ⓘ

1	2	3	4	5	6
II	II		IIII	II	III

41 John has 3 shelves with model airplanes on them in his bedroom. There are 6 airplanes on each shelf. He is going to buy 2 new model airplanes with his birthday money. The expression below represents the total number of model airplanes John will have.

$(3 \times 6) + 2$

Which expression below also represents the total number of model airplanes John will have?

Ⓐ $(2 \times 3) + (2 \times 6)$

Ⓑ $(3 \times 2) + 6$

Ⓒ $3 + (6 \times 2)$

Ⓓ $2 + (6 \times 3)$

42 What mixed number describes point *B* on the number line?

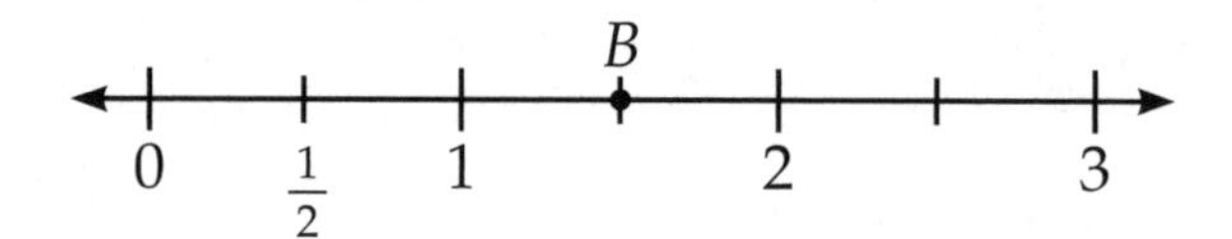

Ⓕ $\frac{1}{3}$

Ⓖ $1\frac{1}{2}$

Ⓗ $2\frac{1}{3}$

Ⓘ $2\frac{1}{2}$

Go On

43 Mrs. Sorenson gave each student in her math class a candy bar. She told each student to divide his or her candy bar into 3, 4, 5, or 6 equal pieces and then they could eat one of the pieces. How many pieces should Martha divide her candy bar into if she wants to eat the biggest piece possible?

Ⓐ 3

Ⓑ 4

Ⓒ 5

Ⓓ 6

44 What figure shows $\frac{1}{2}$ shaded?

Ⓕ 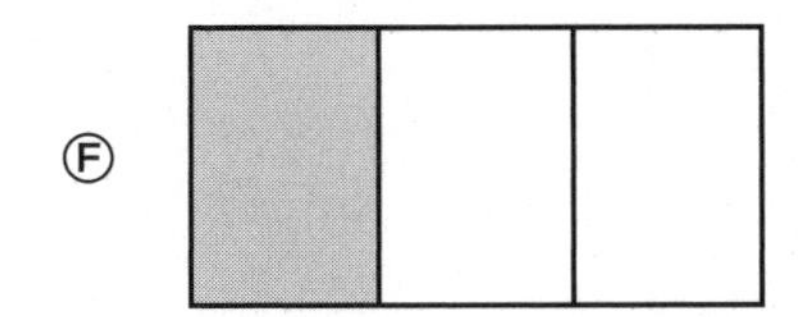

Ⓖ 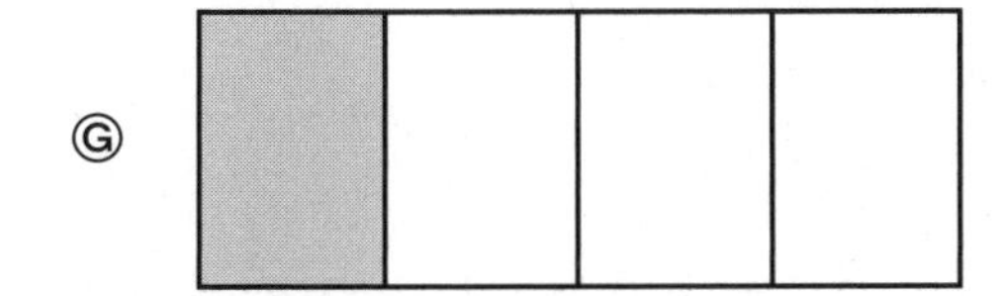

Ⓗ 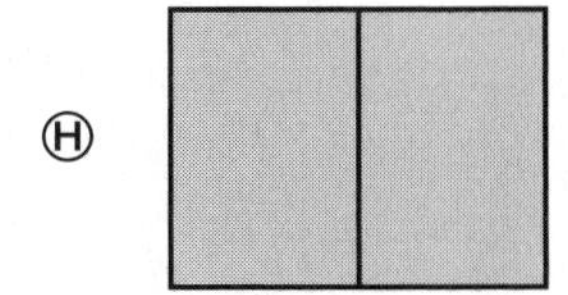

Ⓘ 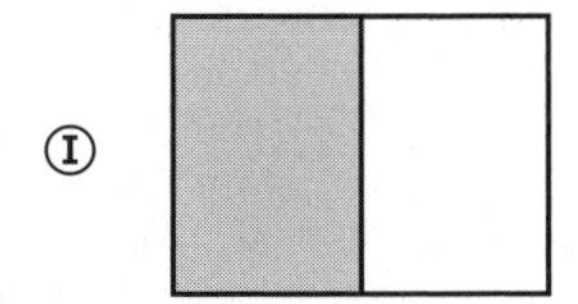

45 How many sides does a decagon have?

Ⓐ 6

Ⓑ 8

Ⓒ 10

Ⓓ 12

46 Jeff is making a bench. He needs to buy nails and boards. The table below shows the number of nails Jeff needs depending on the number of boards he uses. He will use the same number of nails in each board to build his bench.

Number of Boards	Number of Nails Needed
2	16
3	24
5	40
6	48
8	

Based on the table above, how many nails will Jeff need if he uses 8 boards to build his bench? Mark your answer.

Ⓕ 68

Ⓖ 64

Ⓗ 56

Ⓘ 52

Go On

47 The pictograph shows the number of customers served at a restaurant over five days.

Customers Served Daily	
Monday	☺ ☺ ☺ ☺ ☺ ☺ ☺ ☺ ☺
Tuesday	☺ ☺ ☺ ☺ ☺ ☺ ☺ ☺
Wednesday	☺ ☺ ☺ ☺ ☺
Thursday	☺ ☺ ☺ ☺ ☺ ☺
Friday	☺ ☺ ☺ ☺ ☺ ☺ ☺ ☺ ☺ ☺

☺ = 10 customers

How many more customers were served on Friday than on Thursday?

Ⓐ 4

Ⓑ 20

Ⓒ 40

Ⓓ 50

48 Which figure shows a shaded fraction **closest** to 1?

Ⓕ

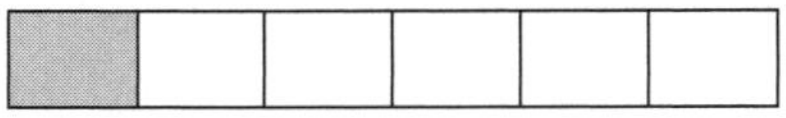

Ⓖ

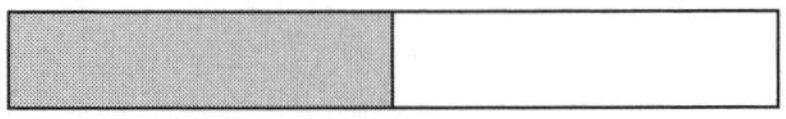

Ⓗ

Ⓘ

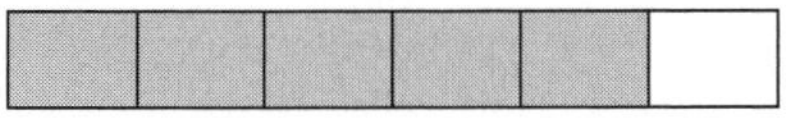

Go On

49 Carlos biked 6 miles last week. Andrew biked 3 times as far last week. How far did Andrew bike last week?

Ⓐ 2

Ⓑ 9

Ⓒ 18

Ⓓ 24

50 What is the name of this shape?

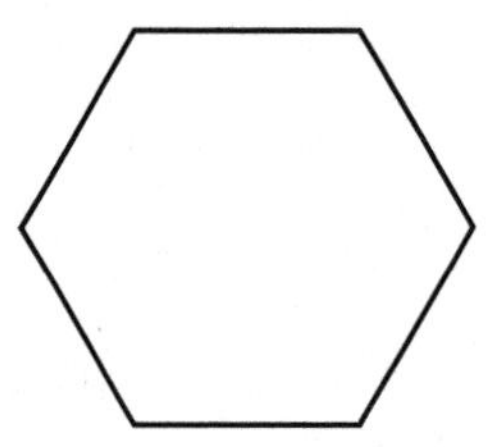

Ⓕ pentagon

Ⓖ rectangle

Ⓗ square

Ⓘ hexagon

This is the end of the Mathematics Test.

Until time is called, go back and check your work or answer questions you did not complete. When you have finished, close your Test Book.